BORN
TO BE
TOGETHER

OTHER HAY HOUSE TITLES OF RELATED INTEREST

Books

ADVENTURES OF A PSYCHIC, by Sylvia Browne and Antoinette May

ASTROLOGY REALLY WORKS, proven by The Magi Society™

AURA-SOMA: Healing Through Color, Plant, and Crystal Energy,
by Irene Dalichow and Mike Booth

COLORS & NUMBERS, by Louise L. Hay

*THE CONTACT HAS BEGUN: The True Story of a Journalist's Encounter with
Alien Beings*, by Phillip H. Krapf

DEVELOPING YOUR INTUITION WITH MAGIC MIRRORS, by Uma Reed
(book and card pack)

*THE LIGHTWORKER'S WAY: Awakening Your Spiritual Power to
Know and Heal*, by Doreen Virtue, Ph.D.

THE MAGI SOCIETY™ EPHEMERIS

*THE STARS IN YOUR FAMILY: How Astrology Affects Relationships Between
Parents and Children*, by Sylvia Friedman

Audios

*CHAKRA CLEARING: A Morning and Evening Meditation to Awaken
Your Spiritual Power*, by Doreen Virtue, Ph.D.

MAKING CONTACT WITH THE OTHER SIDE, by Sylvia Browne

PSYCHIC AND INTUITIVE HEALING, by Barbara Brennan, Rosalyn Bruyere,
and Judith Orloff, with Michael Toms

(All of the above are available at your local bookstore,
or may be ordered by calling Hay House at 800-654-5126.)

Please visit the Hay House Website at: **www.hayhouse.com**

BORN
TO BE
TOGETHER

LOVE RELATIONSHIPS, ASTROLOGY, AND THE SOUL

TERRY LAMB

a Division of Hay House, Inc.
Carlsbad, California • Sydney, Australia

Published and distributed in the United States by:
Hay House, Inc., P.O. Box 5100, Carlsbad, CA 92018-5100 • (800) 654-5126
(800) 650-5115 (fax)

Edited by: Chris Watsky and Jill Kramer   *Designed by:* Jenny Richards
Illustrated by: Mark A. Marsh

Library of Congress Cataloging-in-Publication Data

Lamb, Terry.
      Born to be together : love relationships, astrology, and the soul / Terry Lamb.
          p.   cm.
      Includes bibliographical references.
      ISBN 1-56170-471-7 (pbk.)
        1. Astrology. 2. Love—Miscellanea.   I. Title.
BF1729.L6L35   1998
133.5—dc21

                                   98-9763
                                   CIP

ISBN 1-56170-471-7

03 02 01 00   6 5 4 3
1st printing, November 1998
3rd printing, November 2000

Printed in the United States of America

"Terry Lamb's wise, gentle book,
Born to Be Together, *masterfully disguises sophisticated astrological analysis in terms simple enough for a neophyte to grasp on the first reading. I'm still not sure how she managed to perform this miracle, but it's right there in these warm-hearted pages for anyone to see."*

— Steven Forrest, author of *The Inner Sky* and *Skymates: The Astrology of Love, Sex, and Intimacy*

To all who

dare to let the

light of true,

soul-centered love

shine in their lives

CONTENTS

ACKNOWLEDGMENTS

This book is born out of years of education and experience. Those who have contributed to this growth process have also contributed to this book, so please consider yourself among these ranks if I omit your name below.

I would first like to thank all those with whom I have shared love in relationship, whether intimate, familial, or in another form. I would especially like to thank my sons, Uriah and Aryndel, for loving me and sharing their beautiful souls with me again in this lifetime.

Specifically, I would like to thank Peggy Hoversten and Lou Ann Muhm for their thoughtful editorial input. I would like to thank Peggy, Jean Glover, and Michele Ruiz for sticking by me over the years and helping me bring my vision into form. Finally, I would like to thank Louise Hay for believing in me and giving me this opportunity to give wings to my vision.

I would also like to thank you in advance, dear reader, for reading this book. Your willingness to invest in it makes all our dreams possible.

INTRODUCTION
The Purpose of This Book

Who Can Benefit from This Book

Everyone is involved in relationships. Even those of us who find ourselves without an intimate partner as we read this book have relationships with brothers, sisters, mothers, fathers, co-workers, colleagues, bosses, and friends. In spite of what our experiences have been and what our past has taught us, we all still yearn to love and be loved by another person with whom we share a deep bond. Even if we are involved in such a relationship, we may wish to deepen it.

This book shows how to improve our relationships by understanding ourselves, the others we have shared our lives with, and the way we have interacted with one another. We will explore what we bring to our relationships—from our childhood, our previous adult relationships, our past lives, and the time before this lifetime that we spent out of embodiment. We will use this foundation to explain the patterns of the present and put forth ideas and options for making better choices, if necessary, in the future. It doesn't matter whether you are applying these concepts to a current relationship, one from the past, or one you would like to create. The principles I will express apply to all relationships: partners, family members, and friends.

Why Use Astrology?

As we embark on the road of life, it helps to have a road map. Many people over thousands of years have chosen astrological symbolism to chart their course. The symbols of astrology give us a way to sort out the parts of ourselves, for we are complex beings with many aspects to our nature. We are the Communicator, the Yearning Maiden, the Warrior, the Hero(ine), to name a few. I will introduce you to all the symbols of astrology—the living symbols that lie within us. I will teach you to apply them to your own nature and to your partners' to help you make sense of yourself and your partner-ships. What (or whom) we understand more completely we can love more fully, whether we focus on ourselves or those around us. Deeper, more fully experienced love always improves our relationships.

If You Know Little about Astrology . . .

Then you're in for a treat! Astrology is a wonderful world of myth and mystery, and you are the hero and detective. The myths are within us all, and the mystery is the part of ourselves (and our partners) we do not yet know. Let this book take you on your first (or nearly first) planetary jour-ney into the mystery of our relationships.

If You Are an Astrologer or a Student of Astrology . . .

There's something here for you, too. Inside you will find, I hope, some new ways of looking at yourself and your relationships—and those of your clients, if applicable. It has been my experience that people who know a lot about astrology still gain new insights from this material. Since you know the techniques, stretch your wings beyond the simple formulae that I pres-ent. You may learn new ways of thinking about the basic concepts of astrol-ogy as well as relationships. Apply what you know about aspects and other planetary interconnections, and this book will become more valuable still. I do not use the houses in this work, nor do I rely on the angles except in a minor way. Add what you already know to my work here. I think you'll find a new depth in your interpretation of relationships—your own or those of your clients.

How to Use This Book

Astrology's basic concepts and principles are simple, and anyone can understand them. However, because of the number of symbols involved (11 planets, 12 signs, and 12 houses), there is a certain amount of complexity involved in combining them and knowing which ones are more important than others.

In this book, I will be taking care of the complex part for you, leaving the simpler core concepts and principles for you to enjoy and apply to your life and relationships. This means that we cannot rely just on your "sign" (the location of the sun at the time you were born) to help you discover what's *really* going on. It will be best if you have more information on your chart and that of your partner(s).

Therefore, I will recommend that you have a copy of your own birth chart and those of your partners or a list of where the planets and angles (the ascendant or rising sign and the midheaven) were at the time and place that you were born. This can be obtained in several ways.

Getting Your Charts

The simplest thing to do is to order a chart from an astrological chart service. Nearly every astrologer now does their charts by computer, and most will be happy to run a copy of the charts you want for less than $10 each. There are also nationally advertised chart services. I have listed a few sources for charts in the Resources section at the back of the book (page 313).

If you have a computer, you can purchase one of the astrology programs for beginners. Let price be your guide. If the program costs less than $50, it is not going to be too complex for you to use. An advantage to having your own software is that you can calculate as many charts as you like. Often, the software comes with basic interpretations for the planets in them. Although they are no replacement for the work of a knowledgeable astrologer, who can interpret the astrological language fluently, these interpretations will give you a start. (My recommendations for software are also in the Resources section.)

How to Order Your Charts

For an astrologer or service to cast an accurate chart, it is important to know the birth date, place, and time. Some people encounter a stumbling block when it comes to the time of birth. If you have difficulty finding your or your partner's accurate birth time (recorded to the minute), read my suggestions below.

To order your chart:

1. Have the birth date, place, and time handy for each chart that you want to order to avoid errors. If you have some idea of what your birth time is, but you don't know the *exact* time (for example, it's "around 2:00 in the afternoon"), give your best guess. If you have no real idea, ask for the chart to be cast for 12:00 noon with the sun on the ascendant (solar houses, see #4 below).

2. Ask for a natal chart with all the planets plus Chiron (pronounced *ky-RON*).

3. Ask the chart service if the chart lists your planetary positions (planet in sign in house) separately. If it does not, ask if they can send you an extra report that has such a list. Otherwise, you will have to be able to read the symbols in the chart. This is not an insurmountable task, but it will be easier for you if you have such a listing. The symbols of astrology can be found in the appendix beginning on page 289.

4. If you have your birth time, ask for Koch (pronounced *COKE*) houses, or use what the astrologer or chart service suggests. The house system doesn't really matter too much, but the service or astrologer will ask. If you don't have any idea of your birth time, it is important to ask for solar houses (sun on the ascendant).

If You Don't Know Your Birth Time (or That of Your Partner) . . .

It is important to have your exact birth time to have an accurate chart. Every four minutes, a new degree of the zodiac rises in the east. If your chart happens to be cast to show 29 degrees of Aries rising and you were really born four or more minutes later, you would have Taurus rising instead! So try to be as accurate as you can.

However, it is still possible to gain a lot of insight without having an accurate birth time, especially if you use such a chart in the way I instruct you to below. Often we do not know the birth times of past partners, and the last thing we want to do is call and ask them! For this book, you can get along quite well without a timed birth chart. Just work with what you have, and I promise you that you will learn a great deal.

Here are a few suggestions for finding your own exact birth time:

- Check your birth certificate, even if you think you remember what your time of birth is. In most American states, there are two birth certificates, one for the hospital and one for the state or county. The one for the hospital usually contains the birth time. If the birth certificate you have does not show a birth time, try to order the other one from the state, county, or hospital where you were born.

- If you can't acquire a timed birth certificate, be creative in solving the mystery of your birth time. Sometimes birth times are listed on birth announcements, in baby books, or in bibles. My birth time was not recorded on the birth certificate I had in my possession, but I found it in a birth announcement that appeared in the local newspaper, since I was born in a small town. The article was glued in my baby book.

- As a last resort, use parental recollection. Although it is natural to think that mothers and fathers should remember the times of their children's births, there are many factors that can alter their memory. My experience has shown that many times what parents remember is not accurate. Mothers may have been drugged at the time of the birth. Fathers may not have been present. Also, mothers enter an altered state at the time of birth that enables them to withstand the pain of labor and birth, so their memories may take on a dreamlike quality. Other people who were present may be more reliable—aunts, friends, etc.

If all else fails, it is possible to cast your chart without a birth time as suggested above. Check for accuracy with the following placements:

- The moon. The moon moves very quickly and changes signs every 2¹/₂ days. If you were born on a day when the moon changes signs and you don't know your birth time, you cannot be sure what sign your moon is in. If you have had your chart cast for noon on your birthday and the moon appears after 23 degrees or before 7 degrees of the sign it is in, it could be in a different sign at the time of your birth. If this is the case, read the descriptions of both signs and pick the one that fits best.

- Your angles (ascendant or rising sign and your midheaven) will not be accurate. Don't score the angles when it's time to do so.

- Strictly speaking, the house locations of planets will not be accurate. (However, you do not need them for anything in this book.)

Although you will not need it here, if you are serious about getting accurate results from your journey through the astrological realms and you don't have a birth time, you can have your chart rectified. Rectification is a mathematical process where an astrologer uses information on events in your life to find a chart that works for you. This process must be accomplished by an astrologer qualified to do rectification. It generally costs more than $100 for a good rectification. I have listed some resources for this at the end of the book as well.

A list of resources for ordering your chart, simple astrological software, and rectification services can be found at the back of the book.

If You Don't Want to Wait for Your Chart . . .

If you're eager to learn something from this book and don't want to wait for your chart to be cast, you can use the "if it fits, use it" principle. We always have to filter what we receive from others, even if "the chart says so." We are the final decision makers on what advice to use, whether something applies to us or not, and whether or how we will use it. That is because we are always responsible for our own actions, no matter what we have based them on.

So read about everything, and use the parts that seem to work for you. Chances are very high that a good astrologer will be able to see why that works, even if it doesn't match my portrayal of your chart.

We are the final decision makers on what advice to use, whether something applies to us or not, and whether or how we will use it.

Always remember that there is more to astrology than I can tell you in these pages. I have tried to tread the fine line between oversimplification and too much complexity. I want you to be able to see what is really happening in your relationships without making the information too detailed to understand.

Those Pesky Pronouns and Other Language Issues

Throughout this book, I will use words such as *beloved, partner,* or *partners* to refer to the significant others in our lives. Please take this as a shorthand for "your past, present, and future partners." Nearly all of us have had more than one partner in our lives, and we can learn from all of our relationships at any time. Although we may close the door on a relationship, we never stop learning from it.

Chalk one up to the awkwardness of social change! Language modifications usually lag behind social change, and nowhere is this more true than in the use of pronouns, especially in print. *He, she, it,* and *they*—what to use? *He* is the traditionally acceptable norm. In proper English grammar, it has long been meant to denote people of either sex. Recently, revisionists have either chosen to use *she* to replace *he* as the generic pronoun throughout a work, or to use *he* and *she* in alternate paragraphs. In the first case, the notion of gender is brought up where none is meant; in the latter case, it is just plain confusing!

What is interesting is what has happened in street usage, which is what will eventually infiltrate written language, as has been shown across centuries of time. We have gone frequently to the use of *they* instead of *he* or *she*! Just listen—you may be surprised.

As a linguist by formal education, and as someone who is all for a balanced approach, I have learned to accept language change as a fact of life. It is usually what happens in the street that takes the lead, in spite of revisionist dreams. Therefore, I will give in to the way we all tend to speak more and more and use *they, their,* and *them* in this book, even where only one person is being referred to. Even though some strict grammarians consider this practice a sacrilege, if you look up the word *their* in the 10th edition of Webster's Dictionary, you will see that it concurs with me, or at least accepts this modern change.

Morality and More . . .

As much as I can manage (for I can't entirely control how my words will be understood), I do not mean to imply any specific moral code in these pages—that is, I do not mean to suggest that one form of relationship is better than another, or that all the ingredients of a good relationship are some absolute set of qualities. What makes a relationship good is most definitely subjective. For instance, some people want and need a high level of passion in their relationships, while others place a greater priority on intellectualism. (And nobody said you can't have both!) Also, and I make more specific comments later, the principles found in this book can be applied to any intimate relationship—whether heterosexual or homosexual.

However, I do make one assumption: that all healthy relationships are founded on love expressed in some healthy form, and that we all have a natural desire to experience that emotion. Although in general I will espouse the value of long-term relationships, short-term relationships have their place, and I would never want to urge someone to stay in a relationship that is unhealthy for them. Above all, I would never recommend staying in a relationship if it is abusive in any way.

C H A P T E R   O N E

THE TRUTH ABOUT BEING HUMAN
The Basic Principles of Life and Astrology

While I'm sure you want to leap right into the astrology section and find out what that part of the book has to say about your relationships, I hope you'll read each chapter in order. Astrology can tell us a lot about ourselves and our partners, but it is important to see it in the context of who we are as individuals. Read on, and you'll see why.

What Does It Mean to Be Human?

Before you enter into a relationship with another, it helps to know yourself. I would like to give you some clues to who you are—that is, some things that everyone has in common, male or female, because we are human. They go beyond what you learn in school—too bad, because they're basic things that everyone should know. Some of them you may understand right away because you know them to be true. Others you may have a hard time believing because they are not what you have been taught about yourself. I am going to ask you to be open to those concepts that seem unnatural to you. They are all good things to think about ourselves, things we would probably like to think are true but perhaps are afraid to believe.

I will never ask you to "believe" something that you are not sure is true. Everyone must learn at one's own pace in one's own way. If a piece of information doesn't seem to fit, you can choose to be open to it, but it is better not to blindly accept it. Consider it, be with it for a while, and see how you feel. If the concept is appealing to a deep part of you, chances are good that it is something you will eventually come to accept. But you must first try it out for yourself. Although there are some topics that may be new to you, you might find that they will "resonate" within you and just feel right. I encourage you to acknowledge those feelings as you read on.

Your Inner Being: The Soul and True Self

The part of us we see every day is constantly changing. We may be aware of different moods and emotions from one hour to the next; we may decide we are going to do something one day, then two days later reverse ourselves. We may even feel more than one way about something at the same time!

Who we really are is constant and eternal.

Although this fluctuating, moody self may be familiar to us, that's not who we really are. The real part of us lives beyond this life. It is a part of ourselves that existed before we were born and will continue to exist after we die. I, and many others, call this the Higher Self. The Higher Self has many aspects and can be described in many ways, but it is simplest to picture it as made up of two parts: the Soul, and the Spirit or True Self. The Soul learns and evolves, while the True Self remains constant and knowing because it is always connected to, and a part of, the Great Source. It knows all truths and is within us always, even if we are not aware of its presence. It does not succumb to the unconstant part of ourselves, even though the Higher Self may be masked by it.

What about Past Lives?

If a part of us exists before and after this lifetime, it is not far-fetched to go one step further—to think that the Soul can be born more than one

* 2 *

time—the concept of reincarnation. This is one way of accounting for the fact that people seem to be born with predispositions, a set pattern or a way of doing things that each of us seems to have before we receive any influences from others. It helps to explain why Mozart could write a piano concerto at age four. It helps us to understand why two children born into the same family have different interpretations of their experiences of it and do different things with their lives.

If you find reincarnation difficult to accept, it is possible to think of past-life memories as fanciful stories that help people make sense of the unexplainable. When working with past lives, I advise you to use caution. It is easy to get caught up in the drama of an appealing past life instead of facing the sometimes humdrum or even painful realities of this one. Knowledge of past lives is meant to assist us in understanding the conditions of this life so that we can overcome the obstacles we encounter in the here and now. *This* life is definitely the more important one.

It is useful to work with past lives because if we can see how a misunderstanding may stem from a past-life experience, it may help us to rectify our actions, attitudes, and beliefs in this lifetime. That is, we can develop perspective, purpose, and direction in this life. Our lives make more sense when we see them as organized around a theme, like a thread running through all our experiences, tying them together to make them into a coherent whole. Without that thread, we may feel purposeless and adrift.

We are whole, sovereign beings.

Our True Nature

Most of us search for a way to complete ourselves throughout our lives. Whether we think we can do it in a job, in a relationship, by being a parent, or becoming famous, we look for a way to rid ourselves of a feeling of emptiness—to feel whole, to be fulfilled.

The good news is that we are already whole beings. The reason we don't recognize this is that we are not aware of the entirety of who we are. We have been taught to be less than we are by people who were taught to be less than *they* were. It's truly a case of the blind leading the blind! Although we have souls (and are Spirit), we may never have been taught what it feels like to experience that part of our nature. Thus, it seems separate, unreal, or a part of ourselves that is unattainable. Yet, it *is* attainable, available to each of us. We just have to remember that part of ourselves; then it is ours forever.

When we encounter our entire being for the first time, we stand in humbled awe before the power, love, and connectedness that We all are. It affects our experience and behavior in every part of our lives as we see things from a new, deeper level. In the meantime, we continue to search for that wholeness. On some level, we know it's there. We *know* it. And we'll never settle for less than that truth. We will smell a rat every time someone tries to tell us otherwise—and they do it all the time. We will half-believe them, but something in us reverberates with something in them that knows this truth, and we will search for our wholeness until we find it.

However, we are also taught that wholeness must be found outside of ourselves. We need a relationship to complete us, or some other wave of the magic wand to make us feel whole. *Our wholeness is found within.*

"So," you may say, "if I'm already whole, why do I need a relationship? If I'm already whole, I don't need another person to complete me." Let me assure you that relationships remain important. Once we are whole, we form relationships in a different, more fulfilling way. It is this type of relationship that we all unconsciously seek. It is formed on the basis of things other than "need."

Don't be afraid to be whole. You will still have room for other people.

Before we recognize and live our wholeness, we are like half-people looking for completion, and our relationships are based on (co-)dependency. Co-dependency makes it very difficult to maintain a feeling of love. However, as whole beings standing as individuals, we form our relationships based on healthy interdependency. Healthy interdependency makes it possible to sustain love even in the face of the difficulties that arise as you live and grow together.

We are whole, sovereign beings. To say that you are sovereign means that you own yourself. No one else has the right to determine what is best for you. Your boundaries are yours to keep; you need not take any advice that feels wrong or do anything out of loyalty to another if it betrays yourself. You need not give your power to another person, no matter how they threaten you. You have a right to feel safe, to be loved, to feel and express your feelings, to know what you know, and to be who you are.

You deserve respect for who you are, and you deserve to be allowed to make mistakes. This means that it's okay to respect yourself in your present state, to accept yourself in the weakness of all your flaws and the glory of your gifts. It's okay to express those gifts, to learn from your flaws, and to fulfill yourself, even if it means outdistancing others.

Although these ideas may seem natural, on a subtle level, we are all taught—whether male or female—to deny these rights in many ways. Every person has their own story about this. Yet, these things are our birthright. They are a part of expressing ourselves in a healthy way in all our relationships.

We Carry Symbols Within Us

I remember in the mid-'70s when *Star Wars* came out at the theaters how we all lined up around the block to see it. Everyone loved it! Why did we all respond to the same plot twists with love or terror, laughter or tears?

Well, I believe it's because we identified with the characters to a great extent. In Luke Skywalker, we saw the hero within us; in Princess Leia, we saw the empowered woman. In Han Solo, we saw the renegade-turned-gallant-warrior, the flawed hero who could mend his ways and succeed in the end. We could each identify with at least one of the characters. The "bad" part of ourselves was played by Darth Vader ("dark father" in Dutch) and the Emperor. If we could not identify with the roles, they would not have held us captive, drawn us to them, and made the film such a monumental success.

The symbols of the hero, the empowered woman, the warrior, and the dark father live within us. We play the roles to our delight or horror, or if we cannot accept them in ourselves, we observe them in others. In psychology, a symbol that lives within us in this manner is called an *archetype*.

This is one of the ways that astrology works. If we can name a symbol, we have identified something within ourselves, because we cannot conceive of something that is not a part of our nature. If we can name a planet or a god "Jupiter" and give it qualities, then we have identified the things that Jupiter represents in ourselves—generosity, confidence, and faith.

We all have every archetype within us.

---

* 5 *

Even though we may want to deny that the dark father is in there, he is. We'd rather identify with the hero of the story, even though we may think that we can't really be heroic. But just as Luke came to understand in the ensuing *Star Wars* films that his father was a man who misunderstood the consequences of his choices, or felt he didn't have a choice, we can learn that our own dark father struggles to be understood and loved so that it can grow to love, instead of live in fear.

It doesn't matter who we are—we all have a mother, a father, a hero, a female warrior, and a child within us. We may be aware of some archetypes more than others; we may not be aware of some of them at all until something triggers our awareness, yet they are there. Each has its own life, growing and changing as *we* grow and change.

We each work with these archetypes, learning to understand them, and in so doing, we understand ourselves. We may, for instance, spend a few years working on our inner mother. This means that we think about our mother, we notice other mothers more, and we observe how they interact with their children. We may become a mother by having children or caring for other children. We may also attract women who are mothers into our lives and develop a friendship or professional relationship with them. Sometimes we will attract someone who acts as a mother to us, perhaps providing some of the nurturance we feel was lacking in our relationship with our own mother or those who filled that role when we were children. After a time, our understanding of our inner mother may increase, and we may focus less on her. Our focus may shift to another archetype—our inner father, or our inner warrior, for example.

What's more, we may find that we have a lifelong need to work with one archetype more than another. Some of us, stimulated in part by childhood experiences, may find that we spend our entire lives working on our inner father symbol. We grow a lot by thinking of our father, working for the government (an authority/father symbol), or attracting older men as friends or partners. The evolution and importance of the archetypes we express can be detected, tracked, and enhanced through astrology.

What You See Is Not Necessarily What You Get

I saw a bumper sticker the other day that said, "I wanna be Barbie . . . that girl has everything." Sometimes it may seem as though the world is full of Barbies. Other people have it better, easier, have more, and are happier. Sometimes we may wonder, how can people who are so unconscious and who have made their lives a wreck, have such a good marriage? How can someone who is so hard to get along with have such a fulfilling career? It may seem as though we work and work at something, only to see someone who so easily accomplishes what we have striven our entire life to gain. And they haven't the slightest idea of how they did it! We may feel disheartened or envious because we have worked so hard or seem to know so much more, yet have less outward success to show for it.

Just because we recognize a lack in ourselves and others don't appear to have that lack, it doesn't mean that they're better than we are. It may be that they are just not working on that issue right now. They may have worked on it before (including in past lives), or they may have "the luck of the unconscious." A person who is not working on a given area of their lives is not likely to be conscious of the challenges that arise for others in that area. Those who have difficulty in that particular area usually know the most about it and are most likely to overcome those difficulties in order to be successful. Once they reach this level of awareness, they may be more successful and fulfilled than the person who has unconscious luck.

The fact is that our pain helps us grow. It is part of being human to enjoy comfort. If we are comfortable with something, we tend not to examine it. When we don't examine something, that part of our lives functions okay for us, but it may never be really fulfilling.

All of this is part of the plan. We each have certain things that we have chosen to work on. We can't do it all at once or it would overwhelm us. That is why we observe other people having an easier time than we are in certain areas and at certain times.

If we seem to have chosen a more difficult path than others, it is because we have earned it. This may seem an odd thing to say, but it is true. When we have learned to handle something well in previous lives, we "up the ante." We require more strength from ourselves because we are tougher and wiser there.

In our astrological charts, when we find challenging connections between ourselves and our partners, it is because we want to build on previous strengths, not because we've done something wrong. We are ready to learn at a deeper and more challenging level.

Why Bother?

It is generally true that the more knowledgeable and wise you are, the more challenges you will encounter in your life. It is also true that as these attributes increase in your nature, you will experience more joy and fulfillment.

It is to our advantage to grow, because we will never be completely happy in ignorance. A part of us knows that we are not aware of our wholeness. Even if we experience pain along the path to finding it, this part of us knows that it is worth it, and we will never be content being a half-person.

If it's so painful, why bother taking this path toward wholeness? Aren't we at least as well off in blissful ignorance? Certainly not, because ignorance is anything but blissful. It may appear that way on the surface, but what we are experiencing inside is likely to be anything but bliss—anxiety, fear, anger, and confusion. If we don't realize that our pain is related to our lack of knowing, our pain will be made all the worse because we don't know what to do about it. We won't know that we have the power to change it. We have all kinds of ways of coping with the pain—numbing out; becoming angry; or becoming addicted to a substance, behavior, or activity. We stop recognizing it because we have always had it and accept it as a part of life. We don't realize how radiant and fulfilled we can be once we unite with the other unseen part of ourselves.

Yet, if we dare to embark on the path of wisdom and self-knowledge, we can experience the radiance firsthand. Once we do, we will never consider ignorance a viable option again.

There are always new parts of yourself to know.

You are an infinite being! No matter how much you follow the path of your personal growth, there is still more of you to explore. So even if you feel that you have the perfect relationship with your mother and you have no issues with her, that doesn't mean that you won't be drawn to work on your inner-mother archetype at some time.

We never know what we'll find in ourselves. That's the good news—not something to be viewed with fear. In the modern version of the Greek myth about Pandora's box, the box is opened to find it full of horrible demons—war, death, and disease. However, in the original version of the fable,

Pandora's box was a honey jar filled with blessings, like the cornucopia. The box/honey jar is our inner nature. From the modern version of the myth, we have learned to fear our inner selves—that inside we are terrible beings with pain and evil at the core. Yet, this is not true, as the original version of the tale tells us. To look inside is to embark on an incredible journey through the infinite space within.

As long as you are on the planet, there is more to learn.

The Two Halves of Who We Are

Even though we each identify ourselves as either male or female based on our physical sex, each one of us is made up of two halves—one male, the other female. After reading and thinking about symbols and archetypes, this shouldn't come as a great surprise. If you have mother and father archetypes within, why not male and female?

Each of us is both male and female.

It is useful to think about ourselves as if we have *only* those two halves. But in fact, this is only one of many useful perspectives offered up by psychology within the last 100 years. From other points of view, we might see ourselves in another way—divided into two halves as, say, parent and child. When we talk about intimate relationships, it is especially useful to look at ourselves in terms of our male-female halves.

Within their gender, some people are more male and others more female. It is not hard to see individual differences between members of the same sex. Some women wear frills and lace and soft feminine clothes. Their hair is softly styled, whether long or short. Others wear clothes that are more tailored, even severely cut. Their hair may be cleanly styled, less feminine looking. In between these extremes are many variations, person to person and day to day. For men, we may see some with long hair, loose-fitting Moroccan shirts, comfortable pants, and an earring or two. Others have their hair cut short, wear crisp-fitting suits or casual clothes, and no jewelry beyond a watch.

Within each gender, we can see a range of expressions, some of which would be considered more feminine, others more masculine. So, even though we are physically either male or female, we are really a blend of masculine and feminine characteristics.

Each of us has a side to our nature that is soft, tender, loving, and moody—containing the qualities we call feminine. We each also have bold, individualistic, focused, and objective aspects to who we are—the masculine side. There are many more qualities that are associated with the terms *masculine* and *feminine,* but they are not as important as the recognition that when we have a feeling, no matter where it comes from, it is ours to experience. What's more, we need to know that everyone has both sides so that we know that it's okay to express all qualities as well as to accept them in our partners.

We all tend to respond to these two halves of our nature in the same way. We tend to express the side with which we are gender-identified more. We will tend to acknowledge that side of our nature more fully and freely. We therefore tend to ignore or overlook the other, "opposite" side of our nature. This is the feminine side in men and the masculine side in women. This is called the *shadow*, the part of our nature that we tend to want to ignore.

Our Unconscious Self

We can also call the shadow our "unconscious self." If we don't want to see something, we have the power to hide it from ourselves and make it a part of our unconscious. Any bits and parts of ourselves that we see as weaknesses, we may want to hide, avoid, deny, or disown. We may cover them with a mask of more acceptable behavior. This is a natural part of being human, because we all want to be loved and accepted and feel good about our impact on others.

When we hide or deny a part of our nature, we may not be able to see it, and we may even come to feel as though it has ceased to exist. However, others may be able to be more objective about our nature than we are.

It is a peculiar thing that others may be able to see our shadow better than we. Not only may they be able to see the very parts we are trying to hide, but they may also be less involved in those qualities emotionally and more forgiving when they see this side of us come out. For, the unconscious qualities we have *will* surface. Since they are a part of us, they appear from time to time, often when we least expect it and in spite of our best efforts to control their emergence. These "surprise appearances" make us uncomfortable, but they are inevitable.

Many people are embarrassed by their unconscious "slips," because the needs that this side of our nature expresses are very primitive, simple, and childlike. However, there is no shame in having and expressing those needs if we find a healthy way to do so. They represent basic drives within us to love and be loved, to survive, to unite with others, and to be known as unique individuals. These are never harmful in their simplest form, but if we are taught to feel shame about having any of these drives, then we may decide to deny their existence, and they may surface in more complex, disguised forms.

What If You're in a Same-Sex Relationship?

If you're in a same-sex relationship, it may be more difficult to tell who is playing what role when. Generally speaking, in male-male and female-female love relationships, we tend to take on the same roles as we do in male-female relationships. However, it may be difficult to identify who is taking on the more masculine role and who the more feminine. Furthermore, in same-sex relationships, the roles tend to be more fluid. Partners may exchange roles as the relationship evolves, and they may also share the roles more equally. That is, one partner may enjoy the nurturing role that cooking provides, while the other may tend to enjoy keeping the home well organized. The same partner that loves to cook may at the same time be more aggressive in initiating courtship and love-making. This manner of sharing roles is less common in mixed-sex relationships, where the individual may feel more constrained by cultural patterning to play out traditional roles. However, it is desirable in all relationships, as it is a sign of equality and healthy self-esteem.

Adding Astrology to the Mix

Astrology is a tool. We could even liken it to a hammer. In the hands of a skilled carpenter, it can be used to accomplish great things. However, in the hands of a toddler, it could cause harm to oneself or others. So it is with astrology. In the hands of a skilled practitioner, it can be a great aid to personal growth, fulfillment in relationships, or business success. Poorly understood, it can be a tool of limitation and fear, used to unwittingly curtail potential.

The bottom line is *you*. Once again, you're the boss. No astrologer can tell you what is ultimately right for you. Although astrologers know more about astrology (the tool) than you do, they can't know more about *you* than you do. In the end, you bear full responsibility for your actions, so you must do what feels right to you.

Fear is not an end result, but a signal that there's more to learn.

If something that an astrologer says brings up fear for you, explore that issue more fully, either with the astrologer or in another way of your choosing. Fear is not an end result, but a signal that there's more to learn. Often we astrologers do not realize when we are triggering a difficult emotion in someone. If you speak up, it gives us a chance to help you clear the emotion and achieve peace and balance.

If in reading this book you find yourself experiencing painful emotions, take a moment to go inside and explore where that is coming from. See if you can recall any memories or associations that you have with the thought that seemed to trigger the emotion. Breathe into the feeling, into the place where you are holding that emotion, and ask for light to replace the darkness in that area.

If, in the process, you seem to encounter something you would like help in exploring, it's okay to seek that help. We are not meant to be isolated from each other. We are meant to be *interdependent*. We must rely on each other in this complex world—our strength lies in our relationships with others. It's not that we do not need to learn self-reliance, for we do need to be able to make our own decisions; however, it's okay to get input from other sources before we do. We also need to learn not to rely on any one person too much and to provide a fair exchange with respect to what is given to us by others. That is what self-responsibility and adulthood are about.

In this book, I can use the tool of astrology as wisely as I know how, but I cannot guide you personally as you read it to make sure that we get the meaning right. So if you read something that triggers in you a need to explore your relationships or yourself more deeply, the next step is to have a private consultation with someone who's an expert in using the tool of astrology. With that person, feel free to discuss any questions that have arisen for you.

We can also think of your astrological chart (also called your birth or natal chart) as a blueprint or map. It suggests certain pathways of development, but you do not have to follow them. It refers to patterns that could represent weaknesses, but they may also be used as strengths. The challenge of our lives is to turn every weakness into a strength by removing misunderstanding. The chart also may suggest gifts with which you were endowed at birth, but you are the one who says how they are to be expressed; you alone say whether your artistic talent is to be used for music or sculpting, dance or photography. You also have the power to misuse your gifts or rely on them too much.

The Richness of Astrological Archetypes

When I began talking about archetypes, I mentioned only a few of those that are found in astrology. There are many more (astrology's complete cast of characters will be introduced to you in chapter 6). Astrology provides a more complete, profound, and precise set of archetypes than those which have been presented by any other school of thought on human development and potential.

One of the benefits of such a precise system is that it provides a way to bring order to the confusion of inner feelings and ideas within and around us. Astrology was and still is used as an alchemical tool. Alchemy, the medieval art and science of human development, was based on the premise that we are a mass of confused impulses that, until we sort them out and blend them, make it impossible to fulfill ourselves, to know who we really are.

Is It Fate or Free Will?

Astrology has so much power and is so complex that people see things in it that don't really exist. For instance, they think that astrology can tell their future or that astrologers know everything about them just by looking at their charts. In actuality, it might surprise you to find out that this is not really the case.

One of the objections that the Church has raised with respect to astrology is that it takes away our free will—our right and ability to determine our own path. But, in fact, astrology opens the doors to that freedom.

The most predictable person is the one who does things without thinking about them. If we simply follow our habits or do what is customary, we are not exercising much freedom! Free will is our right to choose our path, and if we don't think about what we are doing, we aren't really choosing. As I mentioned above, astrology is a road map, so it cannot predict your future any more than a road map can. A person reading the map you plan to use may be able to predict which road you are likely to take (the freeway because it's the fastest) if they know where you want to go. But they can't know what your choices will be. Neither can an astrologer. Not only do you have the choice as to which "road" you will take, but you have the choice about how you will take it (by bus or car) and how you will navigate it (fast or slowly, carefully or recklessly). What's more, as you learn about yourself, you will probably choose better and better ways to express yourself through your astrological map, so you may even improve the road system!

Even though this may appear to be nothing more than a clever metaphor, it works. Contained in the chart are a number of processes that we involve ourselves in. As we improve our understanding of life, we change the way we engage in them. Thus, we free ourselves of our "fate," the part of our lives that we believe is bound to happen and cannot change.

One more word about fate. Most astrologers will, if questioned, admit that fate plays a role in our lives. However, the elements of fate are associated with those parts of our lives that we cannot change or that we perceive we cannot change. For instance, one element of fate is who our parents are. Another is the place we are born.

There is another type of fate—that which comes of not knowing that we have a choice. This second kind of fate can be changed, and astrology is one of many tools and techniques of personal growth that can help us to learn how. When we take charge of this type of fate, we experience increasing levels of joy and fulfillment.

Your astrology chart shows the first kind of fate as well, and the challenge for you and your astrologer is to learn to tell the difference. In fact, we're all learning about what we can change and what we cannot. Generally speaking, we can change much more than we think we can, but we are not taught how. As you read on, you'll be learning about some ways to change your approach to relationships. All we have the power to change is ourselves, but that power is everything. If we are willing to change ourselves, that is the key.

Our chart expresses our limitless potential.

From time to time, I hear people mention that their charts don't apply to them anymore because they have grown so much. This is not possible. We cannot outgrow our chart any more than we can make the planets disappear! These individuals are misunderstanding how astrology works. The symbols of astrology have the capability of expressing anything that lies within our potential. The stars are as limitless as we are!

If all we read is the material on astrology that we find in a grocery store or magazine rack, we are likely to get a limited idea of what astrology is and what its archetypes can represent. I have seen doorway after doorway open as people reach for more and more of their potential in expressing these archetypes. Even saints, gurus, and sages use their charts for their self-expression and respond to the rhythms of the planetary cycles in their lives.

What Is the Purpose of Astrology?

The purpose of any tool such as astrology is as grand as our purpose for being alive—to help us know our True Self, to find our connection with the Divine, and to know ourselves as a part of the Source. There are many other tools that can be used for the same purpose, but none in the same way. Astrology shows how the most primal forces of the universe prompt the rhythmic cycles of the planets in their orbits and allows us to see patterns in the stars. Just as the forces of the universe prompt the planets in their courses, we experience them on the planet and respond to them in our own ways.

By understanding the symbols of astrology, we can find our unique role in the world—there is no one else like each of us in the world! Further, we can come to understand who we are in relationships, what each relationship means to us, and how it can help us grow.

Every time that we love, we experience our connection with the Source. Everyone that we love brings that connection to us as we bring it to them. So let's look at what astrology can teach us about loving each other.

Astrology's Bits and Pieces

On the opposite page, you can see a chart with some of the objects found in it labeled. Please refer to this diagram when reading relevant passages throughout the book, if necessary, to clarify what part of the chart I am referring to.

Astrology has four main components: **planets and points**, **signs**, **houses**, and **aspects**. Each planet or point is found in a sign, and each sign is located in one or two houses. Therefore, in Figure 1A, we can say that Mars is in Sagittarius in the 9th house. It is helpful to write down each one of your planetary placements using the form found in the appendix on page 301.

Each component has a specific application in your chart:

- The **planets** tell *what* type of energy you are using and can represent *people* in your life. They are living archetypes. They are the actors of astrology.

- The **signs** tell *how* you are using the archetypes of the planets and what motivates you to do so. They are the processes of astrology—the actors' character roles.

- The **houses** tell where those energies are used. Houses are like the set of the play, such as our neighborhoods, our homes, our career paths.

- **Aspects** tell how the planets relate to each other—do they get along harmoniously, or are they in conflict inside us? They can be thought of as the play's script.

- The **points** in your chart are similar to planets in that they are in a sign and a house, but they are sensitive spots, not bodies that emit energies. They are rather like acupuncture points: We may flinch a little when they are stimulated, but it feels good when they are open and flowing. We respond to points, but they aren't "alive"—we don't act them out—as we do the planets.

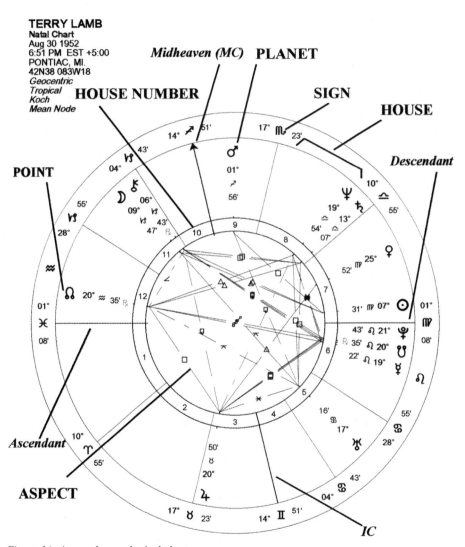

Figure 1A: A sample astrological chart.

Sometimes, the usage associated with houses and planets can get confusing. For example, an astrologer might refer to your moon as representative of your mother, and your 4th house as representative of her as well. Both interpretations are true, but in different ways. The moon is our attitude toward, and experience of, our mother. Since it is a living archetype, it may also signify other mothering people whom we have attracted to us. The 4th house is our home environment and early conditioning, and since our mother is a part of that, we can "read" the mother from the 4th house. However, this house also includes all the things and experiences of our early childhood, so it can also include our father and any others who took care of us at an early age.

Angles and Houses

We will not be using or referring to the houses in this book, so if this statement satisfies your curiosity about houses, you can skip to the next section. The houses are numbered 1–12 counterclockwise around the chart, starting with the lefthand horizontal line (see Figure 1A). These wedge-shaped pieces of the circle are divided by lines called **cusps**. The **ascendant** is the cusp of the first house. It is also referred to as your rising sign, although strictly speaking they are slightly different from each other: the ascendant is the point (literally, shown as a line) in the chart, while the rising sign is the whole sign that the ascendant is in. Each reminds us that this side of the chart is the eastern half, where the sun and all the planets rise every day. The opposite side of the chart is the west, where the sun and planets set. The house cusp shown there, belonging to the 7th, is called the **descendant**.

The cusps for the 10th and 4th houses, found at the top and bottom of the chart, respectively, are the **MC** (called the **midheaven**) and **IC** (just called the I-C). The MC is the south point of the chart, while the IC is the north (backward from most maps). Together with the ascendant and descendant, the MC and IC are called the **angles**. The angles are points of emphasis and sensitivity in the chart. Planets on the angles (within 6°) are more powerful in our lives.

In addition to these points, you will find the symbols [☊] and [☋]. These are called the North Node and South Node, respectively. They are always exactly across the circle from (opposite) each other.

The Planets, Signs, and Aspects

In Figure 1B you can see all the symbols, or glyphs, for the planets that you'll find in your astrological chart. Figure 1C shows all the signs and their glyphs. Although there are glyphs for the aspects, we will not need to refer to them in this book.

I have not covered any of the meanings of the individual symbols in astrology yet. I will cover those in chapter 3 (the signs) and chapter 6 (the planets). There is a brief synopsis of each of astrology's symbols and qualities in the appendix on page 289.

We will talk about the aspects as interrelationships between the signs, which, in effect, they are. See chapters 3, 4, and 5 for information about the various interrelationships between the signs.

The Planets	
☉	Sun
☽	Moon
☿	Mercury
♀	Venus
♂	Mars
♃	Jupiter
♄	Saturn
⚷	Chiron
♅	Uranus
♆	Neptune
♇	Pluto

Figure 1B

The Signs	
♈	Aries
♉	Taurus
♊	Gemini
♋	Cancer
♌	Leo
♍	Virgo
♎	Libra
♏	Scorpio
♐	Sagittarius
♑	Capricorn
♒	Aquarius
♓	Pisces

Figure 1C

C H A P T E R   T W O

THE MAGICAL WORLD OF LOVE[1]

Since astrology is a tool, it can be used either well or poorly. In relationships (as elsewhere), we can misuse our knowledge of astrology and end up just the same as we would have before—or worse! Therefore, it is good to lay a foundation of understanding relationships in general from a soul perspective.

In our culture, we are taught many things about relationships and love that are not true. Most of us are raised on the notion of a romantic ideal that is far removed from the truth of what relationships are like in their entirety. In this chapter, we will look at what really happens when we form relationships. You will find, as you read, that relationships are more profound and wonderful than you ever dreamed possible.

The key to successful relationships lies at the core of our being, the inner life of the heart. We have to relearn how to love by becoming attuned to this part of our nature. We have to learn an entirely new way of loving and being loved.

We do not have to become something special (more special than we already are!) in order to love. By getting in touch with our True Self, we will naturally find love within us and be able to share it with others. When

---

[1] I owe many of the concepts presented in this chapter to the book *Love, an Inner Connection*, by Carol K. Anthony. I highly recommend this book and all her other works.

we connect with the True Self, we are released from the internal struggle that arises when we accept things, or do things, contrary to our true nature. Every time we experience fear, anger, doubt, or hopelessness, we reinforce our separation from others and lose our connectedness. Every time we experience peace, joy, love, happiness, and fulfillment, we reaffirm our connection with our essence and all other forms of life.

It is also helpful to train the mind, because it is the mind that talks us into false love and out of true love; it schemes, plans, and contrives. It is the tool of the ego, also known as the false self, shadow, or wound. If we can teach the mind that it is okay to let go of its hurry-up offense approach to life and love, then it relaxes and allows the True Self to emerge. The ego plays a predictable role in the traditional patterns of relationships in our culture. Even with all the visible advances regarding the empowerment of both men and women to shake off old roles and become Themselves, we have yet to spawn a culturewide movement toward true individuality. Particularly in patterns of intimate relating, we lag behind in the replacement of old patterns with new ones. We know that the old ways don't work, but we don't know what to replace them with. Confusion reigns in modern relationships over who is supposed to do what. Both men and women feel betrayed by each other in our attempt to find a new way to love.

How to Love?

There is a way to love that emerges from the True Self. Even though this means that each relationship develops in its own unique pattern, there are certain stages that all intimate relationships seem to go through due to our common cultural background.

Learning to love from the True Self uproots the entire issue of how to fulfill our roles in a relationship, because when we are in the True Self, we do not require roles—we see them as only orchestrated responses, or ego masks. We can let the roles transform into fluid, living archetypes and become alive in our relationships. We can learn to respond spontaneously to the impulses of the moment from the deepest core of our being.

To free ourselves of the past, we must first examine our roles. What roles are men and women unconsciously asked by our culture to fulfill? How do our relationships get "stuck," stagnating without growth? How can we redevelop the living essence of a relationship once it has died? And how do we nurture a new relationship so that it doesn't fall prey to our old ways of loving?

What Has Happened to Love?

The struggle that we have learned to anticipate in love relationships, whether same- or opposite-sex, has its roots in the "battle of the sexes." The fact that this is a phrase that everyone knows tell us that it is a cultural phenomenon found in, but not limited to, Westernized society. However, in non-Western cultures, this is a foreign notion. Just what is the battle of the sexes, and how did it start?

First, the battle of the sexes is a power or dominance struggle between men and women. It is a sign that we have left behind our natural biological state. In nature, a struggle between the sexes ultimately destroys the species; natural struggles and competition tend to pit male against male, not against female. Thus, a dominance struggle between the sexes of a species is an aberration.

In part, the struggle seems to have arisen out of the "domestication" of humankind and the fabrication of war as a male pursuit. Perhaps it is because we were so successful at civilizing ourselves that we have redefined survival. In a world where biological needs and drives are suppressed, we have relearned what it takes to keep ourselves alive. We have learned to mask our basic need for the opposite sex. All of this is testimony to the power of the mind over our instinctual nature.

It seems also to be linked to the improperly channeled use of aggression in our culture. Whereas early humans would fight man-to-man to win women or territory, this urge has been subverted by civilized behaviors and sophisticated weaponry. Few healthy avenues have been developed for rechanneling the aggressive side of our nature, which is often turned inward in women, creating a pattern of internalized fear and anger. Men's aggression has turned in part into the use of force against women, from subtle forms of dominance to physical and sexual abuse. The ultimate crime is rape—the use of force to subvert the most precious act of love into an experience of terror and victimization.

Yet, in spite of all this conflict, something in us still responds to love. Our ability to connect, to love, somehow prevails. This principle is testimony to our highest spiritual nature.

According to the research of people such as archaeo-sociologists Riane Eisler and Barbara G. Walker, and archaeo-anthropologist Marija Gimbutas, the dominance-oriented culture in which we currently exist arose only in the last 3,500 years. Before that, cultures more peaceful and more directly supportive of life were found worldwide. Only after this more peaceable world culture was overrun did the battle of the sexes begin.

The Lie about Love

Our culture teaches us about love by handing down, through the generations, diverse myths, stories, and traditional ways of interacting, both positive and negative. We learn by watching and experiencing much more profoundly than by any other method. Our notions of romantic love come from the stories we hear in books, movies, popular music, and on TV. Stories of love are found nearly everywhere we turn, and yet what all these examples teach us is often the wrong thing.

In general, modern culture relies upon the use of force to accomplish many of its goals. Since the time that ancient life-oriented societies were overrun by more aggressive cultures, force has been the main underlying dynamic among and between people. Force begets dominance—power over another—and its effects are deep and far-reaching. The notion that we must use force to accomplish our goals became predominant in ancient times, and it is the biggest lie of the last 3,500 years. It is the one that resides at the core of most of our cultural patterns and personal beliefs. Naturally, this extends into intimate relationships. In nearly every place we hear about love, it is portrayed as a hunt, a game, a war, or a struggle. All of these forms are based on the use of force. There are many books available for women on how to get their man, just as there are many for men on how to get all the women they want. These are based on the notion of conquest—dominance through overcoming another's defenses. The use of force is separative because it does not wait for the other—the beloved, adversary, or opponent—to choose to engage in interaction. As sovereign human beings, we all recognize within ourselves that we have the right to choose; and any use of force, however subtle, denies that right. Naturally, love or sex "conquest" books involve the use of force and increase our feelings that the "opposite" sex is our opponent rather than our ally. They are manipulative because the suggested behaviors are based upon hidden agendas and trickery. All of these approaches kill love.

The truth about love is more fantastic than you have allowed yourself to dream, yet it will confirm all the inner feelings that you have had —the things you were afraid might not be true and so denied. It is worth waiting for the right person to choose to love us.

How Can We Find True Love?

Although love appears to be drowned out in our modern culture, there *are* places where it can be found. The fact is, love can be found everywhere we turn, but we have been taught not to recognize it. We have been taught to discount and destroy it when it is sparked. Yet, even though our culture has blunted our senses, blinded us, and maimed our sense of self, love still exists. Once we experience it—and we know we will—we are never the same. Even in the midst of denying our experience, it rises up in us like a wellspring when our mind is at rest.

In learning the astrology of love, we can know the deep
inner purpose of our unions and identify and release the
misunderstandings that separate us from each other.

By learning to understand what love really is, we can reinterpret our past and current relationships or prepare ourselves for the next one. By comprehending the nature of love and our ego, we can learn to develop stable relationships based on trust. In learning the astrology of love, we can know the deep inner purpose of our unions and identify and release the misunderstandings that separate us from each other. Then we can heal them by shedding a compassionate light upon the hurt and fear that create a wall between us.

When Love Begins

Love is an infinitely available, ever-flowing, and healing energy. It rejuvenates, invigorates, awakens, fulfills, and inspires. It brings joy, happiness, serenity, and knowing.

Something happens when we enter the magical world of love. It may happen when we first meet our beloved, or the love may sleep for months, even years, before it is triggered into our awareness. When it is triggered, something beautiful happens: An inner connection develops between the souls of the two lovers. The cord that has always connected them is quickened, and a harmonic resonance is induced. This inner connection opens up a channel of nonverbal communication that results in *mirroring*. Mirroring is a process where we are in constant inner contact with our beloved. Feelings, thoughts, impulses, and experiences are transmitted through the inner channel along the cords that develop. We measure and compare our nature with our partner's. We feel how they will respond to various parts of ourselves, and we try ourselves out on them energetically, shooting streamers of colored light to them and receiving their streamers back, no matter how far away. We know a person energetically long before we know them with our minds, and it is the inner connection through which this energetic knowing develops. We become more and more tuned in to each other as the connection grows. The streamers strengthen and the cords multiply as we come to know each other. This is one of the reasons why we are so eager to know and be with our partner at first. They are great mysteries that we can feel but have not yet come to know with our minds.[2]

This connection actually exists between ourselves and every other person on the planet. However, most of us are not aware of our connectedness. The inner bond is stronger with family and loved ones—people with whom we share more karmic ties, more past-life experiences and current soul agreements. As we mature, the close bonds we form out of free will with our peers assume greater importance.

> *In a healthy relationship, where relating occurs from the True Selves of the partners, the connection grows and supports us, communicating thoughts and feelings.*

The inner connection is nourishing to each partner, which is why we feel so incredibly energized by love. Conversely, when a relationship breaks up, or when it becomes ego-centered, we can feel tired. If a relationship is broken off suddenly, the cords that develop between ourselves and our part-

---

[2] Mirroring and development of the inner connection is part of the meaning found in the Lovers card of the Tarot.

ner are cut; as a result, we may feel adrift and purposeless, tired and empty as the energetic interaction is removed. However, as we heal, we fill in the gaps left by our beloved, and our energy returns.

In a healthy relationship, where relating occurs from the True Selves of the partners, the connection grows and supports us, communicating thoughts and feelings. It is also experienced as mutual attraction. We may feel in awe of the power and depth of our feelings for each other. We feel our beloved is unique on the face of the earth, that we have been guided to meet and fulfill a purpose together. We may sense a soul recognition, that we have known our partner across many lifetimes.

True love relationships are based on deep soul connections. Before we are born, we gather together with those whom we plan to incarnate with, and develop soul agreements. These agreements exist between ourselves and our parents, siblings, children, lovers—all of those with whom we spend an appreciable amount of time have an agreement with us. An agreement carries in it the things the relationship will naturally focus on. Since our souls want to evolve, to learn about how to love and be more whole, an agreement will usually focus on lessons to be learned and challenges to be met. It may involve balancing karma, giving back what has been taken unfairly. It also comes out of the great love that the souls have for each other and the true caring that they have for each other's growth.

It can be challenging to perceive whether or not a certain relationship can truly fulfill the goals of our True Selves. There are ways to decide if we are in a healthy relationship, which I will discuss shortly.

In our love relationships, we may have several people with whom we have agreements, or with whom we can keep an agreement, but they may not all be fulfilled. All our agreements are conditional: We have free will to step into the agreement. We may choose not to participate in the relationship and the agreement it offers us. Sometimes the personality senses that the challenges in the relationship will be great and therefore shies away from the opportunities it offers. In a soul-centered relationship, there is usually a sense that our partner is exactly the right person for us at this time, presenting to us the most important opportunities for spiritual growth that could be imagined. This feeling generally leads us into the relationship despite our misgivings.

For example, a soul may agree to work on its ability to love unconditionally in this lifetime. Other souls to whom it is tied may agree to assist in the process. Once on Earth, the person may come upon one or more of these souls in their life, choosing each time whether or not to fulfill the agreement with this one at the time. Often, it takes more than one relationship (or lifetime) to "get" the lesson, so there may be more than one person with whom we have agreed to take on this great task.

Always, however, we have free will to choose whether or not to step into each true love relationship, or even to learn the lesson. The soul will always urge us to, and we will generally feel drawn to do so. We will feel more joy and centeredness if we enter into such a relationship.

Within each soul-to-soul bond, there are always "sub-clauses" to the agreement, such as: "If we come together, we also agree to work as a team in service to others. And remember that lifetime when you stuck me with the kids while you went to war and never returned? Well, you agree to stick around this time (I know you want to), and I agree to overcome my resentment toward you for abandoning us."

The inner connection is mutual, not one-sided. If the attraction flows only one way, it may be because there is an early intuition of the relationship's challenges, and the other partner decides not to embrace it. However, even here, there will be some initial signs that the bond is mutual. If we feel a love for a person who truly does not share our feelings, we are identifying with a part of them that really exists in ourselves, and the challenge of the situation is to love that part of ourselves and move on to a mutually fulfilling relationship.

Just as the inner connection allows all the great, love-based feelings to flow freely, so too can it carry messages of distrust, fear, anger, doubt, and careless disregard. Although we start out in the magical world of love overflowing, our egos do not support our remaining there. Soon, doubts arise. Our past experiences come back to haunt us. All the strategies and formulae, all the cautions we learned about how to succeed in love creep back in. We want to hold on to the feelings, but we fear loss and abandonment yet again. We begin to back-pedal and become defensive.

The issue is even more confused when the soul-based feelings are replaced by the hope and unrealistic optimism of the ego as white-knight rescuer. We can see all that our love could be, "if only . . ." True, soul-level love neither hopes nor fears. It recognizes what is real, even as it loves completely. It knows how far to go to keep us safe—it never places us at risk physically, emotionally, or spiritually.

When love begins, the false self is temporarily displaced from its usual position on the throne of the self. The True Self comes through, and we experience who we really are for a time. However, the false self senses the power of love and how it has lost control; it creates opposition to the love relationship in the form of doubts. Our logical mind and conditioning from the past remind us of what has gone before, how things turned out badly in the past.

This results in a personal crisis—a choice between the ego-mask and our inner sense of what is real. How we deal with this personal crisis depends on how aware we are of what the real issue is. How we respond and learn to love and trust over time determines how successful our relationship will be. Although we all start our relationships in this manner, sooner or later we learn to set aside the false self in order to meet our true needs. Although it is an on-again, off-again process, we make gradual progress toward dislodging the ego, allowing it less and less power in our lives. Once we begin to turn inside and have faith in our inner reality, our love relationship flowers.

First Impressions

Our first soul-level impression of a person is the most accurate. This ties in with the fact that we first recognize our bond with each other from the soul level. First impressions could also be called *soul impressions*, because, before the ego locks in again, the soul sees deeply into our beloved's nature.

The phrase "love is blind" refers to this phenomenon and the fact that the Soul is not always present in our partner's behaviors. We have a very human tendency to want to think only the best of our beloved, even at our own peril. It is important to connect our soul-level impressions with the present-day reality of our beloved's nature. Even though, upon first impression, we see the other's truest nature, as the relationship develops, it is important—if sometimes painful and difficult—to acknowledge behaviors of our beloved's false self that may get in the way of a true love relationship, or even endanger us.

Allowing Your Love to Blossom

To allow love to flower, we have to be willing to grow beyond what we have already learned in our lives. Once our ego-based doubts arise, we feel conflicted about the opposing realities presented by the two parts of self, and we don't know which way to go. The new path of the True Self seems risky and unreal, but it appeals to something deep inside. The ego-path seems safe because it is familiar; doubt seems to protect us from the pain that could come again through our new partner. Doubts also cloud our perceptions through the inner channel, further masking the love that was so recently born. It is little wonder that we fall back on what we have learned in the past, the reality of the false self.

Yet it is testimony to the power of love that it continues to resurface like a cork on the water. We may try to suppress it, but it comes up again and again. Eventually, we begin to believe in it, to trust our feelings. As we come to know our beloved, we learn to trust them. These occurrences reinforce our inner feelings, and the ego is slowly displaced. Moment by moment, we make the choice between the false and True selves over and over again. It is how we make these small choices that determines whether we reinforce the true love relationship—the soul-level communion—or invoke the ego-based relationship in its place.

The Qualities of Love

It is essential for us to recognize the qualities that must exist for the true love relationship to realize itself. Eventually we come to know what it *feels* like to be in the state of Love, but before we have it stabilized in our lives, it helps to consider what those qualities are.

Trust—The most important quality in a love relationship is trust. Trust is inextricably linked with love, since it is impossible to love without being able to trust. Trust is the knowledge that we are safe with our partner, that they will do nothing to harm us, and that we can show who we are to them without disguise or pretense. This does not mean that we, or our partner, do not make mistakes; only that we are willing to see beyond them and suspend our negative responses so that we have time to see our errors and grow to new levels. Trust allows us to hold a vision of the way the bond can be and to know that all experiences are a part of the process leading to union. Trust is the foundation for all other positive qualities of the love relationship.

Loyalty—Loyalty means respecting and supporting our partner. This quality cannot exist until we are willing to trust that our true inner feelings are correct. If we do not trust and honor ourselves, we will abandon our inner truth about the relationship the first time our partner commits an error in loving. Loyalty allows us to continue to love even when difficulties arise and is based upon loyalty to ourselves.

Acceptance—Acceptance is a quiet form of love that speaks to the openness that must exist for the relationship to flourish. Akin to tolerance, it means to be open to all the conditions of your partner's life, to honor them as they are, and to acquiesce to their right to maintain sovereignty over their own affairs. This does not mean, however, the acceptance of conditions that are debasing to you or that impinge upon your own right to self-sovereignty.

Gratitude—Gratitude is an attunement to what our partner has to offer us and a remembrance that they have chosen to remain in our lives in order to share themselves with us. Gratitude does not mean to fawn over our beloved, but to hold and express appreciation for them and the spark of the Creative that they are.

Equality and Reciprocity—For love to exist, we must hold ourselves and our partners as equals. Just as we must not submit to power plays by our partner, neither must we expect our beloved to acquiesce to any that we might devise, however unwittingly. Equality also means to expect to contribute equally to the relationship. This quality of "coming to meet halfway"[3] is a cornerstone of all true love, which welcomes the expression

---

[3] This term comes from the I Ching, the Chinese Book of Changes, and its application in a love relationship is explained by Carol K. Anthony in *Love, an Inner Connection.*

of each person's unique nature as both part of, and separate from, the love relationship. True love will never dominate or force another in any way. Without reciprocity, the inner love circuit cannot be completed.

Honesty and Openness—Honesty is the ability to be truthful to ourselves in order to nurture an atmosphere of openness between ourselves and our beloved. Honesty does not mean divulging information in an unfeeling or careless manner. Rather, it is a willingness to adhere to our own sense of truth, while being aware that it may not match our partner's. It is being able to look within and face what we see there, and to observe what we see in our partner with truth that does not judge. Without honesty, trust and the atmosphere of openness cannot exist.

Humility—Humility is modesty that stems from a respectful awareness of our entire nature, including our flaws and errors. It is not humiliation, the shame-based feeling that comes from self-judgment or the judgment of others. If we are honest with ourselves, humility is a natural part of our character. When we can see how we have made mistakes and how long it has taken us to grow, we cannot help but approach our partner and their mistakes with an attitude of humility.

Forgiveness—If we approach life with humility, forgiveness will be a natural outgrowth of that attitude, for as we have learned from our own mistakes and forgiven ourselves, so can we be tolerant of others' growth processes and forgive our beloved once they have returned to the correct attitude in relating to us. An ongoing attitude of openness, humility, and forgiveness creates the space for this to happen.

Sensitivity—All of these qualities imply sensitivity, an attunement to our beloved and their inner nature. We must attempt to see into the situations that arise and discover their source. We must try to be aware of our partner's openings and closings to us, maintaining a mindful distance or stepping into the joy of their heartspace when invited. If we are sensitive to our partner's needs, we know when it is important to allow them the time and space to grow on their own.

We must also balance our sensitivity to our partner with our sensitivity to our own needs. Too much attention to our partner's needs can tip the scales away from the equality we need to keep our individuality and our relationship strong.

Justice—A sense of fair play is necessary in any true love relationship. Without a willingness to overcome our own vanity and arrogance, we cannot enter into a relationship on a just basis. We must be willing to be fair, to contribute equally, and to own our own qualities and errors. Perhaps most difficult of all, we must be firm in establishing and holding to our boundaries of what is fair in relating to each other—what we can and cannot do in a love relationship.

Where a partnership is especially deep, the lessons taken on may relate to strongly held misunderstandings, and it may take especially long to understand what is lacking and correct it.

Patience and Perseverance—It goes almost without saying that patience is the glue that holds everything together. The amount of patience required is directly proportional to the depth of the bond. Where a partnership is especially deep, the lessons taken on may relate to deeply held misunderstandings, and it may take especially long to understand what is lacking and correct it. Holding to the relationship through the long adversity that may accompany this process is its own lesson.

Impatience is weak, because in choosing it, we are saying, "I don't believe we can ever get there," and it leads us to use force. We have allowed ourselves to want or accept our partner when our ego is still in charge. Patience allows us to persevere, to see our relationship through to the end and outlast the obstacles that we inevitably lay in each other's paths to loving each other.

Patience is a virtue when it is combined with actions that keep us safe. If we use patience as an excuse to stay in an unsafe relationship, neither we nor our partners can grow.

Self-Responsibility—Being self-responsible means owning what is ours. We take responsibility for our flaws, admit to our mistakes, and face the parts of ourselves that we discover need correcting as we grow. If we can be responsible for ourselves, many of the qualities already mentioned follow naturally. We cannot be responsible for ourselves if we avoid being honest, humble, patient, and persevering—expressing all the other qualities that foster good relationships.

The Ego-Based Relationship

Due to our lack of understanding and training, most relationships start as soul bonds and become ego-based. An ego-based relationship begins the moment we allow the voice of the false self to overrule that of the True Self. While we may not be able to completely silence the false self, we can learn to expect its arguments, to recognize its plaintive tone, and to quiet it. Ego-based relationships have several core characteristics:

- Lack of trust between partners—may show up as suspicions, controlling behavior, or sometimes the creation of a gulf or wall between the partners, resulting in a loss of intimacy or estrangement

- Doubt of self and partner

- Power struggles, where one partner attempts to control or dominate the other

- Forming a faction against the world

- A loss of energy; emotional starvation; a feeling of barrenness

- Unequal energy flow between partners—one person primarily giving and the other mostly receiving; a lack of reciprocity

The Masks of the Ego

There are many disguises that the ego wears in order to hide its true nature, its inevitable hand in the death of love. They are effective because we neither recognize them nor understand how to disarm them. The ego is constantly seeking to protect and perpetuate itself, all the while leading us to think that it is ourselves that it wants to protect and defend, and that it will lead us to love. If we allow it to control our behavior, the ego may:

- constantly seek to justify itself.
- be narcissistic (think only of itself and its interests).
- be ready to quit at a moment's notice.
- want instant results and gratification.
- compare and compete, becoming jealous if it is not "winning."
- be possessive.
- be goal-oriented and want to follow the most direct path to its goal, no matter what the costs.
- fear risk.
- presume more than its due.
- be intolerant and impatient.
- be arrogant when things go well, yet depressed when they go badly.
- be invested in appearances.
- constantly seek recognition, approval, and support.
- try to force matters, however inconspicuously.
- refuse to take responsibility for its own errors; be quick to blame others.
- make threats and/or vows; take rigid positions.
- become mired in the current moment; see things as unchangeable.
- hide its vulnerability behind walls.
- fear rejection, abandonment, and neglect.
- base its value on what others think.
- pose as the great hero-rescuer who can rectify any situation with sweeping reforms.

It is important to recognize our own and our partner's ego masks so that we can avoid encouraging the ego's engagement in the relationship. This is the first step to building the relationship based on the soul level of interaction.

Taking the Soul's Path to Love

A cursory glance at the list of qualities and masks in the ego-based relationship should tell us that the pitfalls are many and the challenges great when we fall in love. How do we avoid these traps? How can we take the Soul's path of love in our relationships?

If you recall, we start our relationships already on that high road. Without that first cosmic impulse of love, we would not have been drawn together, felt so filled with wonder, or been so deeply touched. We would not know what the soul's path feels like without this quickening experience. Although the ego eventually appears on the scene to create the dilemma of which road to take, we can learn to choose that of the soul.

Loving Wisely

At birth, we are pure, unconditional love. However, as we grow, love becomes a conditional experience for most of us, and we develop the false self to meet the conditions for love.

As we mature, it is our duty to ourselves to uncover the True Self. It is a natural part of life, to instinctively seek to unlearn the things that are not a part of who we really are. As we uncover the True Self, we rediscover our ability to love, to be Love.

At birth, we are pure, unconditional love.

True love is experienced and expressed through an open heart. In addition to being an organ on the physical level, it is an energetic doorway on more subtle levels. When we fall in love, the heart opens. It remains open as long as we feel love. When we experience doubt or other negative emotions, it closes. When we are in our heart, we are in our True Self, able to care for ourselves and others in perfect balance.

The challenge in developing the soul-level relationship is to maintain our openness without harming ourselves, to keep the heart an open window for giving and receiving love. However, many people give from an open heart without discrimination. It is good to love others unconditionally, but it is not good to engage in relationships unconditionally. To do so may be to martyr ourselves to a situation that is unhealthy. It is necessary to be aware of how others approach us. If they are not sincere, sensitive, respect-ful, and fair to us, then we throw ourselves away if we love them without restriction. We lose our center, give away our power, and forfeit our self-esteem when we express love to someone who has not earned it through cultivating the proper attitude.

How do we know where to draw the line? The simplest answer is to lis-ten within. There are signals that we all give ourselves when we give our power away, whether it is in a love relationship or in some other arena. In developing the false self, we have learned to ignore those signals. When we throw ourselves away, we may feel alienated, cheated, cheapened, empty, or compromised. We may feel like indulging in an addictive behavior. It caus-es us to seek answers outside ourselves because there is so much emptiness within.

Addictive behaviors and feelings such as alienation and
emptiness signal the absence of something. They tell us
that we have lost the full, balanced heart that is able to
love another and honor the self at the same time.

These feelings and behaviors signal the *absence* of something. They tell us that we have lost the full, balanced heart that is able to love another and honor the self at the same time.

Loving wisely does not mean putting conditions on love. It means to observe what is happening in the arena of love. If what we see does not come from sincerity, sensitivity, and reciprocity—if the heart is not able to spontaneously open and freely give and receive love—then we must simply hold ourselves in reserve. This means remaining loyal to the relationship while sometimes needing to step away when we are compromised or harmed. When we are in friendly reserve, we hold heartspace for our beloved to return to the path of love. Our heart remains open, our love is still there, but we are not required to share that space, that love with the other, until they begin to act correctly. This means that they must return to relating from their True Self so that the relationship can return to complete reciprocity and soul-level interaction.

If we are the one who is harming the relationship, we must go to the root of this part of our ego structure to find how we can correct ourselves.

When we return to the soul's path of love, we feel secure and equal. There is no power struggle, no need to "win" or dominate. Our trust in each other is complete because we approach each other with sensitivity and sincerity. We feel valued and recognized; no strategies or schemes need be applied. Love springs spontaneously and organically from within each of us, and the circuit connecting us is complete.

No relationship can exist between our True Self and the other's ego. We love unwisely when our partner's ego is present and we give in an open, loving way. It sends the signal that the presence of the partner's ego is acceptable, rather than harmful, to the relationship and our self-esteem.

So it is necessary to tune in to where our beloved is. Are they sincere? Sensitive? By tuning in, we keep ourselves physically, emotionally, and spiritually safe, and the relationship is mutually healthy.

There is a difference between sincere and heartfelt regard and the good manners and flattery that the false self may have developed in response to the demands of society. The difference is the depth and intention of the behavior. "Social graces," if they do not come from our sincere need to honor the other person, do not emanate from the True Self; they often have control and desire (ego-based) energy attached to them. When we perform in this way, we mask our real feelings and keep our partner from knowing us as we truly are. In a relationship built on trust and love, there is nothing to fear from revealing the full range of our nature in a responsible and respectful way, and to ask for what we want and need. In the same light, expecting our partner to be polite—or to perform according to any of our expectations—takes away their inner dignity, their right to self-determination. Even if they (or we) fall into a negative pattern, acceptance and holding heartspace for the other will draw them eventually back to the path of love. To be sincere, we must allow our partner and ourselves to give up these rote behaviors.

Difficult Beginnings

Although we may not recognize it, the most difficult and perilous times in a relationship are at its outset. If we do not deal forthrightly with each issue as it arises, our relationship becomes mired before it gets a chance to blossom. In most relationships, trust is never developed, and the egos' struggle for dominance is never quelled. The two people in the relationship work against each other until they finally give up on their love, not understanding what's happening or how to alter the pattern. They may live in a cold war or break off the relationship altogether.

Yet, these difficulties can, and are meant to, be overcome. If we work steadily on clearing our doubts and reservations, our old-relationship pain, and our hopes and expectations, then we can fulfill the promise that the new relationship holds. A long-standing relationship can also be resurrected from the downward spiral begun by our egos using the same method. While it may be difficult and painful at first, a conscious effort by both partners, each sincerely wishing to improve their union, will ultimately clear all obstacles. If we want change and our partner is reluctant, it is necessary for us to hold a loving space for our beloved in reserve, ready for the time of their return to us. This does not mean "saving ourselves" for a person who is not ready to return our love, but to go on our way, prepared to be open if and when the time is right.

We see ourselves mirrored in the other's nature. We also see things in them that we don't understand, which throw us off balance. When we know the other so little, we have no context with which to comprehend their actions. We place their behaviors in the realm of "what it meant when someone did that before" or "what it would mean if I did that." We may take misguided actions personally and feel wounded by our beloved. We may be poised to reject the other before we are rejected.

Once the essential trust is established, on which all soul-centered relationships are founded, we feel safe enough to love and commit ourselves to our partner. During the trust-building phase, we must love wisely. We do not want to give love to our partner without restraint if they are not in the right attunement to us. We hold ourselves in reserve to give our partner the time and space to grow. In this way, they can learn how to love, just as we can. At the same time, we must view our beloved's mistakes moderately, being ready to forgive. We should keep in mind that we, too, have made and will continue to make mistakes. We also hold heartspace, keeping our inner connection intact. We protect the warmth we feel toward our partner from our ego's grievances or the complaints of others.

It is therefore important to let go of our negative thoughts and feelings as they arise. It is a part of being human to have them, but we can choose what to do with them—whether to hold on to them and build a case against our beloved, or to listen to the messages they give us about what we are experiencing and then let them go.

Resolving Trust Issues

Everyone recognizes that when we love, we can experience hurt. Because of this risk, we tend to approach love with conditions and reservations. "She's too beautiful." "He's too young." "I could never have a relationship with someone like him." "She could never accept my kids." "If he tells me what to do one time, I'm out of here." "If she ever tries to stop me from going out with the guys, I'm gone."

These doubts are a natural by-product of the fact that we have not yet learned to trust each other. Trust and doubt cannot co-exist. If the doubts that each of us brings to a relationship are not brought to light and dispelled, the trust that is vital to the true love relationship cannot develop.

We are taught in this culture to rush into our relationships.
Yet, only allowing our relationships to develop over time
will allow all our reservations to be removed.

We are taught in this culture to rush into our relationships. We look on in awe at the friends who boast that they were married three weeks after they met. We are taught to value instant results over the rewards of slow maturation. Yet it is only when we allow our relationships to develop over time that all our reservations—blocks to trust and love—can be removed. As long as our trust remains incomplete, we are on guard against hurt—defensive, even suspicious and possessive.

When we rush into a relationship, becoming intimate too soon, it is because we have learned to disregard our own need to love safely. We have fallen prey to the romantic notion that love can overcome all, but rushing in too quickly overburdens the relationship and causes it to burn out quickly. Our culture has given its blessing to sexual intimacy early on in a relationship, and it is often awkward to delay sexual interaction until trust is built. But when we engage in sex before trust is established, we've given in to the ego's desires. The morning after brings the well-known reaction of withdrawal, and many relationships end there, despite the desires of the partners involved. While such obstacles can be surmounted, it is only with great effort that the damage can be reversed and the health of the relationship restored. It is far better to wait for the right level of trust to be established, preserving the inner dignity of each person and the sacredness of that most precious offering: giving our most private vulnerable self to another through sexual union.

> ***Dominance is the ego's ultimate weapon against loss of control of the self.***

Power Struggles

When egos are involved in a relationship, they lead to a struggle for dominance, or one partner submits to the other's power. This is because egos recognize their vulnerability and seek to protect themselves. This protectiveness closes off the love, the inner connection, between the partners. The power struggle is the effort to maintain or bring back the power we had in the other's life when we were first in love. Dominance is the ego's ultimate weapon against loss of control of the self. If love unseats it, then it must seek to control the relationship if it is to return to its seat of control. When one partner comes to dominate the other, it destroys trust, equality, reciprocity and, ultimately, love. Power struggles can be subtle, unspoken battles—a "cold war" that separates us from our beloved and destroys intimacy. If we experience this type of "walling off" in our relationship, however imperceptible, a power struggle is present.

The beginning of a relationship is when it is easiest to establish things on the right footing. We must be careful to attune to what the other is really offering, be able to focus on it with clarity, and be patient in allowing the relationship to develop, letting go as your partner strays, forgiving transgressions as they return to sincere and sensitive relating. When *we* stray, we know that it is important for us to take the time to grow as well.

Entering Each Other's Heartspace

When we love and are open to another, we readily let them into our heartspace. We share ourselves as we are, without inhibition, without performing. It is wonderful to share our inner heart with someone and to be allowed into their heartspace as well. Here love can be shared without reserve; the ego cannot enter the inner heart.

However, once we have been admitted to our beloved's heartspace, we cannot presume to enter any time we wish. We must wait to be invited. To force our way in—to insist upon intimacy, especially that which is unwelcome—is to invade or encroach upon the other person. This reduces their inner dignity, because they have given up their right to self-determination if we enter without their consent. Encroachment has no place in the soul-centered relationship, since it is a ploy of the ego.

Once we are a partner in a relationship, we cannot presume to be entitled to anything. We do not own or possess certain territory or have certain rights to our partner. We must wait for their invitation to share those sacred rights and territories, even as we trust that they will eventually do so.

If we become arrogant and make uninvited claims, we will be blocked or pushed away by our partner, for they instinctively recognize the injustice of the situation. Stepping back to a respectful distance will allow our beloved's openness to be restored to us at the earliest possible time.

The Anatomy of Soul-Centered Love

Love gives space; it does not invade or force. It is sensitive to what's right for the moment and humble enough to accept that we are not always invited into our partner's heartspace. It trusts the other and has faith that love and the Higher Power can help us to work things out. It also trusts that we would not be led into the relationship for no good reason. It respects the other as an equal and wants to preserve their dignity without throwing ours away.

Love gives space; it does not invade or force.

Love is strong; it is loyal and willing to contribute equally to the relationship. Love is patient and forgiving, for when we remember how long it took us to grow and how difficult it was, we can understand our partner's struggles and the time it takes to grow. Love honors the True Self of each person and does not require us to throw ourselves away in order to preserve the relationship.

The Love Union

After some time, the true love relationship brings the couple together. Where pride and trust barriers are small, this will not take long (although it will undoubtedly seem long to the ego). The relationship will develop in a back-and-forth, meeting-and-retreating fashion that is the natural rhythm of all relationships. Yet there will be gradual, often imperceptible progress toward the love union. In the process, there will be times when it is part of the rhythm to open the heartspace for our partner. At other times, we will need to step back into our own space and close that door until our partner becomes sensitive and open again.

It is the challenge of the blossoming relationship for each partner to develop softness and flexibility in these roles, until each one can play either role in less extreme ways at various times.

We may also find that one person plays the yin (receptive) role, while the other plays the yang (active) role. The yin partner tends to hold the space of the relationship more, to be more attuned to its inner process, and to have a tendency to become dependent in relationships. The yang partner is more likely to focus on outward expression, resist entering into the relationship, have more obvious barriers, and to deny the relationship as a whole.

It is the challenge of the blossoming relationship for each partner to develop softness and flexibility in these roles, until each one can play either role in less extreme ways at various times. By opening to their partner's sensitivity and retreating before their ego, we encourage this flexibility and resilience to develop in the relationship.

The development of most relationships is fraught with mistakes on the part of both partners. We need to have a forgiving attitude in the face of our beloved's attempts to correct their behavior.[4] It is only through making mistakes that we learn to understand ourselves and our partner. We learn through pain how that pain is created and how not to recreate it. We learn to love in a way that we did not know before.

It is not as hard as you think. Throughout all the tribulations of the early stages of a relationship (or later stages in a relationship that has lost its footing in the soul realms), the inner connection holds the lovers to each other. When we are in a positive frame of mind about our partner, we automatically respond in perfect accord to the energy felt through the inner channel. Even if the relationship is one where deep-seated wounds are being healed and a great deal of time is absorbed in breaking these down, the unseen energetic connection that we share with our partner keeps the bond between us flowing and growing, even when we lose touch with it.

When the veils and masks of the ego have been dissolved, the love bond is free to fulfill itself. The inner reality becomes the external reality. We clear the decks for our new love, and old relationships fall away. Each lover stands before the other, unencumbered and open. All the powerful sensations and inner knowing are acknowledged, and the love flows forth into the world.

Our primary job is to maintain our own
attunement to ourselves and to our partner.

Maintaining Our Love

Once established, our work in our relationship doesn't really change. The ego would like to assert itself by saying, "Ah, now I can relax and enjoy. I don't have to work on this anymore." However, our relationship work is never done. Our primary job in it is to maintain our own attunement to ourselves and to our partner. This automatically keeps us in harmony with our partner. We must keep the ego at bay: It may issue its protestations of doubt and its proclamations of final victory, and we will never completely silence it. But if we remain alert to its disguises, we can overrule its attempts to gain control of our life.

---

[4] We must at all times keep ourselves safe, and if any of the incorrect behaviors are abusive, it is essential to seek professional help to protect ourselves and assist us in healing. It is possible to correct even the most difficult relationship, but it must be done in absolute safety.

When we go the way of the ego, we lose our sense of being connected. To regain that connection, we must once again find out how the ego has lured us, and correct our thoughts about our partner and ourselves. We cannot succeed in reestablishing the connection by trying to love the other (feel what isn't there) or find fault with them. We need to look within, not without.

When negative feelings surface, we can choose to follow and feed them, or disengage from them and observe them. With the right tools, skills, and guidance, we can disperse these feelings and find the core fear-based beliefs that underlie them. It is sometimes sufficient, but always necessary, to simply choose to leave the doubts unappeased. At all times, it is important to honor who we are and what we experience as an important and worthy part of our growth process. We all make mistakes; if we are not making mistakes, we are not learning, or growing, or enjoying life.

We are who we are in our partnerships because in some way our partner needs us to be that way.

When We Change . . .

We are always changing. We never stop growing, even when we want to do so. If we feel discontented with our relationship or something else in our life, we have a tendency to want something to change. We have usually been taught to try to change what is around us; if we don't like what is around us, it seems natural to change that thing. However, change in a relationship isn't like changing our living room decor. We can't just replace our partner with someone else and expect a better relationship. Nor can we simply tell our partner what they need to change and expect that to be the end of it.

Relationship means *existing in symbiosis with our partner*—therefore, what one does profoundly affects the other. This is especially true on the energetic level, which is not often apparent to us. Thus, what one partner does, the other experiences in ways they may not be aware of. We are who we are in our partnerships *because in some way our partner needs us to be that way*. Conversely, if we want our partner to change, they may not be able to, since we have in some way, perhaps unconsciously, encouraged them to fulfill that role. Similarly, if we want to change, it may be difficult because our partner needs us to play our current role.

If we want our relationship to be different, it won't work to ask our partner to "just change." We have cooperated with our partner in their being that way. Our behavior is in lock-step with theirs. So, if we want them to change, it is simplest to change ourselves. When we change, it frees our partner to change as well. If it is a change for the better for us, it will feel good to our partner, too, once they adjust to the new reality that is created.

When our partner first notices a change in us, they may feel threatened by the newness of it, because it is not the comfortable (even if painful or negative) old way of being. Even positive changes are unlikely to be welcomed initially by our partner. The first thing they may try to do is to change us back. This is baffling, because they may have said not minutes before that they want us to change in just this way. However, when faced with the reality of it, it feels unsafe *at first*. Give your partner time—they will adjust to the change, and you will be closer than before.

What's going on when a change occurs? One of the most common forms of change occurs when we take back a role given to our partner. Since projection is part of every relationship, as we grow, we must take back responsibility for those parts of ourselves that we have given to our partner. When we take a role back, our partner may feel a little more empty than before because we have been dependent on them to fulfill that role. They may also feel threatened, as if we are challenging their "right" to fulfill that role, or rejected, as if suddenly they are not fulfilling their "job" in the relationship adequately. For instance, let's say that we have been letting our partner take care of all the cooking, and suddenly we recognize that we have not been carrying our share of the effort, in spite of their request that we do so. We decide to help out by doing some of the cooking. Our partner may not perceive this as a sincere effort to help at first, especially if we have resisted in the past. However, by continuing to show how earnest we are in wanting to carry our share of the load, our partner will eventually come to accept our willingness to grow in the relationship in this way.

Even if change threatens the balance of a relationship, it is a must for the relationship to continue to be relevant and alive. Life changes, and we must change, too. Change never stops (and must never stop).

When Love Ends

Sometimes, for whatever reason, love relationships end. The inner connection fades, or to continue in active loving would be unwise. Even if a relationship must end, we can accept it as we do other completions in our life. We remember it, learn from it, and work on resolving our feelings of pain and negativity so we can move on to another love when the time is right.

Sometimes we continue to feel a bond with the person from whom we are parted. Sometimes we know that the bond cannot be fulfilled in the foreseeable future, if ever in this lifetime. It is not necessary to stop loving that person in order to love another. It is essential, however, to resolve our love feelings so that we can move on and make room for a new primary love bond in our life. Knowing that we are bonded to some extent to all people, the old relationship can be placed on the same par as other such bonds.

On an energetic level, especially if the relationship is ended abruptly, the cords that connect us to each other can be pulled out or cut off, leaving us feeling empty, alone, and unnourished. It can take time to heal the wounds left by such an unexpected disconnection. Being aware of what is happening energetically helps in the healing of the wounds. Gaining the assistance of professionals will speed up the healing and ease the pain of the completion process.[5]

No matter where we are or what we've done in our love relationship, we can rectify the situation by correcting ourselves. Rectifying may mean to reestablish the relationship on higher ground—removing it from the realm of the ego is the healthiest thing we can do for ourselves and our partner. If we are in between relationships, increasing our attunement to the inner reality of ourselves and our past relationships can help us attract a new love relationship in its own time.

Love and the Unconscious

Alongside the inner connection that we have with others is our own hidden level of reality. A part of our communication with other people takes place on this level, which we can loosely call the unconscious. Out of this level comes those embarrassing "Freudian slips," times when we commit a

---

[5] Astrologers, healers, and psychotherapists are trained to provide such assistance.

verbal faux pas that reveals how we really feel about something, much to our horror! This level speaks to us all the time in many ways, and if we know how to tune into it, we can read other people as well. In anyone, the needs of the unconscious are basic and simple: to survive, to be loved. The more we accept this part of ourselves and others, the less it will surprise us in unpleasant ways, and the easier it will be to meet those needs.

In relationships, it is important to know that we communicate unconsciously all the time. It's the part of us that spots someone across the room at a party whom we've never met before but who fits all those old relationship patterns we'd rather not remember.

This helps us to understand how we can attract the "same" person to ourselves time and again. The individual may have a different body, but sure enough, they have the same personality and bad habits, try as you might to avoid it! The bad news is that we are the true source of our relationships. But this is the good news as well, because if something comes from within us, then we have the power to change it.

When we are attracted to someone, they will bring a blend of qualities that fits who we are at the time. It is part of the magic of the unconscious part of ourselves that we are able to create a relationship that so exactly matches what we need to learn.

Projection, the process by which we see aspects of ourselves in another person without recognizing them as our own, also plays a role in how our partner is drawn to us. If we cannot accept the part of our nature that is similar to that of our mother, for example, our partner may seem uncannily like her.

Me, You, and Us

When two people meet, a third entity is formed that takes on a life of its own and has its own personality, needs, and purpose. This is the relationship. From the time you meet, it seems to want to go in its own direction. It is as if there were a real third person mediating between the two of you in its own way. We could say that it is created as a result of the cross-section that is formed between the two of you as unique individuals; no two individuals could come together in quite the same way, nor can either one of you go to someone else and have quite the same relationship. If you let the relationship guide you, you will always be in tune with yourself and your partner. To hear the guidance it offers, you must be at the soul level. If you are in the ego, you will not be able to hear it.

Astrology's Role in Relationships

The astrological charts of ourselves and our partners provide a guidepost for assessing how a relationship will work and what its purpose is. It does not tell us whether or not the relationship will work—this truth lies in the realm of free will.

The astrological charts of ourselves and our partners provide a guidepost for assessing how a relationship will work and what its purpose is. It does not tell us whether or not the relationship will work—this truth lies in the realm of free will.

How a relationship works depends on what each person brings to the relationship. The same person can bring much more potential for success to a relationship if at some earlier point they have made the decision to grow toward understanding themselves and being a better person. In astrology, we cannot tell by looking at the chart whether or not that person has made that decision, and how far they have come in realizing their self-knowledge. So, from an astrological perspective, the success of a relationship depends on how each person uses their chart—what choices they make—as much as what the chart says our potential is.

This is good news because it means that we can make positive use of anything the cosmos has handed to us. Although some things in our chart will take more inner work than others, everything can be adjusted to bring about a positive result. This is the work of you and your astrologer—to find the best way to use every part of your chart. In relationships, although no one can assure what our partner will do, our astrologer, and this book can help us to identify those areas where we are likely to project our nature onto our partner, what issues underlie the projection, and how to re-own those parts of self. It can help us identify the soul-level agreement that we hold with our partner—the purpose of our relationship—and discover what makes the relationship work the way it does. It can help us uncover the hidden motivations of our partnership as well. Looking at our motivations in relationships, usually based on lofty ideals and worthy inner goals, can bring us back to the original, unique purpose for seeking union to begin with.

A Working Relationship

Although the factors are more complex on the surface, a soul-centered relationship works on the basis of its inner connection and soul agreement. It is possible and necessary to develop skill in relating to others, particularly our beloved.

Astrology can be applied to assist us in building all of these attributes. We can come to better self-understanding by studying and working with our own chart. We can understand our partner better by coming to know their chart. We can learn about our soul agreement and our way of relating with each other by studying the way our charts connect with each other.

Many relationship counselors, including astrologers, emphasize the importance of communication. It is an essential ingredient to relationship success—but it is not the only one. Sometimes it is as important to know what *not* to communicate, as to know how *to* communicate. Try to become aware of the nonverbal levels of communication as well—in the form of the inner connection (the soul level), touch, visual cues (such as facial expressions or body language), movement, and feeling.

Same or Opposite?

We can become attracted to people in two ways. The first way is thinking that someone is similar to us—and therefore comforting. The second is perceiving that someone is different from us—and therefore fascinating. These forces are actually found on all levels of consciousness and being; they are universals. In physics, they are referred to as the forces of cohesion (like attracting like) and adhesion (unlike attracting unlike). In relationships, we can refer to them as attraction by **similarity** and **complementarity.**

Similarity is easy to understand and explain. We all feel comfortable and happy with someone who shares qualities with us. However, complementarity may not be so easy to comprehend. We have all heard the adage "opposites attract." We see it illustrated in behaviors found in the physical world, from magnets to animals. Complementarity, or "oppositeness," is no less important in human relationships.

To get to the heart of complementarity, we have to look at two related concepts, **polarity** and **opposition.** Polarity can be expressed in two ways, as either complementarity or opposition. Opposition suggests that two things are as different from each other as they can be, and implies that they may be in conflict, at least in human nature. Complementarity implies that, although two things may be different from each other, they are compatible or related. While opposites do not seem as though they are similar to complements, they are.

For example, we all think of black and white as opposites, but they are united as colors. Furthermore, each one defines the other; black would not be black as we know it without white to define it (and vice versa). It is more accurate to describe this way of looking at opposites as a polarity. The notion of polarity includes the idea that the two things connected as opposites are complementary to, or interdependent upon, each other—that is, they need each other and are defined by each other. They can exist independently, but not in the same way. In fact, we can say that a polarity involves different expressions of the same thing.

A polarity involves different expressions of the same thing.

The most important thing to realize about polarity is that the two things that are polarized are inextricably linked to each other. That is, even in their apparent dissimilarity, there is a hidden similarity. This is as true in relationships as in other parts of our experience.

Difficulties can arise, however, when we forget about the similarities between apparently opposite things. When we project qualities onto another person (see chapter 1), we tend to do so because we have two sets of qualities within ourselves that we struggle to reconcile, so we "let" someone else have one set, to reduce our inner conflict. We may, therefore, see ourselves as quite different from that other person, even though they are basically complementary to us, just as the two sets of qualities are equally conflict-free. We can see this quite clearly in our charts.

Since, when we project, we are really seeing our own traits in the other person, our task is to learn about and incorporate them into our nature.

When we see them in another person, we are attracted to this person because they can teach us about this part of who we are.

However, it is not always an easy thing to do. Often we find ourselves fulfilling the negative side of polarity, opposition. We fail to open to the differences in our partner that first attracted us. We resist incorporating those qualities into our conscious nature, unable to see that they are already there. We may even come to resent our partner for having those qualities because underneath we are jealous of their gifts. In the case of characteristics that we view as negative, we allow our vision to be filled with them because we have not yet recognized them in ourselves. Opposition will develop into alienation from our partner—it chases love away.

Opposition is a sign that love is absent; it also tells us that the ego is present. The soul has retreated from the relationship, and the partners feel abandoned by each other.

Complementarity, however, is a natural part of the soul-centered relationship. It fosters all the qualities that support soul-centered relating. It is the successful resolution of polarity, the recognition of the common ground between apparent opposites and the appreciation of their differences. In complementarity, we recognize how our partner makes up for our limitations. If we are aware of projection as an aspect of all relationships, we will know that we can see nothing in our partner that is not present in ourselves. So when we see a quality in them, we look for that quality in ourselves. If we find it undeveloped, we can study and emulate our partner and come to incorporate it into our nature. By taking responsibility for ourselves in this way, we enact complementarity. By "learning" our partner's different qualities, we remain mindful of their value. We continue to appreciate their differences. We open the doorway for our partners to reciprocate by recognizing our qualities in them and growing from those traits as well.

For example, we are attracted to someone. As we get to know them, we find that we enjoy their intelligence, their ability to speak well, and their knowledge. They may be highly educated where we are less educated, and we yearn for the missing quality. So we think we see someone who is very different from us, our "opposite," but in fact we have a great deal in common with them. What we have in common with each other is our interest in education, so we are united more powerfully than we are separated. If we use that awareness to build our own character—to lead us to get a better education, even as we value our partner for what we can learn from them—

we engage in complementarity and support the soul-centered processes in the relationship.

If we fail to respond to our partner's differences by growing toward them, we may find ourselves depending on our partner's intelligence. Instead of becoming more learned, we lean on our partner. The differences multiply, and we may come to resent them. We feel uneasy as we become alienated. We come to fear our partner's strengths instead of appreciating them. We project, and polarity takes the form of opposition; then the relationship becomes ego-centered. Our partner may come to resent us as well for having to be "the expert," not being able to rely on us more. Thus, we become frozen in our roles.

If we think that since our partner is educated we can rely on them, and so put off our own education, we are not using the complementary qualities our partner offers us to develop our own self. We are not using our partner as a guide and example, so opposition emerges. In a soul-centered relationship, where reciprocity has been developed, our partner will enjoy our creative awareness of the world. They will want to learn how to look beyond their formal approach to life—to free themselves, using us as their guide and example, from the need to know everything for their partner.

The positive use of complementarity in our relationship relies upon our willingness to take responsibility for our own growth and wholeness—self-responsibility. If we do not, our complementary aspects become opposed, and a gap grows between ourselves and our partner that drives a wedge into the relationship.

When We Attract an Opposite . . .

When we are attracted to someone who has qualities that seem opposite to ours, we are dealing with the projection of a polarity within us. As we go through life, we notice that there are some things we lack, some ways we are not perfect, and we strive to incorporate new qualities and skills into our nature to make up for our lack. It is natural that we should turn to someone who, we perceive, has those skills already intact—never dreaming that we must have the attributes as well (perhaps undeveloped), or else they would not stand out in someone else. We have projected aspects of ourselves onto our beloved; clearly, complementarity is the mechanism by which projections are worked out. The recognition and development of those desired attributes in ourselves is the healthy working out of projections in relationship.

What's Next?

Love—the true love of the soul—is the foundation of all intimate relationships. Now that you have an awareness about the inner reality of love, it is time to learn how astrology can be applied as a tool to better our way of understanding and working with this level.

All of our relationships are a blend of similarity and complementarity that is right for us at the time. There are many forms that complementarity can take. Astrology allows us to identify exactly what those forms are. We will look at astrology's take on the nature of complementarity in the next chapter.

DIVINE COMPLEMENTS
The Signs of Astrology

As previously discussed, the right balance of similarity and complementarity is essential to a healthy relationship. Just as we are attracted
to someone who is like us, it is a fact of life that we are attracted to others
who appear to hold those qualities that we lack. However, as we have seen,
opposites are not really as different from each other as they appear. It is
more accurate to describe this way of looking at opposites as *polarity*,
where two things are interdependent upon each other—they need and are
defined by each other. They can exist independently, but not in the same
way. We used the example of a relationship where we are attracted to someone who is more formally educated than ourselves. We may have always
wanted to become better schooled, while our partner may be attracted to our
fresh, creative approach to things. The common ground is an interest in education and how we see our world because of it.

Complementarity is a positive part of relationships, while opposition is
a drain on them. Which one we express depends on how we apply what we
learn through the polarity that is found in the relationship. In the example
above, if our partner learns from us while we seek to become formally educated, we strengthen the relationship through complementarity.

Complementarity in Astrology

Complementarity can be found in astrology as well as in life. Astrology is based on a circle, which is a wonderful symbol—complete in itself and never-ending, the ancient symbol of perfection. In astrology as well as ancient symbology, it is really a flat picture of a spiral, or cycle. As the sun draws a circle around us each day in the heavens, it actually describes a *cycle* as well, because each circle is progressive—it is different, and each difference is based upon the cycles that preceded it. The ancients recognized the value of showing some things in circular form, especially where time was concerned. Because the planets appear to travel around us in the "bowl" of the heavens, ticking off the same point every cycle at a predictable "time," they became our timekeepers. Our first clocks were circular, mimicking the planets' movements through the heavens. Although our modern clocks have become more sophisticated, we still use the same technique as the ancient farmer who used to say, "My son was born when the moon shone against the Scorpion, and Venus was in the western sky."

Once symbolism became attached to the pictures and planets that the ancients observed night after night, a blanket of 12 zodiac signs was pictured in the heavens, which are shown around the wheel. Since every square inch of the heavens (and your chart) is in one sign or another, each planet or point found in your chart must be in a sign. In circular images, when something is on one side of the circle, you can find its "opposite" directly across the circle from it. So, each sign has a complementary sign that is directly across the heavens from it. These are astrology's polarities. Since there are 12 signs, there are six polarities in the zodiac. They are shown below in Figure 3A. In this chart, the signs are shown in their "natural" positions—that is, starting with Aries, the first sign, in the "first" position below the ascendant. In real birth charts, however, any polarity can be found anywhere around the wheel. Although the same signs will always be opposite each other and the signs in the same order, their placement as "spokes" on the wheel varies depending on the time of day you were born. Astrologers describe the relationship of each polarity as an opposition, but we can choose whether to express them as oppositional or complementary. We can understand ourselves better by learning about the complementarities in astrology.

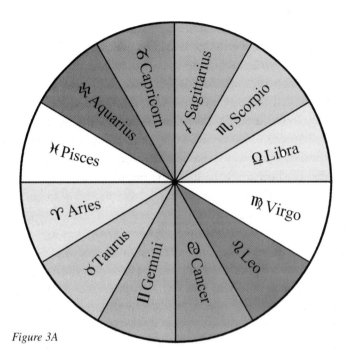

Figure 3A

What's Important?

Unlike universal law, not all signs and sign polarities in our chart are created equal. Some signs assume more importance, depending on the time of day we are born and where the planets are placed on the day of our birth. The signs that contain planets or sensitive points in our chart are more important to us.

> **The signs that contain planets or sensitive points in our chart are more important to us.**

This means that one or two polarities are likely to really sing to you, while others may not seem to be as important. You can tell which ones are more important just by looking at your chart and finding what signs are emphasized. There are several ways that a polarity can be emphasized, arranged in order of importance. Look at Figure 3B on page 59 as an example, and then look at your own chart.

You have an emphasized polarity if there are:

- planets directly across the chart from each other connected by a long (sometimes red) line. They will usually be in opposite signs. Check the polarity chart below.

- two or more planets in opposite signs according to the chart below, but they are not connected by a long line. Their polarity will also be strong in your make-up.

- a cluster of planets in one sign. That sign and its polar opposite are also very important to you both personally and in your relationships.

If you do not have a copy of your chart yet, just read on. The polarities that are significant to you will likely leap off the page!

Keep in mind that even though we do not usually have planets in every sign polarity, they are all a part of our nature. We can find all of them if we look deeply enough. The ones with planets in them may suggest major themes of growth and balance that we work with our entire life.

Polarities of the Zodiac*		
♈ Aries	⟷	♎ Libra
♉ Taurus	⟷	♏ Scorpio
♊ Gemini	⟷	♐ Sagittarius
♋ Cancer	⟷	♑ Capricorn
♌ Leo	⟷	♒ Aquarius
♍ Virgo*	⟷	♓ Pisces

*For signs beyond Virgo, read the columns from right to left.

In Princess Diana's chart (Figure 3B), we can see two prominent polarities. From the long lines drawn across the chart, we see two clusters of planets that are opposite each other. Note, however, that *four* signs are involved: Leo, Virgo, Aquarius, and Pisces. Looking at the polarity chart, we can see that Leo and Aquarius are opposed to each other, while Virgo and Pisces are also paired. What's more, if you look closely, the planets that are in Leo are joined by the long lines to those in Aquarius; the planet in Virgo is joined to the one in Pisces. Therefore, two polarities would have been important in Diana's life. They would have been important in her personal growth, but they would also have played out in her relationships.

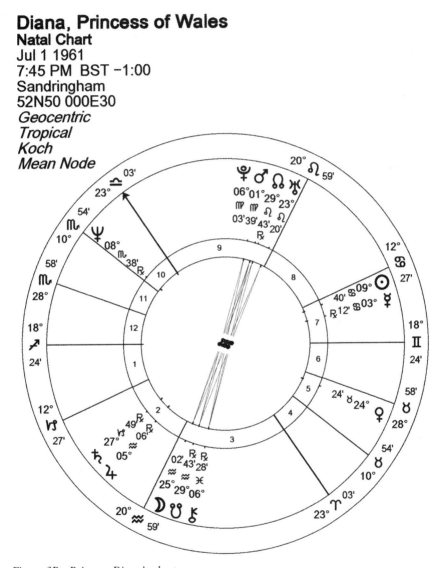

Figure 3B—Princess Diana's chart

Our Life Path

Some of us have polarities measured in the ways I've shown you so far—maybe three or four! Others may have only one or two. However, there is one polarity that everyone has. In addition to the polarities that you have found so far among the planets, you will notice that there is always a polarity shown by the placement of your North (☊) and South (☋) Nodes.

The North and South Nodes form a very important polarity because they show our lifelong direction or path. They form a background, a theme that weaves itself through all our affairs and experiences. We naturally draw people to us through these points.

The North Node is where we want to go to. We are drawn to it with fascination. It seems novel, unique, and alluring. It contains our own specific version of the unknown and how we want to become familiar with it. It is also uncomfortable because it is new, risky. It will take us into realms that we have never experienced in quite this way before. We will learn new lessons on a deeper level, and they will stick with us. We could say it is our *dharma*, or destiny.

The South Node is where we are coming from. It is comfortable, known, familiar, and maybe boring. There are certain qualities contained here that we just take for granted, and we have to learn to rethink everything where the South Node is concerned. We could say that it is our *karma*, the results of our past actions.

Taken together, we can visualize these nodes and the line connecting them as a giant arrow crossing the chart, from the South to the North Node. It is our path, our great journey of life. Everything we do speaks its language; everyone we meet ties into the nodes somehow. When a person connects with one node, they also connect with the other. Isn't this a nice way of saying that anyone with whom we share karma is also a part of our present and future?

In Diana's chart, you'll notice that her nodes are right in the middle of her other two polarities! Since her nodes are on the Leo-Aquarius polarity, they emphasize that complementarity even more than before. What's more, they tell us that this polarity represents a central theme of her life. Take the time now to look up your own North and South Nodes and record them in *My Astrological Profile* in the appendix (page 301). You can do the same for your partner (page 304).

As a Temporary Focus

Besides the polarities that show our personal lessons and themes throughout our lives, we all deal with temporary themes that are suggested by the changing positions of the real planets and nodes right now. If a particular theme leaps out at you as you read, but you can't find it in your chart, it is probably a temporary motif. This is important in relationships because everything that we experience also touches our associations with others.

The Nature of Astrology's Signs

The zodiacal signs are processes that we get better at over time. Therefore, it may be more accurate to say that a person is "Aquarius-ing," or Aquarian, than to say they are an Aquarius. Over time, we become better at fulfilling the deepest inner purpose, the soul level, of the signs under which we chose to be born.

Most astrology books only describe the surface qualities of the personality, the outward behaviors associated with the signs. However, an exploration of the bigger picture, the soul's purpose that lies behind the surface behavior, is needed to truly understand and value the person's nature. Personality changes, but our inner core and soul remain constant.

For example, the sign of Pisces may be associated with behavior that appears wishy-washy or overly sensitive. This indeed may be an issue for Pisceans as they attempt to function effectively in the world. However, there is something deeper going on behind the tendency toward this behavior. To accept the surface interpretation is to sell them short.

There is a deeper level, the level of motivation, and beneath that, purpose. This is the level of constancy, of the soul.

There is a deeper level, the level of motivation, and beneath that, purpose. This is the level of constancy, of the soul. It is what endures within us over time. Every personality impulse springs forth from the well of our purpose. As we go on our way, we try different ways of expressing that purpose. Some work, some don't. We grow. Our personality develops in a different direction. Still, our deepest motivations remain the same.

It is little wonder that the "personality astrology" books describe something about us, but are not entirely accurate. The qualities that are described form a part of the spectrum of the sign's expression. However, they may not be part of *our* expression. We may be further along the road of self-understanding than the author can express. We may not be so far along. The description may fit us in childhood or a few weeks ago. It may even fit us now, at least in part. Some qualities may fit more than one sign, because on the surface, the personality manifestations of different signs can look the same. But if that is all we look at, then we miss the point. We are blind to the deeper well of consciousness that is the *sign* rather than the expression of the sign. We have missed the soul level, and with it the chance to explore the depths of our being. A description of personality will not lead us to the fount of ourselves.

So when we look at the signs in their polarities, we will not be looking at their surface level expressions so much as what lies underneath them. In this way, we can get to the same core point from which love springs forth.

✳✳✳

THE POLARITIES

Aries-Libra

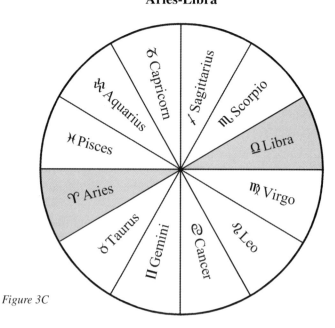

Figure 3C

First of all, it works both ways: Aries-Libra and Libra-Aries. Aries is considered the first sign of the zodiac, so we will start here, but the theme is the same no matter which way you think about it.

Aries the Identity-Seeker

Aries is considered the first sign of the zodiac, because the first day of spring was thought to be the beginning of the year in the northern-hemisphere ancient world that developed the first structures of astrology. Some people say that this is why Aries like to be first and think only of themselves, but this does not take us to the deepest levels of Aries. The Aries in us is deep, indeed; we could say it goes to the deepest of levels—back to the Source Itself. It is pure emanation, pure Self, symbolically the first emanation or spark of life coming from our Source. It is newness, inno-cent of all other things, knowing itself perfectly. It is so new to the realm of all things that it may not recognize its connectedness with other things and people at first. Yet, in its knowing of Itself, it expresses itself with naive confidence, purity of intent, and the force of pure impulse.

Aries goes to the deepest of levels—back to the Source Itself.

There is never any calculation or strategy with Aries. Life is a constant process of exploring new realms. Everything is taken on with a pioneer spir-it. The person with Aries emphasis doesn't care if it hasn't been done before—their "can-do" attitude overcomes the most insuperable odds. Their freshness and optimism beget a talent for success, and Aries will often take the lead in an effort where others fear failure.

The Aries in us has a one-pointed focus that allows them to ignore the slings and arrows that others throw their way. This creates a natural bold-ness that makes them the good warrior and pioneer. While we can admire their boldness, we can sometimes be irritated if Aries has not yet recognized their need to take others into account. The strength of their one-pointed focus can also become their weakness. Yet, this ignorance of others' needs is not ill-willed or selfish, but just innocent oversight—unless other factors suggest otherwise. A person with a wounded Aries nature can refuse to see the need to balance their concern for themselves with awareness of others, choosing to overlook the need to grow.

An Arian may wonder why life seems to go so well and then nothing comes of it, failing to see that what is born out of bright promise, and optimistic faith in their own ability to overcome, dies when they neglect to make the connections with others that are so important to every successful effort.

Perhaps the Aries person's greatest weakness is that their natural self-centeredness (ultimately rooted in centeredness in the Self) can prevent them from thinking anything is wrong—except with other people. The key lesson is to understand that all difficulties ultimately stem from misapplying our own energies in the world. If there is a problem, look within. If one-pointedness is creating difficulties for an Aries, the point of focus is in the ego, not the True Self.

Aries in Our Chart

If we have a strong Aries component in our chart, then in relationships we can be inclined to think only of ourselves. We can unwittingly expect the relationship to revolve around us, our needs, and our ideas. We may truly forget that our partner has wants and needs, also. We may neglect to ask for our partner's advice and may forget to listen or be receptive to them. When there is trouble, we may withdraw, become shy, or feel sorry for ourselves. It may not occur to us to think of the other person.

Aries in Our Partner's Chart

If Aries is a strong part of our partner's nature, their fearlessness in taking on difficult tasks can be refreshing. They tend to approach life with undaunted optimism, unafraid to be themselves and unapologetic for who they are and how they appear to others. However, it may be difficult to bring them into contact with us. When they forget that we exist, remember that standing in their way is not as helpful as standing by their side. If we step back into our own individuality and hold to the relationship, they will eventually return of their own accord. They cannot lead without someone there to be led! Let them see who you are and how you feel—then you become real to them.

How Libra Supports Aries

What's missing in Aries' approach to life and love is Libra, the Harmonizer. Libra's qualities naturally shore up the potential weakness in the Aries perspective. If the Aries self-orientation engenders narrow vision, Libra's natural need to attend to their surroundings—to attract and harmonize—counteracts the Aries tendencies. Libras naturally "glue" themselves to the people and things that they see around them. Just as Aries is oblivious to others, Libra is acutely aware of them. In contact with each other, a great synergy can ignite.

Libra the Harmonizer

Libra is Aries' divine complement. Libra answers all the questions that Aries asks. They uproot all the issues that arise through Aries' approach to life. We will see how Aries, in turn, provides the perfect resolutions to all Libra's questions and issues.

The Libra in us seems to be everything that Aries is not—empathic, other-oriented, interested in partnership, and companionable. But, as with Aries, their surface manifestations range from strength to weakness and arise from a deeper purpose.

Libra's deepest motives lie in their desire to connect and balance or harmonize with other things and people. They can go in the direction of desiring relationships either with people or with ideas, and sometimes both. The symbol of Libra, the balance scale, reminds us that Librans seek justice at their core. Justice is invoked by knowing another's experience from their own perspective. This is what Libra seeks to do.

> *Libra's deepest motives lie in their desire to connect*
> *and balance or harmonize with other things and people.*

At their core, a person with a Libra emphasis is looking for the True Self of others so that they may find their own Self. At their best, Librans uplift all who are around them with a sense of honor, respect, and spiritual love. This happens because when someone sees the highest part of us, we automatically respond at that level, even if we don't consciously know what we are doing.

The popular image of Libra is that of a fence-sitter, a little flaky when it comes to making decisions. We might call this the result of a "developing sense of justice." The Libran wants to do what is right, taking all sides of a matter into account. This innate drive leads them to be concerned with others, often to the exclusion of themselves. If this is taken to extremes, they lose track of, and stop caring for, themselves. Ultimately, they have lost track of their True Self when this occurs. The boundaries that should exist between them and others have been overstepped. The Libran may have given up their sense of self in order to relate to others on the others' own terms.

Librans may also give the appearance of being concerned for others' needs but not really be living that essence. Sometimes, in an ego-oriented moment, Librans can seek to have their own needs met indirectly by meeting another's needs. For example, a Libran and his partner have a disagreement about where to go on vacation. He wants to go to Italy, while his partner wants to go to Greece. So he decides to get his partner a dozen roses as a tool in his persuasive effort. There's nothing wrong with buying a gift for his partner if it comes from the right motives, but here it is used to manipulate. A gift that is meant to convey a hidden message rather than to express one's true feelings is not a gift at all. It has strings and conditions attached, so the impulse to present the gift comes from the ego.

In truth, when meeting our partner's reasonable needs, our own can be met as well, but it has to be done with honesty and mutual respect. If the gift of roses comes from our heart as a sincere effort to show that we have corrected our behavior, then it can be a part of a soul-centered outcome. The roses can be accepted as a true gift, and the vacation disagreement can be resolved without reference to the roses.

Libra in Our Chart

If Libra is strong in our chart, we may have just as much difficulty balancing our needs in relationships as Aries does. We may see a relationship as a goal by itself, thinking that *any* relationship is better than none. We may think only of our partner, forgetting our own needs, until we find ourselves unhappy and our needs unmet; then the relationship becomes a cage in which we cannot express ourselves. We may lose our sense of who we are because we have let our partner's needs take over our own so often that we have forgotten to listen to ourselves.

Libra in Our Partner's Chart

When Libra is featured in your partner's character, they will tend to consider relationships to be very important to them. They will probably feel better when someone is there to share things with. Sometimes they may forget that you are two separate individuals, and that they need to do things without you, if only because it makes your time together more precious. When they stop doing things for themselves, it is time to encourage them to fulfill the needs that you cannot fulfill for them. Help them to recognize that they are all they need; once they see that, they can return to relating as a whole person.

How Aries Supports Libra

You may already sense that the antidote to Libra's "ills" can be found in Aries—not in the selfish side of Aries, but in the side that is centered in the True Self. Librans need a sense of their True Self, or they become lost in the energy of the others around them. Once they find their True Self, Librans can give from that place of integrity and wholeness. They pay attention to the other's perspective, but balance it with their own. Their efforts toward harmony take their own needs into account as well. Even if conflict sometimes arises, they know that this is a part of learning and growing in a relationship. They know that relationships cannot exist if we cannot present ourselves as a whole individual.

Balancing the Aries-Libra Polarity

Although Aries and Libra are opposed to each other in the zodiac, they do not have to act out their polarity as an opposition. Aries is interested in their Self, their own perspective—exploring their nature to see what they are like. Libra is interested in others, the mystery of relationship—exploring the nature of others and how that blends with their own nature. Although the two appear to have very different needs and interests, they are actually rooted in the same consciousness, an *awareness of Self/Not-Self.* Aries' inventory looks something like, "This is me, this is not me." Libra's inventory looks like, "This is you, and this is not you." They are really saying the same thing![6]

When Libra and Aries are acted out as an opposition, they become polarized as *selfishness versus selflessness.* Some of the ways we may think about these signs as opposites are:

Possible Qualities of the Aries-Libra Polarity	
Aries	*Libra*
centered in the True Self	compassionate
focused	diffuse and harmomizing
selfish	selfless
egocentric	self-sacrificial
arrogant	self-deprecating
narcissistic	the martyr

At the top of the table, we can see a healthy expression of the Aries-Libra polarity, while at the bottom is the most unhealthy. When these signs operate in complementarity, partners respond with True Self–centeredness and compassion, *and they exchange the qualities between them.* That is, neither one can say that they alone display the qualities of Aries or Libra. They have blended them into a dynamic interaction, where each one may take the role of one or the other sign in turn. At the soul level, the boundaries between the signs blur, because the highest qualities that are found in one sign naturally lead to the expression of the sign that is its opposite.

Aries-Libra in Our Chart

If we have the Aries-Libra polarity in our chart, we will tend to get caught up in the dilemma of whether we are being too self-oriented or giving too much to our partner. We ask ourselves, "Am I too selfish? Am I giving too much?" We are seeking to find the balance between self and other.

---

[6] In language and logic, this is literally true: I = not-you (or, one of the things that is not-you); You = not-me (or one of the things that is not-me). Our unconscious self recognizes this fact at its very primal level.

Healing an Aries-Libra Split

We must *love ourselves* to heal the opposition between Aries and Libra, no matter what sign we find ourselves in. When we love who we are, we are not fooled by the ego. We do not get caught up in throwing ourselves away in either our false self or the false self of another. We live out the essence of love itself and find room in our heart for our partner in such a way that their True Self is naturally called into play. When we love ourselves, we "marry ourselves." This means that we will hold to who we are, uphold our inner dignity, and respect ourselves no matter what comes at us. We adhere to who we are because the alternative is to abandon ourselves, and then we lose all. In this way, we have the strength to see clearly what is occurring around us and can act from that strength and clarity with peace. We can withstand the petty difficulties that arise moment to moment in our lives, whether they come from our partner or something else in our world. Then we are in a position to relate to—and eventually marry—another.

To heal a gap between Aries and Libra, we must love ourselves.

✷✷✷

Taurus-Scorpio

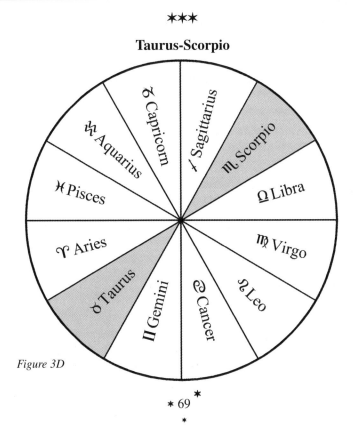

Figure 3D

Taurus and Scorpio are the signs in the next polarity as we spin the astrological wheel. The wheel turns clockwise under our finger, or we can move our finger counterclockwise to achieve the same effect. Doing so takes us from Aries to Taurus and Libra to Scorpio.

Taurus, the Revealer of Beauty

Where Aries is focused and fiery, Taurus is solid and stable—strong, resistant to change, and holding tremendous force within. Taureans are often thought of as slow, even lazy, but it is their inner strength that makes them retain their form, changing only gradually in response to persistent effort.

In its highest form, the Taurus in us is a fountain of creativity, because its true purpose is to bring beauty into manifestation. This can take whatever form Taurus feels is beautiful, and beauty takes many forms. However, if we have Taurus in our makeup, in our grounded solidness, we may want to experience and express beauty in the physical world. Common manifestations are building, architecture, music or song, the arts, crafts (three-dimensional art), and growing living things, whether plants or animals. We may also find the financial world appealing, since money is one product of the material world that has high value. However, without inner principles, the pursuit of money, or anything else, is empty.

In its highest form, Taurus is a fountain of creativity, because its true purpose is to bring beauty into manifestation.

Taureans express and respond to beauty, and although our world often teaches us that beauty lies in appearance, it truly does not. All brides and babies are beautiful because a light glows within them, creating and emanating beauty. When we experience that inner glow, we are beautiful.

It is as if Taurus were the spirit of Mother Nature, overflowing with life, greenery springing forth with every step She takes, life being born with the wave of Her hand. When Taureans live in this vibration, they can bring anything into manifestation; they can be a doorway through which energy takes form, becomes life.

Without an awareness of their inner purpose, of the way life works through them, a person with Taurus emphasis may have difficulty connecting with their fountain of creativity. Our culture generally does not support processes of gradual progress, yet this is where Taureans excel. Slow growth is stable and robust, not flashy or glamorous. It has nothing to attract the ego.

Patient persistence, or perseverance, is one of the Taurean's strong suits. Perseverance is the ability to remain loyal to our inner sense of truth, no matter what assails us. If we are Taurean, a tremendous inner power gives us the capability of persevering.

Sometimes Taurus's patience and persistence (stability and solidity) can be too much of a good thing. In order to be stable and build something long-lasting, it is necessary to be careful about making changes. In this natural resistance to change, they can sometimes come to fear it and get stuck in a rut. They may find the old form too comfortable to leave behind, because it is known and secure, even if they recognize the value of the new. The ego has become enraptured by the appearance of things instead of attending to the well of creativity within.

When the ego takes control, it sees that its attempts at change do not bring the rewards of beauty and growth; Taureans may then come to feel that change must not occur. They may see the present as an eternal, unchanging reality. They may feel as if life keeps them stuck and want to give up. They may revel in comfort, unable to see the value in the temporary discomfort that newness brings. But by letting the light of the True Self shine from within, creativity wells up from deep within, and change occurs smoothly and effortlessly.

Taurus in Our Chart

If Taurus is strong in our chart, we may bring strength and solidity to the relationship. We may want to hold on to our partner too much, become possessive, or fear change. We may cling to our partner, trusting before we know it is safe. We may become focused too much on the physical aspects of the relationship—money and sex or sensuality. We may look to our partner to fill those needs instead of looking within ourselves to feel safe and secure. Well expressed, we may want to grow things or create beauty with our partner.

Taurus in Our Partner's Chart

When our partner has a strong Taurean component, we may admire their stability. They may appear calm as everything around them changes.

Their physical creativity can come out in your relationship as a delicate sensuality. When your partner resists your latest bright idea, it helps to recognize that newness can seem to run against their inner purpose of keeping things stable, until they recognize that rigidity is not stability. Give them time to get used to the freshness that you bring, give them your love, and they will come to understand its value in time.

How Scorpio Supports Taurus

Taurus builds and beautifies, but if we had only the constructiveness of Taurus, we would have too many outmoded, worn out forms of things past—would there be room for anything new? Taurus's processes need the juices of Scorpio to get started. Scorpio destroys the old while transforming it. This makes room for Taurus, the builder and grower, to do its thing. Taurus is naturally counterbalanced by Scorpio, the engine of change.

Scorpio the Transformer

If Taurus preserves form, Scorpio alters it. The Scorpian personality is known to be deep, often intense; there is a strong emotional drive to their nature. They may appear secretive, but only because what they feel and understand is difficult to share with others.

In our depths, the Scorpio in us sits on the edge of darkness, of death. It feels the forces at the very core of existence; it is privy to the world where the gods decide our fate. Scorpio may not even notice what is happening on the surface of things, for deeper levels of awareness draw its attention.

Scorpio is attuned to the need for, and processes of, transformation. All things must change, yet only a part of ourselves is ever altered. When changes occur, they are really on the surface, not the depths of Self—the part of us that always remains unchanged. Only the form changes—the physical, the personality. Our Being, the True Self, remains constant.

The challenge of the person with Scorpio emphasis is to identify with the True Self rather than the ego. When deep change comes to us, we are stripped of all but the True Self, and so Scorpio leads us home. If we identify with the ego, it gets us caught in the drama of change, riding the roller coaster of surface events. If we identify with our True Self, we are in the transformation, but not of it, not consumed by the process taking place before our eyes.

Scorpio is where we deal with death. Death is one half of the process where the inconstant parts of ourselves—our bodies and personalities—change form. The other half is the re-clothing of the Soul, its rebirth into the fluid, fluctuating parts of self that, as an individual with a body, we will come to identify with. No matter whether death takes the form of the loss of physicality, or one of the everyday "little deaths," as long as we are identified with our egos, transformation is not easy to take. It jolts and threatens the ego, unseating it from its position in the driver's seat of the self. No one is more aware of this than a Scorpio.

> *Scorpio is where we deal with death. Death is one half*
> *of the process where the inconstant parts of ourselves*
> *change form. The other half is the re-clothing of the Soul.*

If a person with Scorpio emphasis must choose between ego and the true, constant self, it is not an easy path to follow. Knowing the inner self, seeing the potential for transformation in all that exists, and seeing the necessity of death is not an easy path. It can lead them to feel separate from others. Those Scorpians who are courageous and self-responsible enough to face the truth of transformation do not carry an easy message. They may hide what they know, thus hiding who they are.

There is great power in understanding and accepting the processes of change. With this deep knowledge, Scorpians carry the responsibility to use the knowledge well. For a Scorpian living through their ego, the temptations to use their power for selfish gain are many. The misuse of power is epidemic in our culture, because we are actually taught how to use power against others as self-protection. Generally, it is through the hard knocks of their path that Scorpians learn to use their power as an affirmation of life.

Scorpio in Our Chart

In relationships, if Scorpio is strong in our chart, we may be reluctant to trust. We may test our partner over and over, making them prove their love and reliability time and again, thrilling to the intensity of it all! We may bring the relationship to a crisis point over and over, or we may withhold our love to see if our beloved really loves us. Sometimes, the more we love, the more we withdraw. When we do give ourselves, we want something deep and intense; we may provoke our partner to bring out their feelings. Such a relationship can become heavy and exhausting for both. However, by becoming aware of these possibilities and remembering that to live is to take risks, we can overcome our fears and give the deep love we are so capable of.

Scorpio in Our Partner's Chart

When our partner's chart is strong in Scorpio, we may have difficulty understanding their mysterious nature. The surface may appear placid and cheerful, but underneath they are feeling every impulse at a very deep level. Never mistake their seeming calm for dullness or indifference, for intense feelings lie at the heart of their nature! When they withdraw or seem to test us, it is best to let them have their space. They will open up to us again when they have sorted out their emotions. In the meantime, if we remain true to ourselves and hold a vision of their return, our consistency and self-respect will lead them out of their inwardness.

How Taurus Supports Scorpio

Taurus and Scorpio cannot exist without each other. If all we had were the transformative processes of Scorpio, we would have nothing of form— no things. We would have our constant, living essence, but no world to express it in. Scorpio destroys the old as it transforms what is living. Taurus brings the rebirth after Scorpio's death. They are part of a never-ending cycle, the cycle of life.

Balancing the Taurus-Scorpio Polarity

Just as with Aries and Libra, Taurus and Scorpio do not have to act in opposition to each other. Taurus wants to build and grow, Scorpio to transform and eliminate the outmoded. Their differences are obvious—they are opposites. However, they actually exist on the same axis of meaning, both *operating in the realm of the manifest.* Taurus asks, "How can I bring beauty to this? What can I build or grow?" Scorpio asks, "What needs to be eliminated or updated? What is no longer flourishing and useful (and so worth destroying)? Each really has the same goals—bringing what is of value into existence. They are each fulfilling half of the cycle of life.

Taurus and Scorpio oppose each other as *formation versus elimination.* Some of the ways we may think about these signs as opposites are:

Possible Qualities of the Taurus-Scorpio Polarity	
Taurus	*Scorpio*
manifesting	beauty transforming
fertile	healing
earthy, sensual	intense, deep
possessive	withholding
acquisitive	autocratic
stagnating, stuck	destructive

Taurus and Scorpio can be at loggerheads with each other when the ego gains precedence in our nature. We forget that growth and decay are a part of life. As we rise to the soul expression of either sign, however, we find that it begins to move toward its opposite.

Taurus-Scorpio in Our Chart

When we have both Taurus and Scorpio in our chart, we will play out the polarity in our relationships. Aware of how things change, we will tend to be unsure about trust and safety. We may ask ourselves, "Am I withholding too much? When can I have it all?" We are trying to find safety and depth with our partner.

Healing a Taurus-Scorpio Split

When Taurus and Scorpio are being played out as an opposition, Taurus will want too much, and Scorpio will withhold or withdraw. To heal the gap between them, we must *build trust slowly.* No matter which side of the polarity you find yourself in, building trust uproots the issue that lies within the Taurus-Scorpio polarity. When we take the time to build trust, we build a robust, firm foundation. We do not get caught in situations where we feel unsafe. We do not give ourselves to our partner before we know if they are safe for us. We do not withhold because we fear being overwhelmed. We give ourselves time to develop a knowledge of each other. We are able to go through the difficult beginnings that every relationship experiences without skipping any steps because we know that to deny our doubts and fears undermines the essence of love itself. In this way, we are able to stay in tune with our inner child and that of our partner. We are more able to be open and loving because no demands are being made of us. Once a foundation of trust is established, both Taurus and Scorpio can enjoy its stability. Taurus will not need to grasp, and Scorpio will not need to test or withdraw. Taurus will be able to enjoy having instead of wanting. Scorpio will be able to experience depth and intensity. Both sets of needs will be met because each partner is open when trust is there, and regeneration will spontaneously occur.

When Taurus and Scorpio are being played out as an opposition, Taurus will want too much, and Scorpio will withhold or withdraw. To heal the gap between them, we must build trust slowly.

Gemini-Sagittarius

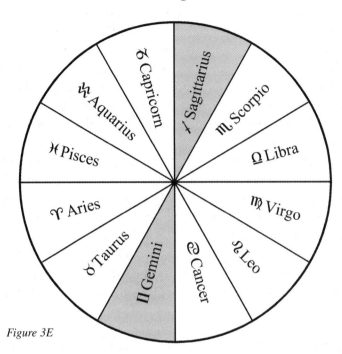

Figure 3E

Gemini the Experimenter

Gemini collects, connects, and communicates. It serves a vital function in our nature, for without it, we couldn't think, or connect ideas and things; use language, to connect words and thoughts; or learn, by connecting actions and experiences.

The Gemini in us is curious and experimental. Geminians can be lively, talkative, and inquisitive. They often love to try new things, just to find out what they're like. However, Geminians may soon be distracted by the next new thing, and dabble rather than develop expertise. This makes them versatile and easy to talk to. They will have something in common with everyone.

Geminians love to learn—to make connections. As we connect new ideas with old, it adds something to our nature. As Geminians, we want to explore things and ideas which are *not* like us. We will examine what we have encountered, turning it to look at it from every angle. As we learn about new things, we slowly incorporate that knowledge into who we are. Eventually it becomes a part of us and emerges from who we are, without thought, organically.

Geminians seek knowledge of everything because
they want to feel whole, connected, and complete.

People with Gemini emphasized apply mental energy—curiosity and logic—to this process of acquiring knowledge. They are not emotional about it or vested in any outcome unless other sign qualities bring that to their nature.

Geminians are often fascinated with people, because after all, when you talk to them, they talk back! They love the feeling of connecting, of communion with others, because it gives them an interface, a way of mirroring themselves. When they get a response (or reaction) from others, they see their own nature reflected in the other person. They are looking in a mirror.

Invisible to most of us, when we have the experience of connecting with someone, we are "vibrating" or harmonizing with them. Geminians want to experience this with many things and people. Each contact brings more stimulation to them. Stimulation is very appealing because it triggers growth and learning. They are a little different with each new thing, each time trying on a little different part of themselves. From place to place and person to person, they may act differently. This can make those with strong Gemini seem insincere. They may tell the same story in different ways to different people, just to see what impact it has, or how it fits. When they try different versions of reality, they can appear hypocritical or dishonest. As they flit from one person to another, they can seem fickle.

If Gemini people seem to lack constancy, it is the natural consequence of their search for communion. They must try many things in order to fulfill the Gemini purpose. Ultimately, they are trying to connect with themselves. They seek knowledge of everything because they want to feel whole, connected, and complete. They search for the piece that will complete them, help them to join the unconnected parts of their nature.

Gemini in Our Chart

If Gemini is emphasized in our chart, we will bring these needs into our relationships. We may want our partners to mirror or stimulate us. We may try a new idea or reality out on them to see how it "plays," consequently confusing or misleading our partner. We may also become bored with our partner, wanting new stimulation and thinking that someone we don't know is more exciting.

Gemini in Our Partner's Chart

When our partner has strong Gemini traits, we will find ourselves stimulated by their curiosity and intrigued by their knowledge. They will love to connect with us, to play "matching and mirroring." When they seem to "lose touch with the truth," let them know how you see things. Communicating openly gives them the contact they crave, and together you can find what is real.

How Sagittarius Supports Gemini

In order to balance Gemini's weak points, we need Sagittarius the Seeker. Gemini's potential for inconstancy is offset by Sagittarius's sense of focus. Gemini's encyclopedic knowledge is consolidated in Sagittarius's universal concepts. Their small-picture, detailed focus is amplified by Sagittarius's broad perspective.

Sagittarius the Seeker

Where Gemini is "up close and (im)personal," the Sagittarius in us deals in the realm of overview and broad perspective. As Sagittarians, we want to find the principles that unite all things—what we call truth.

Our drive is to turn knowledge into Knowing. Knowledge is born of the integration of our experiences into our nature. Knowing is the expression and application of knowledge in the arena of life. Knowledge comes from the mind, while Knowing comes from the deep well of awareness that we all carry inside us. It is not memory or memorized facts.

Knowing is applied in life in part through philosophy. Philosophies are meant to provide an understanding of who we are and how things work. All of us have a philosophy of life, whether or not we are aware of it and can express it to others. Our philosophy is the basis of our principles, the truths that we choose to guide our actions. Principles provide the foundation for our morals of conduct and values. All of these give form to our attitudes. Attitudes have a profound impact on our experiences.

Philosophies, principles, and morals can be lumped together as beliefs. They are things that we feel to be true, but they can't be proven. Still, they are based on something that feels certain within us, the realm of Knowing. Each person can know truth in a different way, because truth has many forms.

> **Those with strong Sagittarius traits are learning about the realm of Knowing. They seek the truth.**

All this is the realm of Sagittarius, and if Sagittarius is featured in our chart, these will be familiar concerns. Those with strong Sagittarius traits are learning about the realm of Knowing. They seek the truth. They want the "big picture," so it is not necessary to experience everything directly. They can learn by observing others or from what others have learned.

Those with a strong Sagittarius nature often extend their interest in big concepts to broad areas: They may love to travel, visit other cultures, or study global and cross-cultural subjects. As they travel, or study and dream about travel, or become part of a new culture by move or marriage, they are unconsciously pursuing a deeper understanding of the universal truths of human society.

They also enjoy experiencing a sense of freedom and wide-openness. This desire can lead them to a wide range of pursuits, from spiritual or religious studies to long-distance running.

In the pursuit of these deep principles, Sagittarian people display many qualities. Their broad perspective gives them a natural insight into the weaknesses that are part of human nature. This they often share as a sense of humor. They are often high-minded and focused in their ventures, shooting for the highest star. This idealism can lead them to set high standards for themselves and others. Their outgoing and principled nature often expresses as a refreshing honesty, especially if it is softened with humor.

However, such high standards can come across to others as judgmental or moralistic. Sagittarians are usually more than willing to share their version of the truth with others. If they forget that their way of seeing things is not the only way, they can appear to be narrow, dogmatic, even fanatical.

They can be too forthright in their honesty, bruising the feelings of those who receive the Sagittarian's direct focus.

They may think that the thing they search for is not inside themselves but outside. They may become a vagabond, looking for the ideal form of whatever they think will save them—bring them truth—now. They may get so caught up in their ideals and universals that they lose touch with the "real world" of people and direct experiences.

Sagittarius in Our Chart

In relationships, those of us with strong Sagittarian traits will look for truth in our beloved. We may project our search for the ideal into our relationship, as a "search for the golden ideal partner." It may be hard for the Sagittarius to settle down with one person if they do this, because no one is going to be able to fulfill their great expectations. We may become a relationship nomad, unable to settle with one person, even if we want to. Until we learn to look within for truth and Knowing, using our experiences with others to fuel our growth, long-term relationship needs may be difficult to fulfill.

Sagittarius in Our Partner's Chart

When our partner has strong Sagittarian qualities, their enthusiasm for understanding the universals of life can be infectious. Their tendency to idealize us can be endearing. However, as long as we are an *ideal*, we are not *real*. By assisting them to get to know us as we really are, we can bring the relationship into the real world of the Soul, where truth and love merge.

How Gemini Supports Sagittarius

Sagittarians need the knowledge of Gemini to feed their desire to Know. If they are willing to experience the world directly, their sense of truth and Knowing will take shape more easily within, based upon a sense of what's in the "real world."

The differences between Gemini and Sagittarius are united by the common purpose of exploring and using the world of the mind.

Balancing the Gemini-Sagittarius Polarity

Gemini's cursory, dabbling approach to life is very different from Sagittarius's in-depth search for truth, yet there is a principle which unifies them. Their differences are united by the common purpose of *exploring and using the world of the mind.* Whether knowledge or Knowing, the mind is involved. Although these two signs have different surface interests, they are really two sides of the same coin. When they act out the polarity as an opposition, it can be experienced as *fickleness versus fanaticism.* Some of the ways we may think about these signs as a polarity are:

| Possible Qualities of the Gemini-Sagittarius Polarity ||
Gemini	*Sagittarius*
exploring polarity/communion	seeking truth
dispersing, spreading	focusing
lively, excitable	idealistic
scattered	narrow
inconsistent	dogmatic
fragmented, split	fanatical

The top of the table shows a healthy expression of the polarity, while at the bottom is the most unhealthy. When these signs operate in complementarity, partners respond with detailed knowledge and deep principles, and, as in all the polarities, they share the qualities between them.

Gemini-Sagittarius in Our Chart

If we have the Gemini-Sagittarius polarity in our chart, we will tend to get caught up in the dilemma of whether we are being too scattered and insincere or too idealistic and judgmental. We ask ourselves, "Am I being honest? Have I said too much?" We are seeking to find the balance between knowledge and truth within ourselves.

Healing a Gemini-Sagittarius Split

When we experience Gemini-Sagittarius opposition, either within ourselves or with our partner, we must understand the nature of truth. Truth comes in many forms, and though it is universal, we each understand it in our own way. Knowing and knowledge are both manifestations of truth— knowing is profound and has broad application, while knowledge is detailed and has specific, worldly uses. We need each in our life. The key to uniting them is *integration.* In learning, we examine what we encounter. We work with it until we make it "ours," or integrate it into ourselves. Then we extrapolate larger concepts from what we have learned, adjusting our concept of the truth and the principles, morals, and attitudes that come from it.

In our partnerships, we must learn *honesty, acceptance,* and *forgiveness.* Having an appreciation of how complicated learning is, we are more able to lovingly accept our partner's learning processes. We can give them the time and space that they need to grow. We can forgive them for their mistakes when they are ready to return to us. We can be gentle with ourselves in our own learning process and face each of our errors honestly because we know we will be forgiven. Yet, we know that most of the time we do not need to say anything to our partner in criticism of their mistakes, because they can find their own way to the truth.

Cancer-Capricorn

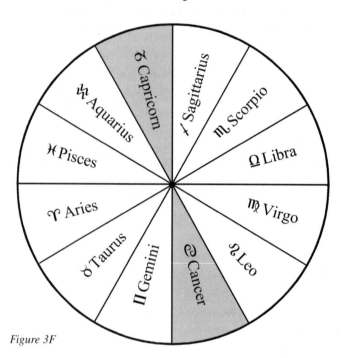

Figure 3F

Cancer the Nurturer

The Cancer in us is the Great Mother, who gives birth to all things of the universe. Persons with Cancer strength in their charts have a great nurturing energy at the core of their nature. They are very concerned with the care and feeding of those with whom they are emotionally bonded.

This is usually the family. For many Cancerians, the family is everything. They will treat others as if they are part of their family as well. Although they may be slow to warm up to acquaintances, they extend a caring warmth to those they feel close to. The Cancerian urge is sometimes expressed as patriotism, or national pride. Here, the "family" is extended to include all fellow citizens.

> *Cancerians are looking for the constancy of the*
> *True Self—what is constant within us.*

At a deeper level, Cancerians are focused on finding and preserving life or what is constant in life. On the purely physical level, they are acutely aware of what it takes to survive, and actively involved in ensuring their own survival and that of their loved ones. The concern for constancy also extends to an interest in the past: Cancerians may study their family tree (the personal past) and history (the cultural past). They enjoy preserving the past as well, whether it means holding onto heirlooms and old photographs, or collecting antiques.

At the deepest level, they are looking for the constancy of the True Self. What is constant within us is the Spirit and Soul—what continues to exist through birth and death.

Cancerians want everyone around them to be comfortable, because that allows them to feel emotionally secure. They experience life as a vivid, often dramatic, ocean of feelings. These feelings are everything from instincts and psychic impressions to the full range of expressible emotions. They feel things on a "gut" level, often feeling that they "just know" something. Their instincts are frequently correct.

As with the other signs, there can be too much of a good thing. The attunement to feelings can become overly emotional, too sensitive, needy. Instincts and impressions can be colored by fears and reactions that have little to do with the present experience. Mothering can become smothering, and family ties can be used to hide from valuable experiences with other people.

It may be difficult for Cancerians to let go of their past. What is tried and true has worked to keep them alive and well, and why shouldn't it work now? When it is time to change loyalties, such as at the time of marriage, they may have a hard time doing it.

Cancer in Our Chart

If we have a strong Cancer nature, we will want to nurture those whom we care for, especially our partner. We must take care to limit our nurturance to what is appropriate for the person. What is good for an infant or child is not right for, or welcomed by, an adult. When we mother our partner, we deny them their adulthood and equality with us. They are likely to feel stifled, controlled, or trapped.

Cancer in Our Partner's Chart

If our partner has a Cancer emphasis, they live in a world of feeling. Even as they notice the ever-shifting world of feeling, they are looking for something that is constant. When they cling to the past or their family of origin, they are holding onto what has seemed stable in their life, good or bad. Their loyalty, once given, is given forever. When they cling too closely, we can help them recognize their capabilities for self-care and -nurturance.

How Capricorn Supports Cancer

Cancer lives in a world of inconstant feeling. Feelings shift and change from moment to moment, and Cancer tries to ride the waves. Cancerians are looking for something solid to hold them, something safe they can rely on. These qualities are supplied by their opposite sign, Capricorn the Protector.

Capricorn the Protector

If Cancer is the Mother, then we can think of Capricorn as the Great Father-Protector, the Governor who oversees all things in their domain. Just as we expect more personal care from those who mother us, we experience more protection, guidance, and structure from the fathering energies of Capricorn.

Capricorn takes a less personal approach to care. The Capricorn part of us tends to see individuals as part of a whole—a society, a culture, a world—within which we must make our way. Such concerns are turned toward creating lasting structures which can sustain us in the world in which we find ourselves.

These structures are found as business, government, and institutions like hospitals and universities. The creation of, and successful existence in, these outer-world frameworks is Capricorn's domain. It is easy to see from this why people with Capricorn emphasis are focused on success in the world. They see things in terms of the big picture, and they want to find out how it works. Capricornians want to place themselves in arenas where they can engage in life on a grand scale. They want a leadership role and responsibility, so they can call the shots and then see the effects.

Applying this to the personal level, they are developing self-containment. This quality is an aspect of keeping the personal world of feelings separate from the impersonal worlds of business and government. When we let ourselves be swayed by our undigested personal feelings, we may not make decisions for the good of the whole. This leads us to hold our feelings close to our chest, and it can become difficult to let go and share with others.

Capricorns are looking for the keys to the Cosmos,
because using those keys they can build any structure, from
the most spiritual cosmology to the most worldly corporation.

Capricornians want to know the rules, so that they can apply them in the building and administration of their structures. For this reason, they are nearly always thinking about what "the rules" are. These rules could be anything from human laws and morals governing the conduct of human affairs, to the physical laws governing nature, to the universal laws upon which all of these are (or should be) based.

Ultimately, Capricornians are looking for the keys to the cosmos, because using those keys they can build any structure, from the most spiritual cosmology to the most worldly corporation.

Taken to extremes, however, Capricornians' interest in rules can become rigidity. They can exert harsh discipline on themselves and others. In their desire to understand rules, they may become slaves to the rules. In their desire for success, they may scheme to control and place others at a disadvantage. As they draw back from the personal to see the whole, they may appear or become cold and remote.

Capricorn in Our Chart

If Capricorn is emphasized in our chart, we may take a "whole-system" approach to our partnerships. We may be focused on the "system" of the relationship—the grand overview of where it is going and what it can be by working on it. We may keep our emotional upsets to ourselves, not remembering that part of loving another is sharing our pain. We may also attempt to show our caring by managing the relationship.

Capricorn in Our Partner's Chart

If our partner has Capricorn qualities, they may bury their love under a businesslike manner. They may guard their feelings and be reluctant to share them. But underneath, they need love as much as anyone. They are just afraid to share their needs with others because they are afraid of being vulnerable, of getting hurt. When they protect themselves behind a brusque or distant manner, they are really afraid to share their tender side. Give them space to sort their feelings out on their own, and they will open when they are ready.

How Cancer Supports Capricorn

Capricorn's businesslike, impersonal approach is naturally balanced by Cancer's warm, personal touch. Without it, Capricorns can become remote, cold, and unfeeling. They can lose touch with the very essence that they are trying to serve with their structures. Each sign has a way to fulfill the other's needs.

Balancing the Cancer-Capricorn Polarity

Cancer and Capricorn are another pair of divine complements. When they act out their polarity as an opposition, they can seem miles apart. Cancer's constant attunement to the world of feelings can be aggravating to Capricorn's larger interests. Capricorn's big-picture view and remote demeanor can threaten Cancer's need for a warm, fuzzy world. They can split into *neediness versus remoteness*. Although they appear to irreconcilable in their differences, they are really speaking the same language. They both find their purpose *in the care and perpetuation of life*. They both want to create and support something enduring. They just take different approaches—one personal, the other worldly. The spectrum of Cancer-Capricorn polarity may be expressed as follows:

| Possible Qualities of the Cancer-Capricorn Polarity ||
Cancer	*Capricorn*
nurturing	structuring
embracing	filling, containing
childlike	savvy, worldly
childish	controlling
needy	remote
smothering	isolated

Once they understand their common purpose, Cancer-Capricorn can begin to turn opposition into complementarity. In complementarity, these signs can provide us with the ability to *give responsible support, from personal to global.*

Cancer-Capricorn in Our Chart

If we have both ends of this polarity in our own chart, we may tend to seesaw between emotionalism and remoteness. "Am I overreacting? Am I opening up enough?" We are trying to find the way to balance our inner and outer worlds.

Healing a Cancer-Capricorn Split

When Cancer and Capricorn express as an opposition, we can heal the split by *taking self-responsibility*. We do not need to focus on the other person or what they are doing, but only on our own needs, for no one can rely on a single other person to fulfill them.

> **When Cancer and Capricorn express as an opposition,**
> **we can heal the split by taking self-responsibility.**

When we take responsibility for ourselves, we face what we bring to a situation and accept that we will make mistakes that we will be able to correct. Then we can learn to sort out our fears and projections from the sensations of the moment. We can learn to draw boundaries between ourselves and others, and consistently give when our partner is open to receiving. We can learn to reach beyond our fears and trust our partner by sharing our emotions. When we are responsible for ourselves, we do not muddy the waters of our relationship with blaming. We are receptive to our partner's openings and closings to us because we respect their need to determine their own path. We know that this allows them to give us the time and space to grow, too. We are also willing to open and share our own tender feelings at the right time, because we know that it enriches the love bond. In this way, Cancer and Capricorn blend harmoniously.

★★★

Leo-Aquarius

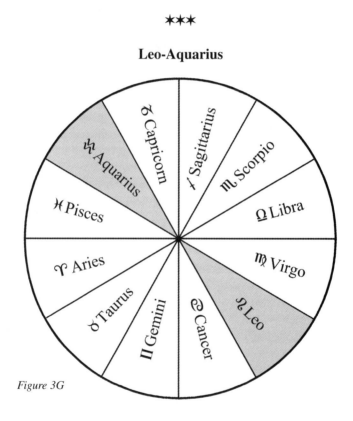

Figure 3G

Leo the Giver

It is Leo's nature to give. With their cheery, outgoing attitude, their sun brightens anyone's day. Everything they do exudes love—love of life, love of others, love of expression.

More than anything, the Leo in us loves to express itself. However, to stop here would deny Leo's purpose, for there is a reason for all that energy. People with Leo emphasis want to find their special role in the group, and their preferred method is to express and measure themselves by the response they get.

It is little wonder that Leonians are responsible for many wonderful creations, from arts and crafts, to drama and comedy, to sports and games. They want to be best, in the spotlight, because when they receive attention from others, they will know that they are unique and accepted as a member of the group.

> **Leo's generous spirit and desire for self-expression**
> **come from a deep inner drive to share love.**

At its heart and in best form, Leo's generous spirit and desire for self-expression come from a deep inner drive to share love. When Leo's pure light shines on us, we know what we are feeling—pure, heart-centered love. The heart is the source of all of Leo's joy for life. No matter what they do, they feel best when they are giving joy to others. They are in their center, the heart that is their home and source of being.

However, the Leonian who is not centered, but rather in their ego, will give just so they can receive. Everything has strings attached to it. The giving is hollow because it doesn't come from the True Self, where giving is out of the pure spirit of love, without thought of what will be returned. Empty giving doesn't get the positive response from others that the Leonain seeks. The giving becomes seeking—the pursuit of pleasure and approval. The fire burns on insincerity, love seems false, and joy is flat. They no longer inspire or incite interest because the heart feeling is absent. At their worst, people with Leo emphasis can be obsequious, seeking the approval of anyone who will listen. They become competitive, as if there's not enough love to go around. If Leos are hurt, they may hide behind an arrogant demeanor, but this is only a way of protecting themselves. Their basic nature is childlike and does not mean to harm.

Leo in Our Chart

If we have a strong Leo nature, we want to shine for our partner. We want their love and approval, and we want to shine our heart love on them and bask in the shared heart light. However, our love may at times become dependent upon our partner's light. Our heart may become brittle, easily broken at our partner's slightest imbalance. We may at times hide behind pride when we feel hurt.

Leo in Our Partner's Chart

If our partner carries Leonine traits, they will want to shine their love light on us. When heart-centered, they will give without concern for love's return. When they are feeling insecure, they may withdraw or pull on us to give them the love and attention they crave, for more than anything they fear being unloved.

How Aquarius Supports Leo

While an essential part of our nature, Leo's loving but self-oriented focus needs a counterbalance. This comes naturally from adding the qualities of Aquarius the Maverick. Aquarius's intellectualism and independence supply a missing link. When both signs of the polarity are activated, the scales come to rest.

Aquarius the Maverick

Where Leo is warm and effusive, Aquarius is cool and detached. Its function is to place the role of the individual within the group as an equal player, not a star. While each of us has a right and need to express our uniqueness, the needs and purpose of the group must also be taken into account. This is Aquarius's domain.

People with an Aquarian emphasis in their chart see themselves in the context of the groups that they belong to. The groups may be actual clubs or organizations, or they may be our ethnic or cultural group, social class, political party, or network of colleagues and acquaintances. Any "affiliations" we have—any groups we identify with—fit into this category.

Aquarians are "political animals," ever mindful of the group function, its purpose, and their role within the group. More than anything else, they have strong opinions about the roles they fulfill relative to other members. They often project into the group their own sense of justice. They are likely to have strong political feelings and be aware of the politics—the sense of justice and power play—of the groups to which they belong.

Aquarius's purpose is to create and develop the balance of individual versus group so that each person can freely express their potential and the group is able to serve its members.

Aquarians are known for plunging into a group with a team spirit. They want to play or work on a level playing field, on a par with others. They prefer a structure without hierarchy in it—they don't want to be above or below someone else in the structure. They will tend to feel that everyone should be equal. But, however much they identify themselves in terms of the group, Aquarians do not want to be considered a mere faceless member. They each want to be an individual, free to express who they are. Often they focus specifically on being different. They may enjoy dressing unusually, have different opinions from the rest of the group, or hold themselves aloof. They may participate without actually joining, preferring their independence over the benefits and responsibilities of group membership. Remember that this can apply to cultural and ethnic groups as well; Aquarians can often be uncomfortably outspoken or violate group rules, from the perspective of more conformist members of the group.

Ultimately, Aquarius's purpose is to develop the balance of individual versus group so that each person can freely express their potential and the group is able to serve its members. Aquarius keeps the group alive and well by looking at it from outside and disturbing the status quo in order to rejuvenate it.

Aquarians can, like the other signs, express too much of a good thing. Individualism can become eccentricity; the sense of fairness and equality can become partisan; objectivity and detachment can become alienation; group revitalization can become rebellion and insurrection.

Aquarius in Our Chart

If our charts have Aquarian emphasis, we will place a high value on equality and reciprocity with our partner. We will want the independence to express ourselves freely, both within and outside the relationship. We will want the relationship to serve the partners, not the other way around. However, we may also find that our cool, detached approach does not always foster the love bond—that more warmth is needed. We may at times have difficulty accessing that warmth. Also, we may react against the commitment we have made if we feel we are being treated unfairly, losing our individuality, or forced to do something against our will.

Aquarius in Our Partner's Chart

If our partner has Aquarius featured in their chart, they will also value equality and fairness. When they rebel against you, it is not because they don't care for you, but because they want to be sure they are free to choose their own way of supporting the relationship. They fear being trapped without choice or the right to act as an individual.

How Leo Supports Aquarius

Leo naturally supplies the qualities that Aquarius needs in order to be balanced. Its warm enthusiasm balances Aquarius's cool objectivity. Its sense of its need for the group balances with Aquarius's detachment. Its warmth infuses Aquarius with the love it needs for each member of the group and a heartfelt commitment to its purpose. Without heart, Aquarius can be cold and alienated.

Balancing the Leo-Aquarius Polarity

Although Leo and Aquarius are opposites in the zodiac, they don't have to behave as opposites in real life. Leo wants to define its specialness and give itself to a group from the place where specialness dwells—the heart. Aquarius wants to define its rights and role as a unique and equal member of the group. Although their needs and interests appear to be quite different, they are actually united in *their interest in how the group and the individual interact with each other.* Leo contributes love and inspirational leadership. Aquarius contributes a sense of individuality, justice, and equality. When Leo and Aquarius are acted out as an opposition, they appear as *specialness versus equality.* Some of the ways they express are:

Possible Qualities of the Leo-Aquarius Polarity	
Leo	*Aquarius*
self-determining	altruistic, humanitarian
enthusiastic	intellectual
dramatic	objective
"the star"	detached
approval-seeking	rebellious
arrogant	reactionary

Leo-Aquarius in Our Chart

If we have this polarity in our chart, we may be at war with ourselves over whether we are being fair to our partner, or to others, if we try to express our specialness. We ask, "Am I being fair? When can I let people see who I really am?" We want to find the way to balance our need to be unique with our need to be part of a group.

> *To mend the gap between Leo and Aquarius,*
> *we must remember that everyone is special.*

Healing a Leo-Aquarius Split

To mend the gap between Leo and Aquarius, we must remember that *everyone is special*. When we know this, we feel confident about expressing our own uniqueness, because we know that everyone has something to contribute that no one else can give. In this way, we open the door to others' unique self-expression because we know that each person is a gift in their own way. When others are allowed to contribute, they are inclined to accept all expressions with a sense of fairness. This sets the stage for the equality of all members of the group, whether it is in your partnership or another, less intimate affiliation.

Thus, when we remember that everyone is special, we naturally feel free to contribute our own creative impulses without fear of overwhelming someone. We can easily allow others to express theirs without the fear of being shut out. In this way, the Leo-Aquarius guise of the ego is disarmed.

✦✦✦

Virgo-Pisces

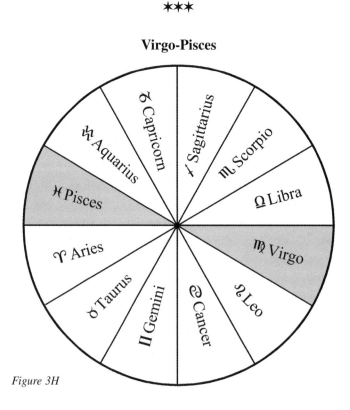

Figure 3H

Virgo the Harvester

Virgo and Pisces are the last polarity of the zodiac, since we started the wheel with Aries and Libra. Symbolically, they complete the process begun by Aries-Libra. Virgo engages in this completion by gathering together, or harvesting, all the things learned in the previous signs, Aries through Leo. It isn't enough to learn the individual lessons and processes taught in each sign. We must put them to use in our life.

This is Virgo's domain, applying the inner nature in the real world. When we do this successfully, we provide support to others in the world in some way, and in return we are supported.

The Virgo in us harvests the crops of understanding planted in the previous signs. In order to do so, we must have skills and techniques. Through Virgo, we develop skills and refine methods so that we can achieve our aims efficiently. We choose what we want from the harvest carefully and logically—only the best will do. With an emphasis in Virgo, our practical and analytical skills are very strong.

The core drive that lies beneath everything Virgoans do is to find and fulfill purpose, to apply the inner nature in the real world.

Virgoans are excellent at making things work. At their best, they can see into the heart of a situation and find a way to accomplish what is desired. They can be expert problem-solvers, taking what others hand them and applying the necessary skills and techniques to find a solution.

Personally, they are often shy, with humility and a "can-do" attitude. They are loyal to friends, family, and lovers, but sometimes they approach their love relationships with intellect and duty. They may forget about the warmer side of loving. However, once they learn to trust, they can be both sensual and sensitive.

In their logical and analytical approach to life, Virgoans naturally see the details that make up the whole. In fact, they may become so overwhelmed by the details of their world that they become stressed and anxious. Anxiety then takes its toll on the body in the form of tension, and they often become concerned with their health, and with learning ways to relax.

At the heart of their nature is *discernment*, the ability to separate things according to qualities. They apply discernment in all that they do. The core drive that lies beneath everything they do is *to find and fulfill purpose*, because that is the best way to distinguish between items. They think, *What is the purpose of this distinction (or this object, idea, etc.)?* After they understand why a distinction is being made, they can properly categorize and use the object(s) of their focus. They can breathe inner life into outer forms—use the harvest for the most appropriate purposes.

When Virgo energy is overused, it loses its sense of purpose. Analysis turns into criticism, discernment becomes perfectionism, and the quest for purpose gets lost in a mass of details. Virgo's warm, sensual side gets buried in the dry world of the overused, anxious mind.

Virgo in Our Chart

If Virgo is a strong part of our nature, then once we give our heart, we stand by our beloved. Our love may not be flashy, but in its quiet under-statement, it is deep and rich with meaning. At times we may forget to love with our heart as well as our head. We feel hurt when our partner doesn't approach the relationship with the same sense of duty and loyalty. Our efforts to seek perfection in ourselves may lead us to project the search onto our partner; then, we may feel that our partner is not good enough. It may help to realize that we are really trying to hide from what we see as our own imperfections.

Virgo in Our Partner's Chart

If our partner has Virgo qualities, they may show their love by doing things for us. They may find deep, meaningful discussions as rewarding as making love. At times they may forget about romantic gestures, but that is only because they express their love by serving us. When they become crit-ical, withdraw into busy-ness, or seem to lose track of what's important, they may be trying to hide from their flaws, afraid to admit to their mis-takes. Sometimes all it takes is a touch, a kind word, or a cup of tea to wake up the warm side of their nature. Then, they will relax and open up to us.

How Pisces Supports Virgo

When Virgoans get caught up in the details of everything they do, they lose touch with their sense of purpose. Caught up in a world of worry and details, what they need is the fluid, healing energies of Pisces to restore them to their sense of purpose and meaning, and to allow them to relax and find their center.

Pisces the Visionary

Pisces is the sign through which we relate to pure energy without form. This is what we all return to at the end of our time on earth. Eventually we all reunite with the One from which we have all come.

No one is more mindful of this than Pisceans. They can feel it, if only because when they are around something or someone for a while, they tend to take on the qualities of that influence!

Pisceans are aware of the subtle shifts of energy that take place in and around them. Sometimes they can see the clouds of color spinning and shooting across the room around and between us. They can feel another person's feelings as if they were their own—in fact, they often have difficulty telling which are their own feelings and which are someone else's.

Pisceans are meant to bring out the spiritual potential in themselves and those around them. They are here to show us how we are all One.

Pisceans are attuned to space rather than time. They carry a vision of what can be, naturally seeing the potential in any situation or person. They may see this potential as real, more real than personality or appearance. Their urge is to bring that out into the world. For this reason, they are often drawn to those who are weak or disadvantaged. They want to assist them in finding their way in life, nurturing their inner potential, encouraging it to surface. At their core, Pisceans are meant to bring out their own spiritual potential, providing an example to those around them. They are here to show us how we are all One. By focusing on the God-Self hidden within us, they inspire us to identify with it. Ultimately they can rekindle the Divine Spark in us, quickening our awareness of who We really are.

If those with strong Pisces traits learn to tune in to their inner sense, they will see into matters far more sensitively than most others. Their awareness can be precisely attuned to the essence of a situation. They can be very good at carefully drawing the best out of those whom they have chosen to serve. On the other hand, when Pisceans look outside themselves for their sense of self, they mold themselves to those around them. If this is the case, Pisceans should be selective in their choice of friends and associates.

Sometimes they get lost in their efforts to be of assistance. Their identity may get caught up in the influence of others—their self may become overwhelmed by others. When they lose their center, they can become confused, vague, and overly sensitive. They may try to be the white-knight rescuer, overstepping their bounds in their fervor to bring out potential in others. They may martyr themselves to a cause, and love the underdog, believing that everyone is worth saving. In addition, their sensitivity may bring them to try to skirt responsibility.

Pisces in Our Chart

If Pisces is strong in our chart, we can bring the light of spirit into our life and into that of our partner. However, we must take care to let them do their own work of growing. We must hold our boundaries, not sacrificing ourselves to a situation that is not good for us. We must take the time to sort out who we are from amongst the cacophony of influences and experiences we encounter on a daily basis. Otherwise, we may become overwhelmed, confused, and oversensitive.

Pisces in Our Partner's Chart

If our partner has a Piscean aspect to their character, we must remember that they feel subtle forces more than most of us do. It is important to honor their sensitivity, yet remain true to ourselves. Even if they want to rescue us from ourselves, we must remember that to be responsible to them and to our relationship, we must stand on our own feet. When they try to avoid facing the music, what they really need is some time and space to sort themselves out. They are most afraid of being overwhelmed—give them your compassion as you stand firm in your Self so they know where they stand.

How Virgo Supports Pisces

When Pisceans are vague, overwhelmed and confused, they have lost their sense of self, their boundaries. They feel limitless and adrift. Virgo's sense of discernment, and ability to put potential into a useful form, is just the cure. By looking for the practical and logical aspects in any issue, Virgo can assist Pisces in coming down to earth and finding natural boundaries. Together, the two signs bring harmony to each other.

Balancing the Virgo-Pisces Polarity

Virgo and Pisces can find the same harmony as the other polarities by discovering their common ground. Virgo brings spirit into matter, molding the forces of the universe together as a service to all existence. Pisces finds the spirit that already exists in things of the physical world, including us, and helps to develop and display their Great Potential. When they split into opposition, they may seem to pit *practicality* against *spirituality*. Although they are looking at things from opposite perspectives, they are really saying the same thing: *Spirit and Matter are One.*[7] They both seek perfection: one on earth, the other within. Here are some of the oppositions found with Virgo and Pisces.

Possible Qualities of the Virgo-Pisces Polarity	
Virgo	*Pisces*
practical	visionary
discerning	empathic/accepting
logical/analytical	surrendering
dedicated/committed	self-annihilating
critical	spineless
belittling	losing the Self

In complementarity, the two halves of the brain work together, really capturing the essence of spirit, of the magical—seeing beyond the ordinary and bringing it into practical form.

---

[7] Nowhere is this better illustrated than in the beautiful spiritual practice of the Sufis known as the *dzikr* (ZICK-er). In the dzikr, one chants in Arabic, "There is nothing but God." This is chanted with two meanings: the "positive" dzikr, where it means that everything we see is God; and the "negative" dzikr, which holds the meaning that all we see is illusion, because only God is real. There are also two words for "the beauty of God" in Arabic, *jemal,* 'the beauty that descends from God,' and *jelal,* 'the beauty that returns to God.' In each case, the first example is Virgoan and the second is Piscean.

Remember that we can find all of these qualities in ourselves, even if only one (or none) of these signs is populated by planets or points in our chart. We do not have to look to a partner to "fill the gap" in our nature if we find ourselves out of balance. Once we develop qualities of both signs of the polarity, we find that we express each one more at the soul level, and they begin to merge in their expression. Whether we are bringing spirit into matter, or finding the spirit already inherent in matter, it will feel like the same thing. We are *integrating* the seen and unseen worlds into One.

Virgo-Pisces in Our Chart

If we have a Virgo-Pisces polarity in our chart, we will tend to be caught up in the dilemma of what's real and how to make it so. We may ask, "Am I being too critical, expecting too much of my partner? Am I living in a dream world?" We want to find the balance between the spiritual and the physical in our life.

Healing a Virgo-Pisces Split

To turn a Virgo-Pisces opposition into a complementarity, we must *learn to accept and forgive ourselves*. No matter what sign we find ourselves in, until we love and accept who we are, we cannot relate to others without criticism, judgment, blame, or loss of self. The harsh eye we turn on others is not nearly so harsh as the one we turn on ourselves. Until we forgive ourselves, we feel as though we are "not-enough." When we are not-enough, we try too hard to be what we're not; we dishonor who we are and deny our divine nature.

To turn a Virgo-Pisces opposition into a complementarity, we must learn to accept and forgive ourselves.

When we forgive ourselves, however, we empower ourselves to be who We are and dislodge the ego from its seat on the throne of the Self. We can admit our mistakes because we are gentle and patient with ourselves. We can heal our wounds and correct our errors because we have faced ourselves and released blame and guilt to the Higher Power. This is forgiveness. In this way, we find that we do not need to hold on to our old patterns.

Only when we can do this for ourselves can we forgive others. When we are empowered by self-forgiveness, others recognize it unconsciously and are empowered as well. We are gentle and patient with others because we remember how long it took for us to correct our own errors. When we live in a state of such open self-acceptance, our Soul naturally assumes its proper role on the throne of the Self and can be brought fully into the world. Thus can the purposes of both Virgo and Pisces be fulfilled.

What's Next?

Now that we have visited each of the polarities, take the time to mull over which of them speak to you the most loudly. Do not be surprised if more than one speak to you—and remember, we each have every polarity in our chart. One or two may leap out at you as lifelong issues (at least so far), while some others may seem to be important in your life only recently.

Each polarity has its turn to be prominent. Every polarity that feels strong in your life will be mirrored at times in your relationships. Even if the polarity is entirely in our own chart, we will still attract people to us—including our partner—who will help us play out its balancing act in our life. Sometimes they will play one sign, at times the other, and we will find ourselves switching to the opposite until we learn, with them, to blend the two signs into complementarity—to take them to the soul level, where they function as One.

The process of growth is always one of fluctuation—never a straight line. As we understand more about our polarities, we spend more and more time in complementarity, less and less in opposition. Every time we feel ourselves slip into opposition, it is because the ego has taken control of the self. A change in attitude is all that is necessary to begin the corrective process, reversing the trend toward opposition. Yet, we cannot control our partner—most often we cannot even effect immediate changes in our own attitude. We must allow change to evolve from the core of our being in complete sincerity. Once we are able to turn the tide toward healing, the forces of complementarity begin to bring us back to equilibrium, union with our partner.

Don't forget that we do not need a partner to provide us with the complementary qualities of a polarity. Even if our chart has planets in only one sign of a polarity, we can supply the missing energies to balance our nature. In fact, we must be responsible for making ourselves whole without reference to our partner. The most we can do is to observe and learn from our partner—allow them to be an example and accept their guidance as we make ourselves whole.

Remember that we are each sovereign beings, complete and perfect within ourselves. When we find a mate, we bring our developing sense of ourselves to our beloved. And so begins the dance of love.

In the next chapter, we will build on what we have learned about the polarities, to see another facet of relating to each other through the lens of astrology—that of how we respond to each other.

RESPONDING TO EACH OTHER

S o far we have talked about relationships and how they work outside the frame of astrology. We have looked at the 12 signs of the zodiac as 6 polarities, capable of being played out harmoniously in our relationships and in our own nature. We have seen how a polarity can be split into an opposition or healed to express divine complementarity. We have found that such complementarity can bring the synergy we all crave to a relationship. In the next two chapters, we will explore how astrology speaks to the time-honored dynamics of all relationships—comfort and conflict.

In the beginning, there is comfort, stimulation, and attraction. But, unless we work on renewing our relationships:

- comfort becomes boredom.
- stimulation becomes conflict.
- attraction becomes difficult lessons.

In this chapter, we will explore how stimulation can turn into conflict. We can do so by looking through another of astrology's windows on relationships—response types. When we stay in tune with our partner, we automatically respond to each other in reciprocity. We appreciate what they present to us and continue to be open to them and to their ideas.

However, sometimes we get caught up in the ideas or experiences that they bring to us, and we lose track of our connectedness. Those who know us have a way of pushing our most sensitive buttons, bringing out our deepest fears and distrusts. Our responses may then become frozen into automatic patterns or strategies that we relied upon in the past, when we felt fear.

As with polarities, we usually have one natural way of responding, even though we have all three response types within us. If we can understand our own response type and also our partner's, we will not be triggered into automatic, rigid reaction, but instead will express fluid, spontaneous, and harmonious responses. This awareness also makes it less likely that we will trigger our partner's automatic reaction pattern.

The Response Types

By grouping the signs in a different way than we have done so far, the response type qualities rise to the surface. There are three groups of four signs each, showing us the response-type qualities—cardinal, fixed, and mutable. Around the wheel of the zodiac, they are shown in Figure 4A.

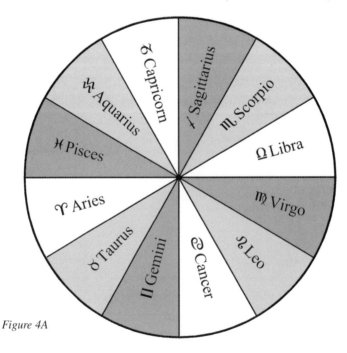

Figure 4A

As you can see, every third sign starting with Aries is a cardinal sign. The fixed signs are next in order, and the mutable signs complete the procession. If you look more carefully, you'll see that each polarity is in the same response type—after all, didn't we discover that polarities can come out as conflict, or reaction? Each polarity is grouped with another to make a response type, and together they form a large cross in the chart if you connect the four signs of a single response type.

Cardinal, fixed, and *mutable* are the terms that astrologers have used for centuries to describe these, but they need a little explaining in modern times.

Cardinal generally means first, most important, or fundamental. In astrology, the cardinal signs are those where each season starts. Cardinal signs are thought to start or initiate action. They like new things. They will tend to have new ideas and want to take the lead. The cardinal signs (in order of the zodiac) are Aries, Cancer, Libra, and Capricorn. (Notice the Aries-Libra and Cancer-Capricorn polarities here.)

The **fixed** signs are stabilizing. They are associated with the middle of each season, when the qualities of the season settle in. Fixed sign people are generally good at following up, doing the substantive work to bring the form or foundation of something into being. The fixed signs are Taurus, Leo, Scorpio, and Aquarius.

The **mutable** signs could be called "flexible," for the time when the seasons are beginning to show signs of changing. They are the problem-solvers, and as implied, they change easily. They work with forms already created, striving to perfect, integrate, fix (heal), and complete them. Their flexibility allows them to work with what is already in place. The mutable signs are Gemini, Virgo, Sagittarius, and Pisces.

Although we may think of cardinal as being "first" in the process, it is not first in order of importance, or in the order of events in life. In fact, cardinal's new ideas come as a natural outgrowth of what the mutable sign before finds out doesn't work, in a conceptual sense. Since astrology is a circle, the cycle can start anywhere and go on endlessly.

Finding Your Response Type

If you have your chart, you can look at it to get an idea of what your response type is. Some charts will sort them out for you by giving you a tally or a "weighted score" for each type. In "astrologese," they are some-times called *modalities* or *quadruplicities*, although the latter term is rarely seen anymore.

If there is no analysis of these for you, you can tally up points for each thing that you have in your chart. Use these guidelines:

- Use the Response Type Tally Grid on page 293 of the appendix.
- Before you begin the above grid, have your astrological chart and your partner's in front of you.
- If your chart is not available, you can learn about your response type by completing the questionnaire, "What Response Type Are You?" found in the appendix on page 294.

Although this is not foolproof, you should by now have a good idea of what your strongest response pattern is, or if you are a mixed type. Before you go on, apply the same rules to your partner's chart. If you don't have their chart and can't seem to figure out their type another way, read on. As you learn more about the response types, you may figure it out.

The Cardinal Response Type

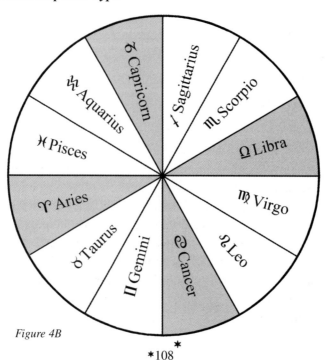

Figure 4B

The Cardinal Signs

♈ Aries
♋ Cancer
♎ Libra
♑ Capricorn

The Cardinal Response Pattern

ISSUE: Identity
EXPERIENCES: Loss of focus, direction, and sense of self
PRIMARY RESPONSE: Make it their own idea
SECONDARY RESPONSE: Action; do their own thing
TO GET A POSITIVE RESPONSE: Make suggestions, let them take the lead

With a strong cardinal response pattern, we may find that:

- our interest arises easily, but lacks staying power.
- we make changes easily if it's our idea or if we have some control or self-interest.
- we may need encouragement.
- we will try new things.
- we need to take the lead.
- we may remake others' ideas into our own.
- what you see is what you get.

Each response type has an issue at the heart of its way of experiencing and acting on something new. "Something new" can be anything from an unexpected phone call, to an environment other than home, to a new idea. Even the smallest interaction contains elements of newness in it, so we are all responding in subtle ways to something new all the time.

If we have a cardinal pattern, our issue is **identity**. When we are under pressure, we may lose our focus, sense of direction, and concept of who we are. We will question our sense of self.

Our **primary response** will be enthusiastic, because we love new ideas. We may think of other new ideas to go along with or replace the first suggestion. In our excitement, we may also try to take over.

Our **secondary response** is to take action. However, our enthusiasm may die quickly. Other ideas and interests emerge and vie for our attention. After all, the new idea has to compete with all the other new ideas we already have!

The danger is getting spread too thin or becoming too commandeering. We may *become unfocused and have difficulty finishing things*. As one project gets piled upon the next, we lose track of what we're doing and lose our focus. Our identity, which we associate with our efforts, gets lost, too.

If our partner has a strong cardinal response pattern, they will exhibit the above qualities. To interact more harmoniously with them, while still maintaining our own sovereignty, we can:

- make suggestions, but let them take the lead on their own behalf. If we are comfortable with it, we can follow.
- be willing to share the limelight, if this is our project or initiative, yet we want their wholehearted participation. Take a team approach. Otherwise, continue on and give them time and space to realize that it's okay for them to take a backseat this time.
- let them know how our idea will benefit them personally.
- allow them to express their enthusiasm and all the new ideas that are generated from it.
- give them their head to approach things in their own way, but give them feedback on the needs of others who are affected by their efforts.
- give them regular encouragement to keep them focused.
- remind them of the team's interest in the project and its outcome.
- be willing to facilitate the fixed and mutable functions.

No response type responds positively to the use of force. If our cardinal partner is not open to our input, giving them the time and space to grow will help them become more receptive.

If we are struggling with our own automatic reaction as a cardinal type, we can:

> • recognize that every new idea doesn't have to be ours.
>
> • remind ourselves that we can still make valuable contributions, even if we are not in the lead.
>
> • think of other initiatives that we are already involved in or can begin in the future.
>
> • look at the situation from another person's point of view.
>
> • open ourselves to what others are trying to tell us.

If we have a strong cardinal response pattern, then when we are in balance, we will be naturally uplifting to others. Our enthusiasm and drive will inspire, and our courage will make others want to follow.

The Fixed Response Type

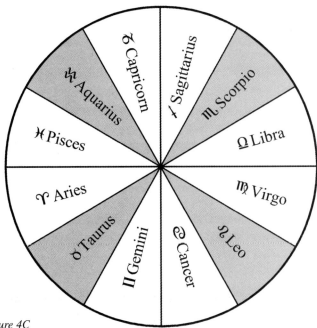

Figure 4C

The Fixed Signs

♉	Taurus
♌	Leo
♏	Scorpio
♒	Aquarius

The Fixed Response Pattern

ISSUE: Self-esteem
EXPERIENCES: Loss of foundation, stability, and self-love
PRIMARY RESPONSE: Resistance, withdrawal
SECONDARY RESPONSE: Probing, testing
TO GET A POSITIVE RESPONSE: Be patient and give them time to respond

With fixed response pattern tendencies, we may find that we:

- have a tendency to hold things in.
- are slow to change.
- need time to get used to new ideas.
- will naturally resist change and newness; however, once accepted, we will be committed to it.
- need initial support and trust.
- will become stubborn if pushed or manipulated.
- may not overtly respond.

The fixed signs' function is to sustain what is already established. If we have a fixed response pattern, then when we encounter something new, our **primary response** is to resist or withdraw. We need time to think things over, to see if the new concept fits with what is already established. We will not mind making improvements if the new thing is really going to make things better. However, we will need to test, examine, and investigate to find out if it will. This is our **secondary response**.

With fixed signs, if we become overwhelmed by new stimuli, we may experience a loss of **self-esteem.** Since we think of things in terms of their value, we may feel as though who we are and what we stand for isn't worthwhile. If we give ourselves time to consider a new idea carefully, we will be able to sort things out, consider all the possible results of the changes it will bring, and make a decision. We do not make decisions lightly: Once we have made a choice, we will remain true to it.

The danger lies in closing ourselves off to newness. Nothing ever remains the same; the nature of life is to grow and change. Although we can keep our filters up so that we are satisfied that the changes we make are right for us, we must remain open to new things. If we completely reject newness, we *get stuck in a rut and begin to die.* Being open does not mean giving automatic acceptance. It means being ready to consider the new things that we encounter as we go through life. We will not accept all of them, but by considering each, we will find that some new things are right for us.

If our partner has a strong fixed response pattern, they will show the above qualities. To interact more harmoniously with them, while still maintaining our own sovereignty, we can:

- be patient and give them time to respond.

- hold ourselves open to their input, even though it may not come right away.

- try not to flood them with a lot of new ideas all at once.

- be willing to discuss a new option and its repercussions with them, but wait for their openness.

- allow them to safely and sensitively test, explore, and examine the new idea.

- be open to alternative proposals.

- once they have made a decision, expect them to stick to it. If this doesn't work for you, find ways to achieve your goal individually, if possible. If you need their participation, patiently standing in your truth may engage them in further negotiation.

- be willing to facilitate the cardinal and mutable functions in the initiative.

People with a strong fixed response pattern will react to the use of force by digging in their heels. Giving them time to consider and adjust will bring out the best in them.

If we are struggling with our own automatic reaction as a fixed type, we can:

- give ourselves the time and space to sort things out to our own satisfaction, to let our best decision emerge.

- communicate about our need to proceed slowly.

- be willing to discuss our thoughts and feelings with others.

- recognize that when someone offers a new idea, it is not because they think something is wrong with us or what we have done.

- remember that change is an important part of maintaining stability.

If we have a strong fixed response pattern, then when we are centered, we will be naturally stabilizing and comforting to others. Our reliability and perseverance will feel like an anchor, and our willingness to resist outside pressures will hearten others to obey their own inner truth as well.

The Mutable Response Type

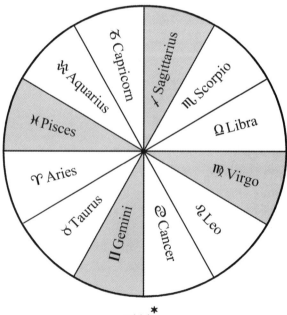

Figure 4D

The Mutable Signs

♊ Gemini
♍ Virgo
♐ Sagittarius
♓ Pisces

The Mutable Response Pattern

ISSUE: Wholeness
EXPERIENCES: Loss of completeness, completion, and self-integrity (scattering)
PRIMARY RESPONSE: Agreement, accommodation ("Okay, whatever")
SECONDARY RESPONSE: Reconsideration, regret, avoidance
TO GET A POSITIVE RESPONSE: Don't accept the first response; wait for the expression of their true feelings

With a strong mutable response pattern, we may find that we:

- are basically flexible, wanting to make things work.
- have frequent ups and downs.
- easily take on and cast off new ideas and situations.
- are open to newness but have to work at discipline, may live chaotically/arrhythmically.
- are sensitive to outside stimuli.
- want instant results, becoming easily discouraged.
- may not follow through due to distractions, scattering.

With a mutable response pattern, our **primary response** to something new will be to accept or agree to it. We are flexible and sensitive, often overly receptive to others' input. However, not every idea is right for everyone, and we too need time to decide if something is right for us; while the fixed sign person needs time to come to a first decision, the mutable sign person needs it to reconsider their first decision. So, while our first response may be acceptance, our **secondary response** could be reconsideration, regret, and anxiety.

If we feel overwhelmed by newness, we may experience a loss of **wholeness.** We may have difficulty in maintaining our integrity.[8] We may become fragmented, anxious, overcome, and confused. We may feel as though we are split, and we may attempt to avoid new ideas rather than deal with them.

If, instead of facing the issue we are dealing with, we simply say something agreeable to end the discussion as soon as possible, it festers in our consciousness. Others may perceive us as hypocritical when we find it necessary to shift our stance. If we slow down and resist the urge to agree instantly, we can avert the loss of wholeness that comes with changing our mind. This is how we can assist our own integration process.

If our partner has a strong mutable response pattern, they will exhibit the above qualities. To interact more harmoniously with them, while still maintaining our own sovereignty, we can:

- recognize that their first response may not be their true response.

- wait for their second response, for their true feelings to be expressed.

- encourage them to think things over before agreeing.

- make suggestions gently; then they will come to know their own desires more quickly.

- once they have made a decision that you feel comes from their True Self, support them in sticking with it.

- assist them in facing, and then holding firm with, others who wish to push their ideas on them.

- If the newness involves establishing a new routine, help them remember to follow it until it is an automatic part of their life.

- be willing to facilitate the cardinal and fixed functions in the initiative.

---

[8] Here, *integrity* means not "honesty," but "completeness."

If we use force against someone with a mutable response pattern, they will go into deep avoidance. Essentially, they will leave or disconnect from us in an attempt to regroup or find themselves. Outwardly, their cover-up may be so skillful that the forcing person will never know that they are no longer present or that anything is wrong. They may actually lie or change their mind without telling us because of their sensitivity.

If we are struggling with our own automatic reaction as a mutable type, we can:

- recognize that it is important for us to honor our own needs before someone else's.
- choose to disagree if that's right for us.
- change our mind.
- slow down long enough to pull ourselves back together, into a whole and centered person.
- face the music and tell the truth.

When our mutable nature is in balance, we will find that our flexibility and fluidity allows us to flow around life's obstacles. Our ability to solve problems and heal imbalances contributes to the completion of processes begun by others, and they appreciate our input.

Response Types—Ours and Our Partner's

We have talked about response types in our own or our partner's charts as if they were unrelated. However, we can also use them to relate the two charts to each other. Ironically, if our chart has the same overall response pattern as our partner's, it is more difficult for us, not less. This is because our response type is often a blind spot in our nature. Whenever we experience something new, the way it changes us is called our response. Our responses are the result of a stimulus plus our attitudes or expectations of life. We may respond mildly, without emotion, to "Please pass the salt," but if someone throws angry words in our face, we may have a reaction, full of emotion. Strong emotions turn responses into reactions; reactions are often perceived by others as an attack. When we become defensive, or react, to something our partner has said or done, they perceive an attack as well. We became defensive because we perceived our partner's first action as an attack. The cycle goes on until someone recognizes that *what appears to be one thing is actually another*. With care and sensitivity, we can disarm ourselves and clear the air. This will reduce our partner's defensive behavior, and reactions can return to responses.

Planets and Response Types

As discussed in chapter 1, planets can be related to each other by what astrologers call **aspects.** Here, we will call them **planetary interrelationships.** Two planets share the same response type when they are three or six signs apart from each other. The "Sign Interrelationship Chart" found in the appendix relates each sign to every other sign and tells what interrelationship exists between them (pages 299-300).

When two planets, whether in our own chart or between ours and our partner's, are in signs of the same response type, friction may develop because of the same response→reaction→defense-triggering process described above. However, as I have emphasized before, nothing difficult or unpleasant needs to stay that way. When planets do not have intrinsic harmony, we can develop or learn to apply an uncommon harmony through the creativity of our soul. At the soul level, we can see the common and harmonious function of all things. By applying an open, innocent (unprejudiced) focus to our experiences, we can break through to that level.

What's Next?

The six polarities function at the foundation of all relationships. They tell us about the major dynamics in our partnerships. The response types give us the little picture that means so much and affects everything—they show us how we and our partner respond and react to each other on a moment-to-moment basis. If we misunderstand our partner's response type, we can think they are trying to block our love, when all they are doing is honoring it in an unfamiliar way.

Next we will look at the ways that we are naturally similar to each other. By focusing on the harmonies of our love, we can keep our love strong and the hard parts in perspective.

C H A P T E R   F I V E

OUR NATURAL HARMONIES

We have looked at the challenge of relationships; similarity is their other major dynamic. Every relationship is founded in part on what we have in common, what works naturally for us in our approach to life. This is the basis of similarity, where we feel like our partner. Natural sympathy and agreement arise. Similarity is our foundation and our harbor during stormy periods in the relationship or in outer life. When we need comfort and safety, it can be found through our similarities. In astrology, they can be discovered by exploring approach types, the elements in our astrological charts.

How Similarity Works

Through similarity, we see ourselves in our partner, the parts of our self that we enjoy and accept. Unlike complementarities, which are a mixed bag, our ability to enjoy our partner through similarity is unfettered: Since we generally like the parts of ourselves that we identify with in our partner, we have no difficulty sharing those qualities with them. What we accept in ourselves we can love in another.

We can freely harmonize with our beloved through our similarities. This is literally true—we energetically resonate, or find harmonic resonance, with our partner. Like two strings on a guitar in perfect tune, we amplify each other's best qualities and bring them out in each other. We create new expressions through the "overtones" of our relationship. The more time we spend with each other, the more these qualities are enhanced.

The building of resonance is rapid at the beginning of a relationship; then it tapers off. This is part of the "high" of first love. We adapt to our partner and they to us in roughly equivalent amounts, if our relationship is based on reciprocity. It feels good—it is healing—to have our best qualities acknowledged and brought out by another, and to do the same for them. Energetic healing takes place in the same way, and active loving is a healing experience.

After we have spent some time with our partner, the building of resonance levels off. We reach a plateau, and unless we each keep growing as individuals—learning about ourselves and developing new qualities to introduce into the relationship—the relationship will remain at the same place. When this happens, what at first feels exhilarating and self-affirming becomes stagnant and deadening. Similarity brings comfort, and, in our humanness, we can't continually find pleasure in the same way all the time. There is a freshness as well as something familiar about what is pleasurable to us, and something that is the same all the time induces boredom, not comfort.

So it is not enough to rely on similarity—comfort—to sustain a relationship. It is an important component in giving us a feeling of safety with our partner, but we must also have enough excitement, enough newness to hold our interest.

So, we need a balance of complementarity and similarity. Now that we have an idea of how complementarity (polarity) works in our partnerships, we can explore how astrology shows us the qualities of similarity in them.

Finding Similarity in Our Charts

There are three types of similarity in our chart: *resonance, companionship,* and *harmony.* They describe the interrelationships between planets, whether the two planets are in the same chart, or whether one planet is in our chart, and the other is in our partner's, as follows:

- **Resonance** occurs when two planets are in the same sign. Here, the energies of the planets involved blend, or resonate at the same tone.

- **Companionship** flows when two planets are two signs apart from each other (one sign in between them). Here, harmony is created because the signs are both considered either masculine/active, or feminine/receptive. Both planets will tend to have a generally active or a generally receptive approach to life.

- **Harmony** is induced when two planets are of the same **approach type**, or four signs apart (three signs between them). Harmony does not involve the same tone as resonance does, but rather two different tones that go together very well. This is the case when two planets share the same approach type.

We will be exploring the companionship and harmony combinations as we develop our understanding of similarity in this chapter. Before we go into approach types, let's take a quick look at resonance.

Resonance in Our Charts

When two planets, whether in our chart or between ours and our partner's, are in the same sign, we experience a pure blending of the energies represented by those planets. Both will exhibit qualities of that sign. However, each planet will express the sign in a different way and deal with it somewhat differently. *More than any other planetary interrelationship, resonance is by far the most powerful.* We can place resonant planetary combinations at the top of our list of important links between ourselves and our partner.

If we have two planets in resonance in our own chart, we may have more success with one planet in the sign than the other. We may not be able to tell them apart—they may blend in our consciousness if they are planets that are not unlike each other in natural energy. However, if the planets are by nature unlike, we may express mostly the one we prefer, struggle to express them as a blend, or alternate between the two planets.

If the resonance lies between our chart and our partner's, we again look to the "blendability" of the planets. If they go together well, such as the sun and moon, or Mercury with anything, we can expect the resonance to be very pleasant. If the blending is between planets that experience some difficulty with each other—say, Venus and Saturn—we may need to work at refining their blend. Venus is very warm and bonding—the goddess of love. Saturn is structured and sets boundaries. They do not blend well without practice. The comfort of the blend depends mostly on the planets being blended, since resonance is neutral. That is, it does not add or subtract anything from the planets being blended. Since the planets share the same sign quality, dissimilarity in outlook is not an issue, only in their qualities.

When three or more planets are found in the same sign, we may experience extreme expressions of that sign. Even between partners, we must be careful to take into account other parts of our nature, even though the resonant interrelationship is so comfortable.

The Approach Types

There are three types of similarity in the birth chart: resonance, companionship, and harmony, or approach type. All are expressed through the interrelationships between the planets. In astrology, approach types are called **elements**. In addition to each sign having a response type (modality), discussed in chapter 4, it also is assigned an approach type (element). The elements are not those of modern chemistry but those found in the ancient sciences such as alchemy.[9] The ancient elements are **fire, earth, air,** and **water**. Since there are four approach types, three signs are given to each. Like the modalities, the approach types alternate in order with each other through the chart, so the first sign of the zodiac, Aries, is a fire sign, and every fourth sign after it—Leo and Sagittarius—are also fire signs, and so on.

The signs, differentiated by element, are shown in Figure 5A. If we were to draw lines joining the signs of a given element, they would form a triangle around the chart. These signs have qualities in common; they harmonize with each other.

---

[9] Alchemy is the parent of chemistry. Alchemists studied the various substances of matter, seeking to find ways that they could be combined or separated to enhance the qualities of the soul. They felt that if they could do something with physical substances, the soul would "copy" that process—by the law of harmonic resonance. As they became more focused on the physical properties of the substances they were investigating, their studies eventually became known as chemistry, and they lost the inner, soul component of their studies.

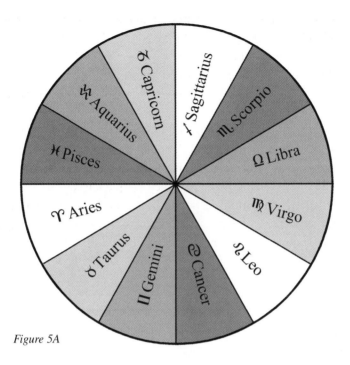

Figure 5A

Each of the signs gets along quite well with the other signs of its approach type because they have the same approach to the things they encounter in life. They are likely to see things and then come to understand and experience them in the same way. For instance, air signs will think about and apply ideas to deal with things they want to affect.

By understanding our chart and that of our partner in terms of their approach type qualities, we can find where we mesh with our beloved. We can discover what approach type is strongest in our charts and find out what kind of blend we have with our partner.

Finding Your Approach Type

If you have your chart, you can look at it to get an idea of what your approach type is, your approach to life. Some charts will give you a tally or a "weighted score" for each type. In "astrologese," they are sometimes called *qualities* or *triplicities*, although these terms are less favored than just being called "elements."

If there is no analysis for you, you can score yourself for each thing that you have in your chart. This is similar to what you did when you evaluated your response type (cardinal, fixed, or mutable). Use these guidelines:

- Use the Approach Type (Element) Tally Grid on page 296 of the appendix.
- Before you begin the above grid, have your astrological chart and your partner's in front of you.
- If your chart is not available, you can learn about your response type by completing the questionnaire,"What Approach Type Are You?" found in the appendix on pages 297-8.

After you have determined your own approach type, apply the same rules to your partner's chart. If you don't have their chart and can't seem to figure out their type another way, read on. As you learn more about the approach types, you may determine their predominant approach type.

The Four Approach Types and Our Chart

Let's look at what the approach types are, the signs that are assigned to them, and how we approach life if we are dominant in that element. This will give us a foundation for understanding how we are similar to our partner. We can and need to build on similarity; similarity will get us through the tough times of sorting out polarity issues and other challenges in our relationships.

The Fire Approach Type

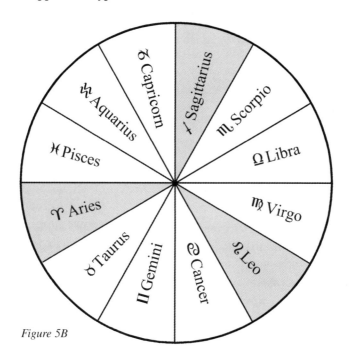

Figure 5B

The Fire Signs

♈	Aries
♌	Leo
♐	Sagittarius

PRIMARY QUALITY: Action (Outward expression)
RESPONSE: I'll do it!
PERCEPTION OF TRUTH: Internal (I am my own truth.)

The fire in us:

- expresses the energy of will (yang force).

- relies on its own fuel for sustenance ("the clinging"[10]).

- moves upward.

- expresses itself positively as high spirits, enthusiasm, humor, intensity, or joy.

- expresses itself negatively as impulsiveness, anger, reckless-ness, or lack of empathy.

- finds it difficult to express passivity, receptivity, patience, sensitivity, or stability.

If we think about the qualities of the physical element itself, we can see a great deal about how the fire signs behave in common. Fire is hot and volatile. Its movement is upward. It does not flow along its own lines but relies on the qualities and characteristics of its fuel for its direction and even its heat and volatility. A fire fueled by gas is very different from a fire fueled by wet wood. If a line of gunpowder is placed on the floor, the fire will fol-low the gunpowder, not go off on its own someplace.

If we take these qualities to a more symbolic level, we can see that fire is motivating and invigorating. It is the energy of life itself—it is how we move or animate ourselves. For all that it appears independent and self-motivating, it is actually dependent on its fuel source.

Fire in Our Chart

If fire is predominant in our chart, we tend to be energetic, energizing, and motivating. We also tend to be excitable, passionate, and spontaneous. We express our self directly, without strategy or falsehood. Emotions that we can express easily are anger, joy, enthusiasm, and humor. However, we are more self-oriented than empathic when expressing the fire side of our nature.

We generally have high spirits and an optimistic approach to life. We have great faith in ourselves and need freedom to express ourselves without

---

[10] In the Chinese five-element system, the element of fire is known as "the clinging" because it is dependent on its fuel source.

inhibition. Our flaws come more from insensitivity to others or a lack of self-control than from bad intentions. Our vigor may at times be overpowering to others. We may have difficulty being receptive, patient, sensitive, or stable.

Fire in Our Partner's Chart

If our partner has strong fire qualities, they will light up our life with excitement. They may be pushy at times, or burn brightly and then need to spend some time recuperating for the next flare of enthusiasm.

Remember that they need a fuel source, and it may be the people around them. If we feel that they are tiring us, we must let them know and then talk with our feet! Actions speak louder than words when they are in a fire mood.

We can help them to sustain their energies, rather than experiencing so many highs and lows, by distracting them from their "high passion" pursuits after a time. In quiet moments, or when they are exhausted from the latest "energy binge," enlist their support for more moderate behavior. Then, when they are in the moment, remind them of the benefits of moderation—for they are not likely to remember on their own.

Sometimes we will just have to wait to get their attention, because when they are burning brightly, we will not get a word in edgewise. If they seem to expect the world to revolve around them, it is unintentional. We must not get swept away by them and forget ourselves, for our own interests and pursuits are just as important.

How Fire Relates to the Other Approach Types

Each approach type does best with itself or with the approach type that is most like it. Fire does best with fire or air, because they are the "masculine" (yang or active) approach types. Air fans the fire—in fact, it provides another fuel source. Earth and water are not as good a mix with fire. Fire may feel "put out" by water's sensitivity and smothered by earth's heaviness.

✶✶✶

The Earth Approach Type

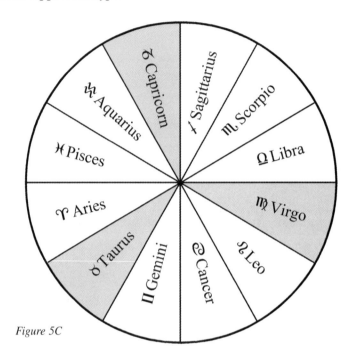

Figure 5C

The Earth Signs

♉	Taurus
♍	Virgo
♑	Capricorn

PRIMARY QUALITY: Sensing
RESPONSE: I sense it.
PERCEPTION OF TRUTH: Concrete (what you see is what you get)

The earth in us:

- provides sustenance (yin).

- resists movement.

- expresses itself when in balance as perceptiveness, sensuality, resourcefulness, practicality, or stability.

- expresses itself in extreme as depression, stubbornness, conservatism, or sacrifice of emotions for "reality."

- finds it difficult to express emotions, be flexible, or to have a sense of initiative or enterprise.

The element of earth relates to the physical world. It is solid and stable, resisting change or movement. It provides support, sustenance, and physical reality. Earth is in everything we see around us, from the forms of nature, to our relationship with the world, to anything associated with having a physical body. Things that we can touch and feel have form and are of the earth. Material or financial concerns are an extension of earth into our lives.

Symbolically, earth tends toward passivity, conservatism, resourcefulness, and roundedness. Earth people have a practical, "what you see is what you get" approach. They can take a very direct approach to life, without preconceived ideas, beliefs, or prejudices. They may not see the symbolism or deeper levels of intention, but their world is concrete and comforting. They are especially attuned to the sense of touch; they are sensual and perceptive of others, and can often physically feel sensations in their bodies that other people experience in a different way.

Earth in Our Chart

If earth is predominant in our chart, we will be practical, stable, receptive, and resourceful. We may tend to be creative, nurturing, and passive. We may approach things cautiously, mildly, and rationally. We are comfortable expressing our perceptiveness, sensuality, and nurturance. However, we may be less able to change, and even resist it, not knowing how to adapt. We may break down rather than change.

We generally have a steady, slow-burning energy level, experiencing neither high highs nor low lows. If anything, we may tend toward depression when we feel mired in the solidness of our approach type, or lose track of how we feel altogether. Generally, we are loyal to our causes, and have great faith in ourselves. We can make do with what is available. Sometimes, however, we may sacrifice emotional needs for "reality" or what is practical. Our faults are mostly self-inhibiting, but they may affect others if we become immobilized through lack of movement and change. We may be too clinical, efficient, practical, or conservative to be aware of what we feel or what we need emotionally.

Earth in Our Partner's Chart

If our partner has earth strongly in their nature, they will be an anchor to those who know them. They may be stubborn at times, or passive. If their energy level drops, it is because they have lost track of themselves in their concern for the forms around them.

Remember that they are sensitive and sensual, and that the sense of touch is one sure way to reach them, as it will bring them back to their center. If we become frustrated with the slow, deliberate way in which life seems to move around them, we must remember that this is another way of describing stability. When we encounter inflexibility, we can assist them by giving them time and space to open themselves—eventually they will. Take advantage of the slow, steady burn of their energy—once they're focused on something, nothing will keep them from it!

How Earth Relates to the Other Approach Types

Earth does best with itself or water, since both are receptive or yin (feminine) elements. Earth and water combine to create the potential for growth, because they combine gentle movement and structure. Air's impracticality and lack of seriousness may wear on earth. Fire's lack of concern for others may mean that earth allows fire to take advantage of it, creating resentment.

The Air Approach Type

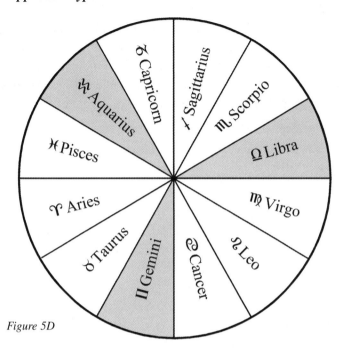

Figure 5D

The Air Signs

♊	Gemini
♎	Libra
♒	Aquarius

PRIMARY QUALITY: Thinking
RESPONSE: I think (about) it.
PERCEPTION OF TRUTH: External (comes from society)

The air in us:

- carries the energy of connection (yang).

- connects, transports, catalyzes other substances.

- moves across (horizontally).

- expresses itself when balanced as objectivity, sociability, flexibility, inquisitiveness, or quickness.

- expresses itself in extreme as insensitivity, remoteness, split nature, or shallowness.

- finds it difficult to express intimacy, intensity, emotion, cr stability.

The air element relates to wind, the atmosphere, and breath. It is a step closer to reality than its nearest cousin, fire, although it is still abstract. Where fire rises upward, air moves across, horizontally. It brings seed to soil, moisture to plant, and scent to predator. As it blows across the land, it is a vehicle for transport, a connector.

On a human level, air has to do with thinking, logic, and social interaction. Here, air connects thought to lips, concept to word, and people to each other. Air is objective and impersonal. It takes a perspective outside the self and accepts truth based on the concerns of others. It wants to cover as much ground as possible, to get the idea of the whole, and to connect all the parts into one understanding. Thought is the process that air uses in solving a problem.

Air in Our Chart

If air is a strong component in our chart, we will tend to be logical, objective, and socially oriented. We will enjoy being around people, talking, and engaging in other forms of communication. We may enjoy language for its own sake and love to engage in argument because it allows us to see things from another point of view. We are not likely to be invested in our own perspective any more than someone else's. We may love to flit around, exploring a variety of interests, getting to know a wide range of people. We are willing to change, but the most compelling motivation comes from the world of others.

We generally have a steady energy level but a short attention span. Our energy is often expended in short, regular bursts, like little gusts of wind. We enjoy short-term contact with just about anything, but may be at pains to stay with something for long, even if we are initially quite intrigued by it. This includes relationships: we may not do as well with intimacy as we do with initial acquaintance. Since air is impersonal, emotions may seem foreign to us; we may not be sensitive to others' needs beyond how they think. We have a quick intellect and are good at planning, observing, and communicating; however, we may be at pains to be practical, feeling, patient, or stable.

Air in Our Partner's Chart

If air is an emphasis in our partner's chart, they may tend to be all over the map in their efforts to understand what makes everything tick. Intensity is not a part of their nature—in fact, we may have a hard time getting them to do anything for long. Although they may seem insensitive, it is only because they live in the realm of thought and idea, not feeling. It may never occur to them that emotions enter into the picture until we give them feedback and they learn that other people have different ways of seeing things.

Our air partner may also be, or appear, fickle. The best way to counteract that is to keep our own life interesting. As long as we continue to grow for our own reasons as an individual, we will always remain intriguing to them, and intrigue is what they like best.

We must remember to value them for the "up" side of their nature. They have no prejudgments of us; they will tend to look at everything with openness, and they are easy to talk to when functioning through the air part of their nature. So, even if they seem insensitive, talking is one of the best ways to let them know how we feel. Eventually, because of their interest in understanding all there is to know, they will come to know feelings, too.

How Air Relates to the Other Approach Types

Air does best with itself and its cousin, fire. Both are active and can join forces in externalizing their energies. Air can fuel fire's passion. However, air can feel dampened by water's emotionalism, and confined by earth's concern with the real and practical.

The Water Approach Type

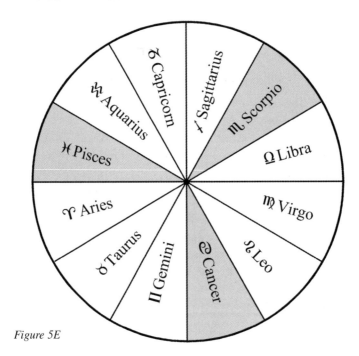

Figure 5E

The Water Signs

♋	Cancer
♏	Scorpio
♓	Pisces

PRIMARY QUALITY: Feeling
RESPONSE: I feel it.
PERCEPTION OF TRUTH: Personal (based on what I feel)

The water in us:

- emanates the energy of flow (yin force).

- assumes the form of what contains or influences it.

- moves downward.

- expresses itself in balance as sensitivity, subtlety, psychic perception, compassion, or serenity.

- expresses itself in extreme as moodiness, depression, possessiveness, or insecurity.

- finds it difficult to express objectivity, liveliness, stability, or practicality.

The element of water is the most yin (receptive) of the elements. Its motion is downward: Water flows to the lowest point and takes the shape of whatever it has flowed into. Until it reaches the point where its receptacle is stable or level, it will continually move. So we have rain falling from sky to land, brooks running into rivers, and rivers flowing into oceans. Water in motion is irresistible in its force, as the danger of tides, rip currents, and floods remind us. Unlike two ideas (air) or two objects (earth), when two bodies of water meet, they merge rather than remaining discrete. They lose their identity as separate bodies.

Symbolically, water is nonlinear, nonrational, and nondiscriminating. It is intrinsically difficult to communicate, because it does not lend itself to separate ideas or thoughts. Everything flows together into one mass. Art rather than thought communicates water's nature. Its reality is deep and deeply personal. Like fire, water experiences passion and intensity.

Water in Our Chart

If water is emphasized in our chart, we tend to be empathic, compassionate, and sensitive to the subtle flow of energies around us. We sense things that others call intangible or unreal, and it is all in the irrational realm of feeling. We are likely to be intense and changeable, as subtle energies change and flow around us. We respond to unseen forces and may express them through talent in the arts, healing, or psychic perception. We are most comfortable and do best in a clean psychic environment, as we easily pick up others' energies. Strong personalities are difficult for us, and we may desire time alone in order to sort out our own nature from those that we most recently encountered.

Communicating what we experience is difficult using words, and so we may often prefer to remain silent, or to rely on nonverbal communication. Our sensitivity may make us crave security—an environment where we can be sure of protection from strong energies and emotions. We are more comfortable with intimate relationships than less personal ones, because we need to develop trust in order to feel safe with our associates. Sometimes any social environment is difficult, and we would prefer to spend our time alone. We are good at nurturing, healing, and deep inner attunement. We may find the skills of objectivity, logic, practicality, and spontaneous expression more difficult.

How Water Relates to the Other Approach Types

Water is most comfortable with other water signs or with earth, its most similar approach type. It may find fire's passions too strong or overpowering, and air too dry and analytical for water to be at ease. Earth, on the other hand, provides solid containment that feels comforting and supportive to water's sensitive nature.

Water in Our Partner's Chart

If our partner's chart emphasizes water, they live in a world of flowing, drifting feeling. They will be sensitive to a reality that we may find hard to perceive without their help unless we have a strong water component in our nature. Their intensity and compassion may lead them to pick up and carry others' feelings long after contact is made. When they hold on to these energies for too long, they may become moody or depressed. We can help them to sort things out by pointing this out to them in a delicate way and helping them to talk about what is bothering them. Their sensitivity to unseen influences may lead them to know what we are thinking and feeling before we know it ourselves.

If our water partner feels insecure, they may become possessive, clingy, or withdrawn in an attempt to bring themselves back into their comfort zone. When we remember where this is coming from, it makes it easier to reassure them and show by our stability that they are safe.

Which Approach Types Are Compatible?

> **COMFORTABLE:**
> Fire ~ Air
> Earth ~ Water
>
> **STIMULATING:**
> Fire ~ Earth
> Air ~ Water
>
> **CHALLENGING:**
> Fire ~ Water
> Earth ~ Air

As noted above, some approach types seem to go better with each other than others. When we mix fire and air, or earth and water, the blend brings companionship. The box above shows how we may think of them. Sometimes it helps to think about how the real elements in nature may behave if combined:

> Fire + Earth = clay brick
> Fire + Air = bonfire
> Fire + Water = steam
> Earth + Air = dust(storm)
> Earth + Water = mud (arable soil)
> Air + Water = mist (fog)

There are also other ways in which the elements combine in our world to produce every thing and action imaginable. The ancients thought they blended all the time and in different ways, which gave us all the laws and effects of nature.

When the elements combine in the human nature, the result is more complex. We are never simply a product of one element, and we are all striving to balance all the elements in ourselves. So, even when we have a dominant element in our chart, we will not always behave according to that element's nature. What's more, as we learn to balance the qualities of one element against the others, the qualities will come out in our nature more subtly, with fewer extreme expressions. Others may have a hard time seeing which approach type is strongest in us when we express all four in balance; however, they will surely notice the enrichment we bring to life if we are acting from the most healthful expressions of our predominant approach type.

When we're in a partnership, sometimes the combination of two approach types is more balancing than both partners predominating in the same approach type—which can be too much of a good thing. When we come to the approach types that present challenge or stimulation, sometimes these approach types contribute to conflict and misunderstanding, especially at first, but eventually any combination can be mastered.

Fire and Air

Fire and air are most compatible with each other because they are considered most expressive or active. They tend to understand each other's basic approach to life, and balance each other well. Fire's personal, passionate approach is balanced by air's impersonal objectivity. Air's tendency toward diffuseness is adjusted by fire's single-minded focus. Either within our own nature or in our nature in relation to our partner's, these approach types tend to harmonize easily.

Fire and air in combination may lead to pioneering intellectual pursuits, such as research or research projects, retail entrepreneurship, or writing adventure stories, to name a few. In relationships, both partners may always want to take on new things, being adventuresome and outgoing.

As one of the companionship combinations, fire and air can combine planets in signs connected as follows:

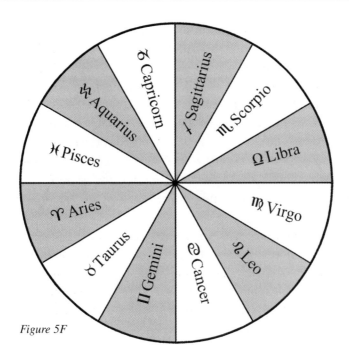

Figure 5F

Earth and Water

This is the other most compatible combination, linking the two receptive approach types into a companionship mode. Earth's solidness contains water's fluid nature. When mixed, they create the fertile environment needed for growth. They understand the nature and value of creativity and receptivity. Earth's practical nature can help to balance the extremes of emotional behavior and contain water's flowing power. Water's imagination can keep earth from becoming stagnant and dry, and its sensitivity can broaden earth's practical perspective. Either within our own nature or in our partnership, these approach types assist each other.

Earth and water may express through one of the nurturing arts and sciences, such as gardening or farming, nursing or child care. They may combine in the development of a craft like carpentry or mechanical repair. Architecture is also suggested by the earth-water combination. This combination can stabilize a relationship and make the partners want to grow things—a family, an art gallery, a garden.

As this is the other companionship combination of approach types, the following chart shows the regular interrelationship that exists between companionship signs connected by earth and water:

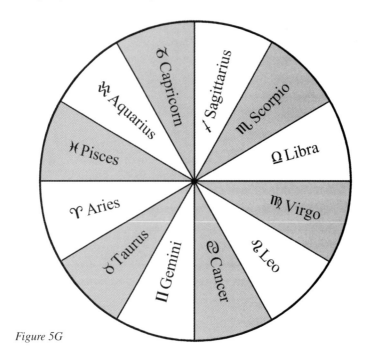

Figure 5G

Fire and Earth

A little less comfortable, but still a good mix, are earth and fire. Here the immovable object is met by the irresistible force, and they combine for effective action and powerful forms. When fire gives its passion and energy to the stable forms of earth, they balance each other. But too much earth can kill fire's zest, while too much fire can turn earth into ashes. This combination can be difficult, but kept in balance, we can be very effective movers and shakers in whatever we take on.

In our partnerships, we need to be careful to keep either fire or earth from overpowering the other. Otherwise, one partner can overwhelm the other's good influence, and the partnership will lose its balance and effectiveness. In harmony, however, fire and earth partnerships are very well suited to having an impact on the outer world. They may take on a great cause as a team and have the productivity to succeed with it. This is a good business combination; the partners are likely to be naturally drawn to build and create new things.

Air and Water

Air and water can also be blended in a helpful and stimulating manner. Air can help water to articulate the intuitive impression which water knows to be true but has much difficulty expressing. Water can deepen air, opening their awareness beyond logic, and helping them see underneath the surface appearance. Air's intellect lightens the sensitivity of water, while water's sensitivity gives air the compassion it needs to soften its intellect. Although water and air can "fog" our mind or create giddiness (think of champagne), at best they produce a head-and-heart balance.

This mix can give us the balance we need to heal or counsel others. It is especially good at tasks where social skills are important. However, in romantic partnerships, air-water may keep us from being effective. We may lack boundaries or a sense of the practical. However, if we take the best of what this combination has to offer, we can focus on developing the qualities we lack.

Fire and Water

This combination is one of the most challenging to work with. Fire's motion is upward, but water's is downward. They either flow away from each other and act separately though side by side, or they flow into each other and change each other's nature: water puts out fire, and fire changes water to steam. Both fire and water are passionate and personal, with nothing in their individual natures or their interaction to temper these qualities.

However, they do have mutually supportive qualities, even if they do not appear to be able to blend with each other. Water is naturally attuned to others in a way that fire is not. Fire has the ability to march to the beat of its own drum, which water does not carry in its essence. Just as water and fire can be brought into cooperation with each other in nature, we can bring them into balance in our self or in our partnership. Fire and water can bring passion and personal interest to our endeavors.

In our partnerships, the water person can bring awareness of the world around it to the single-minded fire person. The fire person can ignite the water person's creative energies. *We must remember to incorporate qualities from outside the two approach types in order to get this challenging combination to work.* Fortunately, since everyone has all four approach types in them, this combination can be made to work. It will just take more conscious effort to do so.

Earth and Air

As with fire and water, earth and air have very little in common—except a basically objective, impersonal approach to life, which can be too much of a good thing. Earth smothers air, while air disperses earth, so that neither can be effective. Since their respective ideas and structures are intrinsically dissimilar to each other, relating may be a difficult task.

We may, however, be able to blend these approach types if we learn to moderate the impersonal nature of earth-air. Adding a dose of feeling from the less dominant parts of our nature can do much to soften the edge that this combination can have. For instance, earth-air can bring thought into form through writing, but we have nothing to write about until we have passion or feeling. Adding emotion (water, fire) allows us to bring our writing to life.

In a partnership, the air person can be scattered and disjointed, and the earth person can help them become grounded. The earth person may yearn to break out of their mold, and the air person can show them how, stimulating them to new ways of thinking. Our own and our partner's energies may seem to connect very little. But if we take the time to feel, to get personal, the connection occurs.

The Approach Types and Polarities

With our new understanding of approach type qualities, we can look at the polarities in a slightly different way. In each polarity, the two signs have "comfortable" approach types. That is, they are either fire-air or water-earth. Knowing that these are the most natural approach types to combine makes it easier to see the similarity and innate balance within each polarity. Once we recognize this, we are more able to create complementarity and develop harmony by becoming conscious of what we have in common with our opposite.

What's Next?

Until now, we have been dealing strictly with the signs of the zodiac. While they tell us a lot, there are also the planets! Working only with signs is a bit like having costumes and roles for a play. We can see how the actors are supposed to behave, and we know what they are supposed to wear, but we don't know who the characters are and how they really interact. We don't know if the baker is sunny and outgoing, or sly and sullen. We don't know who the heroine and the messenger are.

The planets fill the costumes. They give substance to the roles that the signs represent.

CHAPTER SIX

ENTER THE ACTORS!
The Planets and Relationships

Everything we have covered so far has dealt with the signs of the zodiac. Now let's look at the planets. Until we know which planets are in what signs in our chart, we don't know who the actors are, where the action is, or what costumes they wear. The planets create the action. Unlike most plays, the action is improvised, except inasmuch as we rely on old habits and ways of doing things. The planets fill the costumes and roles that the signs provide.

In chapter 1, we talked about the planets as *archetypes*. Where they fall in our chart—what signs and houses—and how they relate to each other will determine what patterns we bring to life and to relationships.

As with the signs, some of the planets can be grouped into pairs or polarities. Since they move independently of each other, they will not often (and some, not ever) be across the chart (opposite) from each other. For instance, the sun and moon can be anywhere around the wheel of the chart with respect to each other. They can be next to each other, across the wheel, or somewhere in between. All the same, they are naturally paired as complements because of their meanings. Other planets can be grouped in a similar manner. When we look at our charts in terms of relationships, this is especially important.

First we will look at the planets that work in pairs. Then we'll explore the ones that "stand alone." Finally we'll talk a little bit about relating signs and planets to each other.

All Planets Are Created Equal, but Some Are More Equal Than Others

Although in school you probably learned to think of the planets as all being similar to each other, astrologers have ways of grouping them that makes their archetypal meanings clearer. The first way of categorizing them is by whether or not they relate to our personality. The *personal planets* are Mercury, Venus, Mars, the sun, and the moon.[11] The "invisible" planets— Uranus, Neptune, and Pluto—are referred to as the *transpersonal planets*. The planets in between, Jupiter and Saturn, we can call the *impersonal planets*.

Within the personal planets, the sun and the moon form a pair, as do Venus and Mars. Mercury is considered a neutral which can blend with anything. The two impersonal planets, Jupiter and Saturn, can be paired as well. The transpersonal planets do not form pairs, but act independently.

There is another body that is used by some astrologers called Chiron. It orbits between Saturn and Uranus. Discovered in 1977, it was at first called a "planetoid." Now it is thought to be a captured comet.[12]

As you saw in the charts in chapter 1, astrologers use glyphs to identify the planets, just as they do the signs. The planets are known by the following symbols:[13]

---

[11] The sun and moon are technically regarded as luminaries, since they cast or reflect light. However, they are grouped with the inner planets and are included when we refer to "planets" in general.

[12] As comets travel through our solar system, their path is frequently altered by their contact with the gravitational fields of the sun and planets. Sometimes they burn up and disappear, but from time to time they begin to orbit the sun along with the planets, instead of following their customary orbits. Chiron is thought to be one such captured comet.

[13] Although the symbols for the planets through Saturn are generally known and used throughout the world, the glyphs for Uranus, Neptune, and Pluto vary from culture to culture. Please refer to local sources if you do not find the symbols shown above on your chart.

The Planets	
Glyph	**Planet**
☉	Sun
☽	Moon
☿	Mercury
♀	Venus
♂	Mars
♃	Jupiter
♄	Saturn
⚷	Chiron
♅	Uranus
♆	Neptune
♇	Pluto

There are other symbols that you may see in the chart, but the only other ones you will need as you read this book are those for the North (☊) and South (☋) Nodes. If you recall from chapters 1 and 3, these are "points" in the chart, not planets. The planets are briefly introduced below.

The Sun and Moon

The sun and moon represent the basic male and female (respectively) parts of self. The sun/moon duality can also represent other dualities within ourselves, including active/receptive and conscious/unconscious. Just as these bodies are the brightest in our sky, they are the most important symbols in our chart.

Venus and Mars

In a way, Venus and Mars are, respectively, the "wannabe" female and male parts of ourselves. They operate at a less profound level than the sun and moon, but are still part of the balance between masculine and feminine in our nature.

Mercury, the Great Mixer

Mercury is the last of the personal planets. Any way you look at it, it is neutral, and it is not paired with any other planet. Actually, it can be "paired" with any planet in any sign. When it is paired with another planet, it carries the energy of that planet into its function—communication and connection. Although we can experience difficulties with Mercury's function, it is nearly always due to another planet's interrelationship with Mercury, not to Mercury by itself.

Jupiter and Saturn

Jupiter and Saturn are neither personal nor transpersonal planets; rather, they bridge the gap between the two sets. We see them in the world around us in the form of society (Jupiter) and its rules (Saturn). In our personal nature, Jupiter represents expansion and Saturn the opposing force of contraction.

The "Wild Cards"

The three transpersonal planets—Uranus, Neptune, and Pluto—could be called "wild card" planets. They stand alone and above the rest, rather than in pairs. They represent energies that we cannot feel directly within us until we accept that a part of nature is unseen or unfelt except in subtle ways. Until we become conscious of their activity, these planets will intrude on our lives in generally unwelcome ways. However, once we learn to understand the forces that they represent, we can make our way through the passages they bring to us with strength and purpose.

Chiron

Chiron is the new kid on the block. It was discovered in 1977, and astrologers have embraced it as the "wounded healer." It is neither wholly transpersonal, nor is it impersonal in the sense of Jupiter or Saturn. It seems to bridge the gap between the visible (the planets through Saturn) and invisible (those beyond Saturn) planets.

★★★

The Sun and Moon

No discussion of astrology would be complete without including the sun and moon. These bodies, so immediately visible to us, provide a deep reflection of our nature. By identifying where the sun and moon were in the heavens at the time of our birth—and the relationship that existed between them—we can learn a great deal about what makes us tick. By ascertaining where they are placed in our partner's chart, we can learn about the essentials of our beloved's nature as well. When we look at the sun and moon of each chart in combination with the other, we can see the foundation upon which the relationship is built. The sun and moon are so important that by knowing how they work together, we have laid the groundwork to which all the other planets only provide adjustments.

The Sun, Our Expressive Self

The sun is the eternal part of us, the God[14] Self. If we are truly in our sun, we are connected with the universal, the abundant source of creativity from which stems the eternal life of the Soul. Just as the sun lives forever (in human terms), our Self lives above and beyond each lifetime. To identify with it is to live the Divine Source in us. To be at one with the sun is to be at One with The Source. When we are able to express our sun in even the most basic way, we can tune in to our purpose and see the way to fulfill it. When we feel the sun within us, we are united with all life. We are in our most natural state, simply being. Time does not exist, only an eternal present. We are relaxed, yet vibrantly alive.

However, we do not always live in or express the sun in its fullness. But even then, like the sun that is always with us, providing life and nourishment whether we know it or not, so does our God Self exist in us. We express it unwittingly, often clumsily, in our innocence and misunderstanding. So, even though they are unconscious of their purpose on the planet,

---

[14] Here I intend the word *God* to mean "the Infinite, the Divine, the Source of all life, the great Mother-Father Founders of the Universe." I am as comfortable with *Spirit, Goddess, Cosmos, Universal Being,* or whatever other name for a supreme consciousness exists. Feel free to substitute the name of your choice.

the child with sun in Taurus will unconsciously display Taurean traits. They *are* this Self, even though they don't know it. We can't stop being who We are, no matter how hard we try. Even if we "blow it"—lose track of our divine nature—we are close enough to that Self that we can still find inside us a child crying out to be loved but filled with fear. We are still that part of us that will live eternally and return to rectify the karmic imbalance created by our lack of understanding; someday we will come to know that God Self, no matter how deeply we have buried it.

If you felt a glow inside as you read the last two paragraphs, you were feeling the sun in your nature. You were tapping the force of your God Self, the depths of your truest, eternal nature. We all get glimpses of the sun in ourselves—it is always available to us—but we have learned to overlook it. Yet it shines forth clear and true whenever we need it most, because that is when we will allow it to happen.

We feel the sun in our heart. It is the center of our body and our being. Through it we radiate love—love for ourselves and love for all other forms of consciousness. When we are heart-centered, we are bursting with joy and radiance; nothing can penetrate that glow and daunt us in our expression of that love. Others are drawn to us like a magnet, and our impact on them is pure and good, in spite of whatever weaknesses or flaws we might have. When we are in our hearts, we can give only from our purest, divine essence.

The sun is the heroic part of ourselves. When we feel challenged and rise to accept the challenge (rather than fight it), we are responding with our solar force. Whenever we encounter something new, in a very simple way we will use our solar force to conquer and integrate that newness into our life. The hero archetype is found throughout our culture. Learning the stories of our culture's heroes is the primary way in which we learn to express our sun. As the hero, we take on new experiences with our whole being. We embrace whatever obstacles lie in our path. We learn new lessons that are central to our life's success, and in so doing, we fulfill our purpose. Myths often take a hero through birth, growth, self-discovery, success, death, and the resurrection/rebirth cycle. The stories of King Arthur, Jesus, Harriet Tubman, John F. Kennedy, and any number of Greek myths, from Hercules to Odysseus, amply illustrate this cycle. The key is self-discovery, which is not just the discovery of our personality and purpose, but of the ego-death which brings resurrection, the rebirth of the True Self.

We see the sun in the world around us through those people we regard as modern examples of heroism, as leaders of broad vision. For some of us, this may be our father (or fathering person), a mentor, stars of film and television, the president, or Princess Diana or Mother Teresa in their roles of world service. Anyone whom we admire is a projection of our solar force, and can show us something about ourselves if we contemplate what draws us to them.

Tapping the Force of the Sun Within Us

We can tap the force of the sun in our nature by going into the core of our being. When we feel deep down into our center, we find the sun. Its glow shines forth; its light fills us. If we have difficulty feeling it or finding it within, we can access it by focusing up through the top of our head (our crown center); reaching into the heavens; and drawing down light, the Universal energy, like a cascading waterfall.

We can also tap it by asking ourselves questions such as:[15]

- Who am I?
- What kinds of experiences help me strengthen and clarify my self-image?
- Where do I naturally find and express my personal power?
- What unconscious biases shape my world view?
- How do I want to be a hero(ine)?
- Where do I want to shine?
- Where does my motivation to shine come from?
- What qualities do I see in the people I admire?

When we are in touch with our solar force, we feel, without the bravado of ego-involvement, as though we can take on any challenge. Even though we know we will encounter difficulties, we feel confident that we can overcome them. We feel whole and radiant, in touch with and filled with the love of life. We are energized.

When we lose touch with our sun, we may become tired. We may look to someone outside ourselves to acknowledge us or to fulfill our goals for us. We may become brittle, like an empty shell, because we have lost touch

---

[15] My thanks to Steven Forrest, author of *The Inner Sky,* for suggesting this approach. I have paraphrased some of his questions and added some of my own.

with our essence. We put too much effort into what we do, trying to get what we don't have instead of letting our native worth shine and call those things to us. We may feel empty.

We always express the sun—and understand it in our nature—in terms of the sign in which it is found. When we are "in our sun," the qualities of that sign will naturally show themselves in how we act and experience things.

The Sun in Our Partner's Nature

Our partner's sun is shining forth when they display a lot of natural energy—not the energy of physical action, but the energy of vibrant life. They will naturally draw others to them from this place; they will display qualities of the sign in which the sun is placed. They will have a sense of purpose, be fulfilled by what life presents, or be challenged to find fulfillment; but they will not feel defeated when they are in their sun—failure is only a temporary setback in this mode of being. When life pushes them, they will press back, attempting to influence rather than be influenced. If our beloved is truly in touch with their God Self, we will feel the radiance of their presence when we are near them.

If our partner loses touch with their solar essence, they will lose some of their shine. They may appear tired or listless and lose their sense of purpose. It may be difficult for them to take even the simplest action, big projects too much even to contemplate. They may want to get energy from others, to fill their emptiness with some of our light. They may be more vulnerable, and want our acknowledgment.

When our partner has lost that solar glow, we can help them by doing things that prompt them to remember what the solar field is like. We can remind them of a time when they were in full contact with the sun's energy. We can share our solar energy with them, letting them feel it without letting them drain it from us. We cannot fill their emptiness with our solar energy, since everyone is a unique expression of the sun—no two of us are identical.

The Moon, Our Inner Self

The sun gives so much light that it is easily reflected back to us. Earth's largest satellite, the moon, gleams silver even in the day. At night, she lights our way; she even casts shadows when at her brightest. However, the moon's light is uneven, changing from day to day and hour to hour. Some days we do not see her at all, and every day that she is visible, she looks different. Furthermore, the light that she brings us is not hers. When she passes into the shadow of the earth (a lunar eclipse), her glow is lost altogether.

These facts about the moon's physical appearance and behavior tell us a great deal about what it represents in our nature. It is the strongest receptive, reflective force within us, yin to the sun's yang nature. As the sun seeks to influence, the moon is influenced easily by external forces. When we observe the moon by itself in our nature, we see constant changes, representative of our moods, momentary feelings, shifting awareness, and ways of sensing the world. It is the source of our habits and attitudes, formed out of the totality of our past experiences and what we have learned from them. Just as the physical moon is the way that the sun indirectly lights our nights, the astrological moon is the way that the sun indirectly lights the darkness of our being.

If the sun represents our conscious, outward-directed side, the moon portrays our inner self, who we are when others get to know us well. The moon describes our emotional nature, our unconscious self, habits, motivations, and need for nurturing. The moon also speaks of our mother and the mothering influences in our lives. In partnerships, people are often attracted by other factors, but in long-term relationships, the moon forms a major part of their connection.

When we are in our moon, we will be more open to impression from the world around us. However, the impressions that we receive are greeted by our attitudes, our "knowledge" of the world that we have already experienced. When someone does something that reaches our consciousness, we (often unconsciously) decide how to interpret that encounter based upon our past experiences. For that encounter to have an impact on us, we must accept it into our energy field, for nothing enters without our (often unknowing) permission. Once in our field, we "make sense of it" by interpreting it in terms of what we already know. If the action we perceive is very much unlike anything we have perceived in the past, we will still interpret it in terms of what we can relate it to, even if it is far-fetched. This is why the native people of the West Indies called the ships that transported Columbus and his men to the Americas "clouds." It was the closest they could come to describing what they saw. They were familiar with the storms that boil up from the eastern Atlantic and blow their fury onto their shores, but not with the white-sailed flotilla of galleons that bore Columbus to them from the same direction.

No matter what we encounter, we will interpret it in terms of our past experiences, unless we have taught ourselves to be truly open, a "blank slate" when we meet something new. This concept is fostered in many of the world's spiritual traditions. One of the first lessons of any path is to let go of our past impressions so that we can experience the present moment with openness, to be in the "now." From the Buddhist who learns to see value and purpose in the life of every being, large or small, to the Sufi or Christian who learns to dwell in the heart,[16] this lesson needs to be learned if we are to reside in the True Self (sun/God Self).

It is essential to learn to blend the solar and lunar forces in our lives, because it is by achieving a balance of these energies that we integrate old and new in our day-to-day existence. It is not easy to clear ourselves of our past impressions; however, it is important to take on the task all the same. Once cleared, it allows us to experience life through our moon without the stress that expectation and the resulting fear bring to us.

The moon allows us to make sense of our world in terms of our past experiences. This opens the doorway to the world of intelligence. Without the moon, we could never learn anything, because at its core, it has to do with memory. When we remember our impression of an experience, we do not have to relearn it. Learning takes our entire focus. Without retained memories, we would encounter each situation as if it were new, and have to use our solar focus to deal with the "new" challenge each time.[17]

For example, let's say that we have just gotten a new job and we're trying to find our way to work. The first time, we tackle it with our sun: We ask for directions, perhaps get out a map, develop a plan to meet the challenge and give the drive our undivided attention when it is time to make our way there. For the next few days, we may still give our active attention (solar focus) to the process of driving to work, but with each passing day, our consciousness will wander more and more. Soon, we will not even notice the familiar features of the drive, "automatically" turning at the right corner,

---

[16] The heart is considered the crossroads of heaven and earth (God and man) in Sufism. It is called the seat of Christ in Christianity for the same reason.

[17] This is what happens to people with Alzheimer's disease—they lose their ability to retain experiences, so they encounter each situation as if for the first time; they have lost their lunar awareness.

shifting lanes on the same stretch of highway. In short, we have moved "the drive to work" into our lunar awareness; we have turned much of it over to our unconscious mind. We have put it in the background of awareness so that we can pay attention to more complex activities and functions.

Since the moon is where we receive our impressions of the world, this is also where we will naturally seek to adapt to the world, so that we are more comfortable. The moon is where we seek comfort, and nurture ourselves and others. To nurture ourselves, we will naturally want to be in an environment that we perceive as friendly and secure. This allows us to "recharge our batteries," to get ready for the next foray into the world of the sun, of challenge and unfamiliarity.

When we were born, the first impressions that we received came to us through the moon. These first impressions happily include the care we received from our mother and other caregivers. The support we received fulfilled one of our biggest needs, and left the most profound impression on our nature. It's little wonder that the moon is associated with our mother—and the care we received as an infant.

The moon is an important part of our consciousness, one that we couldn't do without. However, we must understand the coloring brought by our past experiences. Until then, prejudices, fears, and misapprehensions may color our perceptions of the world. We may lose track of the sun in our nature and identify so completely with the moon that we see ourselves as caught in a capricious and fluctuating roller coaster of life's emotions.

The moon gives us the warm glow of comfort, lets us know how the world is affecting us, and gives us the signals that keep us alive. It grants us sensitivity, compassion, and appreciation for others. Without it, we would be unable to experience the peak experiences of our life—those based on love and the thrill and comfort of connecting with others.

Tapping the Receptivity of the Moon

When we feel like curling up in a blanket with a cup of hot tea, we are in our moon. Anytime that we do something "on background," without our direct focus, we are relying on our lunar consciousness.

To get in touch with our moon, we can tune in to every minute sensation or feeling that we have. When we do this, we will find ourselves naturally focusing also on what stimulates those feelings: We will relate them to the experiences we perceive and accept from the outer world. We will become aware of whether we are comfortable or uncomfortable, and what emotions pass through us at the time.

Another way to get in touch with our lunar awareness is to ask ourselves questions such as:

- What kinds of experiences do I feel are necessary for my happiness?
- What makes me comfortable?
- What makes me retreat into my comfort zone?
- How do I express my moods and irrational side?
- What emotional needs, conscious and unconscious, motivate my behavior?
- What qualities do I see in my mother?

When we are in touch with our lunar force, we are aware of our feelings and are comfortable with them, even in environments that we perceive as unfriendly. We are able to truly experience our emotions and to express them appropriately. This will help us to remain centered and to interpret fewer experiences as emotionally charged. We will go through fewer ups and downs—what we experience will have lower highs and higher lows.

When we lose touch with our moon, we may become withdrawn and numb. We may not be aware of our feelings. When we lose touch with our moon, we may need to retreat, to go inside. This gives us the time and space to reconnect with our feelings and our True Self. If we give our moon enough room to grow, accepting and respecting whatever we feel, we will soon be back in touch with our entire nature and ready to engage with the external world again.

We will understand and express the moon in terms of the sign in which it is found. When we are in our moon, the qualities of the sign it is in will naturally show themselves in how we react and respond to things.

The Moon in Our Partner's Chart

When our partner is expressing their moon, they can show many faces. They may be soft and sensitive or warm and cuddly. They may be nostalgic or loving, sad or anxious, fearful or withdrawn. When these qualities come out, they are relating to their feelings, even if they are not aware of it. They may want to connect, or they may want to retreat. Whatever they are experiencing, we know that it will change just as the moon changes throughout the month.

At times, we all shift our lunar perceptions onto others, especially onto our partners. When this happens, we have no idea that the qualities we are projecting truly reside within ourselves. For example, we may transfer our perception of our mother (a lunar archetype) onto others, particularly other women. Our unconscious holds a concept that it seeks to confirm: All women will behave like our own mother, and if we do what we did to please our mother, we will gain their approval.

A projection of our emotions may also occur when our emotions become too painful to bear. At these times we may wish to avoid our moon and all that it represents. We may repress these overwhelming feelings and project them onto others—so, for instance, everyone else is jealous, not us. We may also project feelings onto others if they are unacceptable to our conscious mind. For example, a person who declares that they are never angry may unconsciously leak anger onto others through a constant, low-level irritation and then notice how angry others seem to be.

Therefore, it is helpful for us and our partner to be in touch with the full range of our feelings, and to give ourselves permission to have them. Having feelings is a wonderful part of being human.

If we are female, we are likely to receive the projection of the moon from others, both male and female. When this happens, we may feel pulled to behave in ways that are unusual for us at first. However, as the projection continues, we will fall into a pattern of response that the other person unwittingly expects, even if they don't like it. We may find ourselves being the partner who feels more or seems to care more. We may find ourselves taking responsibility for the feelings in the relationship if our partner cannot relate well to their own moon and we do not know how to gently redirect that projection.

Blending the Sun and Moon

The sun and moon, the conscious and unconscious, are both important to our nature and so basic that we may have a hard time perceiving them as separate parts of ourselves. Even though it feels wonderful when we shine through our sun, we can't maintain it, or even feel it, without the relaxation and nourishment we get from our moon. We need "down time," time to be in our comfort zone, sort out our impressions, feel our intuitions, and integrate them. We need to replenish after meeting those situations that take all our focus and keep us on our toes. We need to nurture ourselves and others, and to be nurtured in return. Only then are we prepared with new knowledge, a fresh outlook to express purposeful action from our center.

We can neither deny our feeling (lunar) nature nor suppress our True Self (solar nature). We must find a way to blend them, balance them. *The key is to be aware of our solar selves as the observer; what we feel is "the observed," the lunar.* It is our True Self that does the observing, the solar work; it is our personal, lunar self that experiences the feelings. Both are vital parts of who we are; we can embrace and enjoy each side—the light that shines and the light that receives. They are what make us human, giving us heart and the capacity to love.

The more we can blend and balance the sun and moon in our own nature, the less difficulty we will have with the basic nature of our partner. Even if their sun and moon are not naturally harmonious with ours, if we take responsibility for ourselves—developing our own inner harmony—our relationship will not be hindered by the lack of natural harmony.

Venus and Mars

You have probably heard that "men are from Mars, women are from Venus."[18] While this is not the whole picture, there is some truth in this statement. Venus represents our ideal of the feminine, whether we are male or female. Mars represents our ideal of the masculine, regardless of our gender. If we are female, we will tend to want to be like

---

[18] From John Gray's book, *Men Are from Mars, Women Are from Venus.*

our Venus and want our partner to be like our Mars. If we are male, we will often want to be like our Mars and want our partner to be like our Venus.[19]

Venus, Goddess of Love

Venus represents the force that brings and keeps things together, what science calls cohesion and what poets call love. This is love in the sense of natural affinity, not the modern romantic (ego-centered) notion of love. With Venus, when two things are joined through affinity, the whole formed is greater than the sum of its parts: Something is added to the essence of the new whole that did not exist before they were cojoined. The creation of beauty or life (also Venusian functions) operate on the same principle. When an artist paints a picture, it is greater than the sum of paints plus canvas.

Reciprocity and equality lie at the heart of Venus's energy field. More than anything, she wants to bond with another in true, spiritual love. When we feel her breath in our ear, we know that the Goddess has spoken for us— that love has come.

Love could be called "the creator of harmonic resonance" on all levels of being. That is, when we come to love another person and that person returns our love, our energy fields gradually blend and merge. The process by which we do this is called harmonic induction. This creation of harmony between two beings is a Venusian process.

We can come to vibrate at the same rate with a living being, or even with inanimate objects like rocks and soil. Since everything that has a form vibrates, we can change our vibration by coming into contact with something and accepting its energy. For instance, we can allow the vibration of a quartz crystal's structure to assist in energizing or healing us.

In a partnership of equality and reciprocity, the process of harmonic induction will occur roughly equally between the two partners. If the relationship involves a dominance structure, the submissive partner will change more than the dominant partner. This is natural in relationships such as boss-employee and parent-child, but it is out of place in a love relationship. The creation of such a balance between equal partners is a part of the great

---

[19] This is not always true in same-sex relationships. It is often the case that same-sex partners will both "compete" for the role most closely identified with their physical sex, male or female. However, eventually, most same-sex partnerships will tend to cast one partner as "Mars" and the other as "Venus," although the partners may exchange the roles with more fluidity.

work of building a soul-level relationship. Although the harmonic balance may ebb and flow from one partner to the other, as the relationship deepens and matures, the balance will come to rest at the center and stabilize the relationship in trust and love.

Venus has to do with the love side of sexual interaction. On the surface, she beckons and is the object of desire; in ancient times, she was the torch, the siren, as well as the preserver of true love. She has allure and charm for her pursuer, and she enjoys being seductive in the right circumstances. Yet, for Venus, sex without love is not worthwhile. While she may also desire that her senses be seduced by her beloved's outward appearances, Venus wants a true knowing of her partner's inner self. Even if Venus is in a sign which by its purpose does not create things of long duration, like Aries or Gemini, we still want love, even if it is only in the moment. The sign she is in shows how the stage must be set to encourage us to feel loved so that we open ourselves to making love.

When we experience Venus within us, we feel beauty and love welling up from our depths. We feel inspired and creative and seek to express what we feel. We are naturally beautiful because love flows from us. This is not something that we can feel only in response to the love of another—in fact, we must be able to feel it for ourselves, independently of another's love.

On a more mundane, daily level, Venusian feelings of this depth may come and go as we turn our consciousness over to the different forces within us that the planets represent. Venus is our natural feminine nature—and thus, the way we see ourselves if we are female, or the way we want to see our partner if we are male. It may represent the person we want to be—the way we want to be seen by others, especially our partner.

Tapping the Well of Venus Within Us

To get into the flow of Venus's love, we can go to our hearts. The heart is the crossroads of the human and the divine within us, and the expression of that union is love. Begin by bringing the golden light of the heavens in through your crown like a waterfall. Allow it to flow into your heart and pool there as a great golden lake. Then drop your consciousness down through your seat into the center of the earth. Bring up the silver light of the earth into your heart like a fountain. When the two streams mix, their light turns to luminous white. Allow this light to flow from your heart, front and back and all sides, radiating in all directions. Feel the love that Spirit has for us as you allow it to flow.

To tap Venus in another way, we can ask ourselves questions such as:

- How do I want to be loved?
- What do I want from life—what values and qualities do I cherish?
- What do I want in a partner?
- What do I want my partner to see in me?
- What do I bring to a relationship?
- What do I find beautiful?

When we are in the flow of Venus, we radiate love. We naturally attract others to us through love's magnetic power. We naturally find a balance with the forces that we encounter on our path. We excite harmonic resonance with those we meet, since they can be open to us when we are in a loving place.

When we lose touch with our Venusian force field, our inner beauty and feelings of love fade. Beauty loses its attractiveness, becomes hollow. We feel less inspired and lose touch with the creative flow.

The sign that Venus is in shows how we love and want to be loved. It shows what opens the doors of love for us—what moves us in a loving way.

Venus in Our Partner's Nature

Regardless of their gender, Venus is how our partner expresses love and wants love returned to them. When in their Venus energy field, love will flow freely. Our partner will be generous and caring in their unique expression of the sign their Venus is in. They may tap into and exhibit creative inspiration by bringing beauty into the world around them. Beauty will well up from within them, a fountain of radiance to share.

When our partner loses touch with their Venus, they will seem to have stepped out of love's flow. They may seem a little empty, less able to give from their own fullness. They will not be as attuned to harmony and balance with us as when in Venus's field.

To bring love and beauty back into our beloved's awareness, we can love them in the way they long to be loved, as long as we give from our own fullness in a safe way. Even if they are not open, or are preoccupied with other concerns, by holding our heartspace open for their return, we prepare the way for them to reattune to Venus's flow.

Mars, the Warrior

Brisk and bold, Mars steps onto the scene, fully clad in armor. He is hard-edged and tough, ready to go toe-to-toe with anyone. He is the Warrior, Rogue, or Pioneer.

Mars represents our ability to act and assert ourselves based on what we desire. He is yang to Venus's yin, but he lacks the global and altruistic perspective of the sun. He is self-centered and maintains a single focus. This is his strength. If he is always focused outward, impervious to external influences, he will not accept anything into his energy field. This is how he protects himself—his real armor. A warrior who is not open is not vulnerable to attack. Nothing can touch him, including love, which requires vulnerability.

In everyday life, Mars symbolizes our ability to act, and to remain who we are in the face of pressure to change. It is our will to survive—it is even the kinetic energy that makes our muscles move. Through Mars, we act alone, without reference to others; we emphasize our differences from other people when we are in our Mars. At its extreme, Mars is a source of conflict and aggression. When we are threatened, Mars brings us the "fight or flight" adrenaline surge that can carry us to safety and give us superhuman strength. Emotionally, Mars is associated with anger or fear. Anger is the emotion by which we throw off another person's energy. Anger can help to keep us whole and safe, if we use it to signal when we are being challenged to let in an energy that feels threatening. If we let in forceful energies, our emotional response is fear, which can be turned to anger if we decide to cast that energy off.

However, kept in balance, Mars is an essential part of our make-up, one at the core of our ability to relate well to others and to survive. Without Mars, we would lack the ability to act, to protect ourselves, to remain a unique and separate spark of the Divine Being. Without it, we constantly would lose our nature in that of others. We would be merged with others, without distinction. We would not be able to engage in a soul-level relationship, which is based on the willing union of two whole individuals.

Mars is the counterpart of Venus; where Venus wants to merge and blend, Mars stands strong and separate. We need both skills to relate in balance with others. Just as Venus is "the woman" and the feminine in relationships, Mars is "the man" and the masculine. So, Mars is a man's self-image—how he wants to be seen; and it is a woman's image of what she wants her partner to be (whether same- or opposite-sex).

Mars also has to do with sexual desire and interaction. Mars represents penetration, the active part of sexual activity. The partner with the more active Mars might initiate sexual activity more frequently. Our Mars will show how we like to initiate lovemaking and what is sexually stimulating to us. Mars is also the part of us that wants sex for its own sake. It is not concerned with whether there is love or responsibility, unless we have learned to temper Mars's self-centered tendencies in our nature.

Although every planet has ego manifestations, we associate the ego most closely with Mars. The ego creates a mask to protect against perceived threats. Each time the ego senses a threat, we put on the mask, until we learn to let go of our fear and so cease to feel threatened. So, even though we may mask any planet's true expression within us, it is our misuse of Mars's energy causing this. Although Mars may lead us to develop the ego mask by natural extension of what it is, we do not have to identify with the ego. It is only when we allow the ego to have supremacy in the self (over the True Self) that it is in the wrong place. Allowing the True Self to have supremacy, and keeping the ego in its place, permits the best quality of Mars to shine through, that of *inner independence*. This is a quiet self-assurance that aligns with our sense of truth. It does not react with fear or anger, because it is not easily threatened. It is independent, not seeking others' approval or living by their rules or values. This side of Mars allows us to act only in reference to what we deem important. Because our reference point is our sense of truth, which comes from our True Self, the ego cannot take control or corrupt our behavior.

Tapping the Force of Mars

Mars is activated by movement of the body. When we work out, get out of the house, do something strenuous or energetic, we are activating our

Mars. Deep, powerful breathing also brings us into Mars's force field. By breathing deeply and powerfully, in through the mouth and out through the nose, we can also trigger our Mars nature.

It is also possible to bring out our Mars through questions such as the following:

- How do I express my assertive energies?
- What triggers anger or fear in me?
- How do I show my anger?
- How do I show my fear?
- How do I pursue what I want?
- What am I willing to fight for?
- Where do I feel competitive?

When we are in our Mars, we feel strong, able to compete. We enjoy competition, the testing of our courage, strength, and skill against others. We may be playful or assertive, ready to move or attack. In Mars's force field, we feel vibrant, alive, and triumphant. We feel as though we can do anything, win any contest. We approach any challenge with vigor. We want to be active, to *do* things. We may feel like engaging in sports or besting our latest record in a skill we're building. We want to try new things, and we are inspired to action by the vigor and power we feel.

When we lose track of the Mars in our nature, we start to lose our sense of how we are different from others. We may be unwilling to assert ourselves, to challenge another's point of view. We may become insecure, or even domineering or bullying to cover up our weakness. We will also stop wanting to engage in physical activity.

Mars in Our Partner's Chart

When our partner is in their Mars force field, they will be independent, even a bit prickly. They will want to do things their own way and not listen to us. They won't be particularly open, and they will want to take the first step in anything they do. Sometimes the ego will be unusually evident. They may become angry or defensive if you approach them.

To bring out the best of their Mars side, give them lots of space! They want to be self-reliant right now, to push their boundaries. Perhaps they let their Mars slip too far away from them, and began to feel lost in the identities of others. To be able to contribute fully and equally in our relationship, they must be allowed time to feel their wholeness. Being patient and giving them space is the best thing we can do to help our partner balance their Mars energy.

Considering Venus and Mars

While the sun and moon are the basic archetypes of masculine and feminine in our nature, Venus and Mars also contribute to the way we balance our masculine and feminine energies. The sun and moon are our frame of reference, showing how we define ourselves; Mars and Venus show what we're striving to become. They are more likely to be how we describe ourselves, or try to appear to someone we are trying to impress. Once that person gets to know us over a longer period of time or through constant contact, they will see our inner sun and moon.

When we first meet someone, our contacts with them are usually relatively brief, and we feel at our best when we interact with them. At those times, we are usually in our Venus if we are female and our Mars if we are male. This is true, even if we are not "courting," but meeting a friend, whether same- or opposite-sex.

Venus and Mars in our own nature show how we see relations between the sexes—is it battle or play?—and between us and our partner. These planets also show how we play out the process through courtship—stabilizing our relationship until we know each other through the sun-moon roles that emerge with trust and familiarity.

In mythology, Venus and Mars (in Greece, Aphrodite and Ares) had many dramatic interactions. They came together and fell apart many times during their long relationship. This is much like the process of courtship, where we have brief interactions ("dates") and then separate. It also describes the dance we engage in when we respond to each other's openings and closings.

If we have not learned to blend Venus and Mars in our nature, we will have difficulty initiating relationships or allowing someone else to initiate one with us. We may not feel that we deserve to be loved. *To blend them, we must acknowledge and accept both the masculine and feminine sides of our nature.* Women must accept their fear, anger, and aggression; men must accept their fear, vulnerability, and their need for a partner. In this time, when it is also often difficult for us to accept our own basic sexual nature, we must also fully accept ourselves as a woman if we are female and as a man if we are male. We must allow our own unique version and balance of femininity and masculinity to emerge and express itself. Once we have found peace with our own masculine and feminine sides, we will find peace in our partnerships.

Mercury, the Great Mixer

Mercury stands alone, not because it is insular, but because it blends so easily with everything that it can't be paired with any one planet! Mercury is the life of the party, able to talk to anyone, getting even the shyest wallflower to laugh, flitting around and touching base with each person.

Mercury is the hottest and fastest planet. Its physical speed matches its speed in our nature. It has to travel fast to symbolize the neural pathways that keep our lungs and body functioning, our mind working, and our tongue wagging.

Mercury is very important to us because it represents the way we think, talk, and interpret our world. It shares some qualities in this sense with the moon, although the moon's perceptions are more those called "feelings," which are either sensed in the body or felt as emotions. Mercury is more the realm of logic and the intellect. It has to do with the connections we make between objects (as in travel) and between thought and the desire to communicate it (as in language).

It also has to do with our power to see more than one meaning in a single item. This gives Mercury its role as the trickster. In dreams, poetry, and jokes, ambiguity and double meaning are easily found.

Mercury is associated with young people, students, messengers, and counselors. The UPS delivery person who whisks into your life and is gone in a half-minute, leaving something with you that is not from them, is the essence of Mercury in action.

Since Mercury rules communication, its importance in relationships is unquestioned; however, its communicative capacity is generally associated with verbal skills, although communication takes place on many other levels within Mercury's domain, and through other planetary forces as well. Still, there is often no substitute for speaking our heart and mind.

Tapping the Zest of Mercury

To tap the force of Mercury, we need to quiet our environment for a moment and listen to our inner voice. When our mind is still, it becomes clear. Our emotions quiet, and we let go of what's happening around us; then, we can hear the voice of Mercury speak to us. As long as we let the chatter of our subconscious continue, we can't hear the voice of the Messenger. He never speaks for himself, but always for another—another planet, person, or part of Self. Once we can hear our inner voice, we can speak with clarity and be heard. We come to understand the value of silence, or of waiting for the right time to speak. We can find our focus and empower our mind. We will engage in all forms of Mercury interaction more meaningfully.

Any mental pursuit will stimulate our Mercury function. Writing, reading, deep conversation with a friend, studying, and hanging around with a three-year-old are a few more ways to tune in to Mercury.

Another way to come into contact with Mercury is to answer questions such as:

- What really draws me out in conversation and gets me to talk?
- What do I know a lot about?
- What are my communicative strengths and weaknesses?
- What do I like to talk and think about?
- Who do I like to talk to and why?
- What stimulates my curiosity?

When we are tuned in to Mercury, we feel light and quick. Our mind traps new concepts and absorbs them with spongelike facility. We are articulate, our thoughts are clear, and our sense of humor is on the money. We are curious—we want to explore the world of knowledge and communicate it to others.

When we overdose on Mercury, we feel brain-tired, even headachy. We may feel like going into isolation to rest our mind. We won't feel like talking, writing, or listening—we may not feel as though we can absorb another thing! We are likely to feel overwhelmed and overstimulated by life.

On the other hand, when we lose touch with Mercury, it may be because we have gotten too caught up in our feeling-emotional side. Logic naturally counterbalances feeling, and if we become overly involved in an experience, we lose contact with the voice of the Messenger, because the ocean of emotion drowns it out.

Mercury in Our Partner's Nature

When our partner is tapping Mercury's flow, they are likely to be talkative, friendly, and spunky. They may be playful and humorous, or open and serious. They are listening to Mercury, but we must remember that they carry the message of another part of Self, another aspect of who they are. If it is the moon, they will be seeking comfort; if it is the sun, they will be on stage; if it is Venus, their words will be soft and loving; if it is Mars, they may throw sparks as they speak.

We must listen, not only to their words, but to their intent—to the planet that wishes to be known through the message. We must give our beloved time and space to speak, to get their words right. They, too, need time to listen to their inner voice, to quiet the chatter, and to find clarity. If we can be open and patient with our partner, that is the best way to engage them in dialogue.

When our partner has overdone Mercury, they need a break. Let them have a time of silence—it is the greatest gift you can give them. If they just can't seem to tap Mercury's flow, a note or card may help to open the gates of the intellect for them.

Jupiter and Saturn

Jupiter and Saturn are our last pair of planets. However, unlike those that came before, they are not part of our personal nature, our personality. They have more to do with how our personality meshes with the world around us. Can we make a living? Can we succeed? How can we serve others, make ourselves useful so that we can receive the wealth of our culture? What rules must we follow? How must we prepare? What plans must we make and stick with? Together, Jupiter and Saturn balance to give us our ability to make our way.

Jupiter, God of Thunder

His jovial, booming voice precedes him as he enters the room. He is the uncle that has a smile for everyone, the car salesperson that has just the right vehicle for every person, the teacher that always has a hive of students around her. Jupiter is everyone's Santa Claus, handing out goodies—whether they're good for us or not. He says to us, "Come on! The world is a friendly place just ripe for the picking!" He has supreme confidence in his ability to overcome all odds. Like the large, brightly striped planet that symbolizes this archetype, he comes in neon colors, bright lights, and the glitter of gold.

In our nature, Jupiter also represents the impression we have about the world and what we can expect from it. This is the role that society plays for us on one level, and our religion or spiritual path on another. If we have learned that the world welcomes us, we will approach it with more self-confidence, maybe even foolish grandiosity.

Because Jupiter stays in a single sign for one year, it gives the same general perspective on these things to everyone of the same age.[20] So we will share an outlook with others in our high school class, for the most part. Although we may have a unique idea of what we need to do to be successful—and different tools and skills to make it happen—we will tend to agree with those of our age about what the world and cosmos are like.

---

[20] Naturally, since Jupiter does not change sign on the same date each year, we don't know for sure whether or not someone shares our Jupiter placement until we see their chart, unless their birth date is very close to our own in the same year.

At its core, Jupiter is about expansion. Our desire to expand comes when we are born. On the one hand, we discover that we are no longer the great, limitless beings united with all things that we were before taking on a physical body. On the other hand, we find this body that we have taken on to be ill-suited for containing the spirit that is attempting to wedge itself in there! It flails and flops uselessly at birth, and we must rely on others with more control of their bodies to keep us alive. These two discoveries cause our deepest nature to desire a return to that state of expanded well-being, and we spend the rest of our life trying to achieve it, whether through religion or wealth, education or travel, eating or gambling. Expansion is the natural outgrowth of our need to go out into the world and make it a part of ourselves again.

If we understand and use Jupiter well, we are more likely to make it work for us by developing skills—educating ourselves. To do this, we may travel, attend school, learn through apprenticeships or work experiences, read, and listen to those wiser than us. We expand because we are assimilating more of the world into our nature, through learning about it.

Jupiter may lead us to expand in other ways as well. Its instruments in our nature are knowledge, faith, and optimism. If we direct its energies toward the physical, we may engage in activities like enterprise (expanding through business), gambling (attempting to expand wealth rapidly), or overeating (expanding our body). Naturally, some of these are not healthful ways to expand ourselves, and so we must have a way of tempering the desire for limitlessness and union with the whole, a way of harnessing our faith and optimism and returning to realism. This ability is granted to us through the energy field of Saturn, the other impersonal planet. Faith is our willingness to accept things that we do not yet know, and optimism is our trust that things will turn out well—neither of these is a replacement for knowledge. With Jupiter, we sometimes want to believe something so much that we will hide from knowledge, replacing it with faith and optimism. Herein lies the pitfall of Jupiter, because in these circumstances, we often end up taking risks that are too big.

Tapping the Wealth of Jupiter

To get in touch with Jupiter, we need to stimulate ourselves with newness. Newness brings awareness, and awareness naturally expands.

Awareness can come in many ways, but whatever action you engage in to increase awareness, *it must feel fresh*. Anything stale will not trigger awareness. If it feels new to us, we can expand our awareness through things as simple as taking a walk, playing with a child, reading a book, or making love with our partner.

To tap Jupiter's field, we can ask ourselves questions such as:

• How do I see the world and cosmos?
• What do I expect from the world I live in?
• How do I expand my awareness?
• How do I want to grow?
• Where might I be taking too high a risk?
• Where am I overdoing it?

When we are in our Jupiter, we feel upbeat and happy. The world is our teacup—we feel open, and our awareness is broadened and sensitized, as if we are plumbing a deeper well of consciousness than we ourselves can contain. We *know* things, more than just having knowledge.

If we overdo Jupiter, we may feel as if we can do no wrong; everything is coming our way. We can surmount any obstacle. We are eager, even impatient to achieve our goals. We may set unreasonably high goals for ourselves in this frame, or deny reality. We may feel compromised or unsafe because of a high level of risk.

When we have lost touch with Jupiter, we may lose our zest for life. We may feel as though life gives us a set of diminishing opportunities. We may lose hope and faith in what we do not know. We may become depressed, feel helpless and abandoned by providence.

Jupiter in Our Partner's Nature

When our partner is in their Jupiter, they will be warm and magnanimous. Their generosity and optimism are lovely to bask in. Watch for signs of overconfidence and overextension—the grand gift, the get-rich-quick scheme. They may want to overindulge or engage in risky behavior.

When this occurs, it is helpful to hold ourselves in reserve from their enthusiasm. Even though it is tempting, if we are clear about what feels safe to us and what does not, we will by our own sincere example be able to help our partner balance their overconfidence.

If our partner seems to be out of touch with Jupiter, we can do things that could lead them to an expanded awareness, to living in a world of possibility again. Although we can open doorways, we cannot make them walk through, nor can we anticipate what will feel fresh and new to them, what will actually open their awareness and expand their horizons. If we keep ourselves in Jupiter's flow, then in returning to us, they will return to Jupiter as well.

Saturn, Father Time

Saturn is the natural counterpart to Jupiter in our quest to make our life work. Just as Jupiter represents our expansiveness and what we expect from the world, Saturn brings structure and limitation, showing what we think the world expects of us. Saturn is often thought of as the taskmaster, the one who makes us do what we don't want to do. Yet, he is nothing more than the time-keeper. He just marks the passage of time, and through it we see the results of our actions. We see that our hard work is not for nothing, or we find that our irresponsibility eventually catches up with us.

Time exists because we have a physical body. Without a physical form or structure, we would not be subject to the cycles of the planets, marking off our time. Time brings us to our full potential; it also ages us and brings us eventually to the point when our physical form must die. The same process operates with our projects and endeavors.

Our projects and activities go through a sprouting, growth, flowering, harvesting, reward, and death process as well. If we realize that this is true for all things—that time is not of the essence, time *is* the essence—we will understand how to work with Saturn.

Saturn is associated with structure: laws and rules, both natural or cosmic, and those concocted by humans. Time and the cyclic revolution of the planets are the result of cosmic laws. The laws of motion and physics are natural laws to which all of us are subject. We can choose to ignore them with little effect but self-harm; or we can choose to work with them with a greatly self-rewarding effect.

We can see, then, that where Jupiter is associated with expansion, Saturn has to do with contraction and limitation. Most of us have negative associations with the Saturnian concepts, but they are both natural and necessary. We appreciate them when we understand what they really are.

Limitation is a natural result of structure. We could also call limitation "boundaries" or "structure." Without boundaries, we would have no separate identity. Without the structure of bones, we would be shapeless blobs. Structures also support us. It is much easier to gain speed while swimming when we have something to push off against. We feel comforted by drawing a blanket around us because we feel embraced and enfolded. These are forms of limitation.

Limitation feels good when it is the right amount for us. With too much limitation, we feel restricted or trapped. With too little, we feel unstructured and unfocused.

The best form of limitation—the one that feels best—is the one we place on ourselves. The key is knowing how much is good and what it feels like when we haven't got it quite right. When we have mastered this quality of self-responsibility, we will be in harmony with Saturn.

Tapping the Structure of Saturn

To get in touch with Saturn, we need to look at the big picture. We need to see our life in terms of the long-range process of growth and development that we have achieved through our own efforts over the years. To tap this, first look at what your biggest issues are now. Also look at what you have accomplished or are working on constructively. Then look back to ten years ago. Where were you then? What you did then has given birth to your accomplishments or problems right now. If we are working well with Saturn, we will see the rewards that have come to us. If we have "room for improvement," we will see very clearly where that improvement can be made by adjusting our attitudes and actions. Chances are very good that we will see some solid development when we look at our life in ten-year chunks. We can also look back 20 years, 30 years, and so forth. It is also helpful to think of a very important time or experience in your life, look back 10 and 20 years before it, and then look forward 10 and 20 years after the experience.

With Saturn, we are sure to get the rewards if we do the work and face the facts. This is Saturn's law. Another way to tap Saturn's stream is to think about the following questions:

- Where must I learn to stand on my own feet?
- Where will a lack of self-discipline hurt me most?
- Where am I most aware of my need to be responsible?
- Where do I have the most difficulty with fear?
- Where do I struggle with ambiguity—not knowing what some thing means?

When we are in touch with our Saturn, we find it easier to face the music, because we know that being continually responsible is the best way to be free. We walk our path without fear because we know that we are doing the best we can, and the universe supports us when we do our part. We feel wise and have deep insight into the problems that exist in our world. We can see humor in the paradoxes of life.

When we overdo Saturn, we may be a wet blanket, pessimistic and depressed. We may feel caught in a world that is not of our choosing, that controls us. We may feel trapped and want to rebel. We feel sorry for ourselves. The future looks dark.

When we are out of Saturn's stream, we lose touch with our need to be responsible. We may lose our drive, or feel as if we are outside the law. However, it is not possible to really be out of Saturn's energy field, only to think that we are. Such an illusion will catch up with us soon. We cannot defy the laws of the universe, and we do not have a choice about living with them.

Saturn in Our Partner's Chart

Saturn in our partner's nature can come out as the (self-) responsible individual who knows their limits and abilities. They know how to use their strengths and weaknesses, and apply wisdom in making decisions. They are realistic, unafraid to be patient and to allow things to develop over time.

If our partner is overwhelmed by Saturn, they may feel burdened or depressed. They may be tired, worried, and fearful of what the future holds. They may be taking a serious look at all that they are, and all that they want to be, measuring one against the other. They could also become controlling or concerned with rules.

If they are ignoring Saturn, they may exhibit some of the same traits as with too much Jupiter—overconfidence, overindulgence, taking big risks. They may be heedless of limitation and responsibility.

To bring Saturn back into balance in your partner's life, it is important to bring it into balance in your own *without taking on the responsibilities your partner is shirking*. The sincerest form of support is often setting an example and being ready to forgive our beloved when they have opened to what is missing. By being self-responsible, we can open the door to the self-responsibility of others.

Blending Jupiter and Saturn

Jupiter and Saturn must live in peaceful balance within us if we are to live in harmony in our world. We must be able to move forward (expand) and retreat (contract) as circumstances demand—to dream, and to live within reality. We must accept limitation, yet be able to take a risk and expand when the time is right. These are essential skills in relationships as well as in work or business.

We need to be able to build our relationship, to accept Saturn's structure in it. We also need to be able to feel Jupiter's self-assurance so we can learn to trust. We need to learn how to use the time and cycles of Saturn to enhance the development of our love.

Comparing the interaction of Jupiter and Saturn in our chart to that of our partner's will show us how we will forge our way as a couple in the world. Will we see eye-to-eye on religion and philosophy? Will we both enjoy travel? Will we have a growth-oriented approach to our relationship? Will we want to go into business together? No matter what the answers to these questions may be, we can see general harmony or potential discord (that can be worked out) by seeing how they mesh with each other by sign.

The Wild Cards: Uranus, Neptune, and Pluto

Uranus, Neptune, and Pluto all represent energies that are clearly beyond our personality. Their energies are intense and can feel overwhelming, but we can learn to channel them into our lives in constructive ways. In relationships, they are responsible for the feelings of spiritual depth and recognition that we encounter in a soul-level relationship. They are the source for our knowledge of the soul and spirit in ourselves and our partners. When we come into contact with these planets through our partner's chart, we are affected by our beloved more than influencing them. The wild-card planets represent ways that our partner brings us into contact with these great forces. When our partner contacts these wild cards in us, we become the vehicle for transformation in their life as well.

These planets are wild cards, because they bring the unexpected. There is a part of us that expects life to go on without ever changing. Even though experience teaches us otherwise, any change is treated with surprise, since it challenges our concept of reality. Even when we know change is coming, it rarely turns out to be exactly as we had expected. Since change is the stock-in-trade of these planets, we're nearly always in for a wild ride where we encounter them.

Our experiences with these planets make sense only from the perspective of the soul. From the level where we live eternally, the pain and obstacles on the physical plane seem insignificant, merely serving to push us toward what we need to learn. Pain is an instrument of our education, with meaning and purpose.

When these planets are significant in our chart or our partner's, we have to deal with them continuously. We may feel an uneasy peace with them, but they demand the best of us when we are under their influence. We must learn to really understand and work with their powers and the tasks they bring. We become accustomed to them in our own chart, although we may project them onto others. However, when our partner brings the wild card planets to us, they often come to us in an unfamiliar package.

Developing our ability to direct these planetary energies with our beloved is the Great Work of our relationships. It is where all the action is. These planets show where we have left processes incomplete from past lives, where we have issues, preconceived notions, and incomplete understandings. They show us the nature of our soul agreements and how we plan to fulfill them. Because they are so powerful, they usually present us with both the allure and the "problems" of our relationship. It is these energies that sustain a relationship, because we need something to work on together in order for the relationship to last. It's not so much that we need to have problems if we want to stay with our partner, but that we come to the planet to learn, and this person is one with whom we can fulfill that task. Once the obstacles are overcome, we can team up with our beloved to serve the world in those capacities suggested by the planets that challenged us before. It is where we have been wounded that we become most able to serve.

Uranus the Awakener

Uranus is the planet of "mishaps and miracles." I like to think of it as the "Life Path Adjuster." That is, if we can think of ourselves as having a path to complete fulfillment, Uranus is the planet that nudges us back toward the path. Since most people tend to forget that they even have a path, it is not surprising that Uranus must jolt them back from time to time. Uranus brings us back into alignment with our True Self in shocking, unsettling ways. They can be pleasant as well as unpleasant.

From the soul's perspective, shock is good. Since we learn to be ego-centered in this world, anything that unseats the ego from its role of supremacy is good. Shocking events jar us and thrust us into situations where we cannot apply the familiar schemes and orchestrated responses that we are used to using. Once the ego is unseated, we respond naturally and with strength from the True Self. Even if it is only a brief time before the ego resumes its familiar controlling position, the shock has succeeded in revealing a part of ourselves that we may not have known existed, or may have forgotten about. Every time we are shocked, the True Self steps into its rightful role more easily, until eventually it has dominion most of the time. Once we are familiar with the feel of the True Self and its response to the world, we can begin to discern whether it is the ego or the Self that is steering the ship. As we learn from shocking events, we find that it takes less and less of a shock for us to unmask the ego. Eventually, we just have to sense that a shock is coming for us to allow the True Self to assume its central role in our consciousness. This allows us to correct our course and defuse the situation before something more dramatic occurs.

Flowing with the Force of Uranus

We cannot truly control Uranus's energies, at least from the perspective of the personality, but we can work with them constructively. If Uranus is a planet that is prominent in our chart, we will be challenged throughout our life to "be real." This means being conventional or unconventional, as it suits our true nature—we cannot merely react against what other people are doing or want us to do. Periodically, we all experience a certain amount of chaos as Uranus upsets the status quo to introduce a new, more genuine reality. We may find ourselves going through periodic awakenings and having that effect on others as well.

Uranus in Our Partner's Chart

When we come in contact with our partner's Uranus, we may be surprised by their actions, their attitudes, and what is happening in the outside part of their life. It is here that they are attempting to be unique, to be who they really are. Just as this is a learning process for us, so it is for them. They may be unpredictable in this area, and we may misunderstand their behavior.

This behavior may trigger feelings of rejection or abandonment in us, although this is not usually their intent. They may be simply coming from a deeper reality than we are used to experiencing. Or, they could be casting about inside, trying to find their true nature within all the chaos they feel. Whatever it is, to remain closely engaged with them when we feel unsafe can cause us to lose our self-esteem because we are not honoring our needs. It is necessary to pull back to "safe territory" until we feel safe and loved again.

Neptune, the Divine Mind

Ψ Neptune is truth. However, most of the time we don't experience it that way because its truth lies in the unseen, often unacknowledged, realm of spirit. In fact, in many astrological books, Neptune is related to illusion. The key lies in understanding that what we see in this world is the tip of the iceberg. We cannot see the whole truth—the entire iceberg—even though it sure seems that way, until we look beneath the surface. Once we do, we're in unfamiliar territory. Looking down into the water, the iceberg looks larger, fuzzy—all proportion is lost. Until we come to know this world in its own right, Neptune does seem to be illusion. However, once we understand that it— truth—shifts and flows, we will know that Neptune shows us what is real.

The key is to become familiar with its realms. It is the lord of subtlety, and its soft voice may go unnoticed, except as a whisper in our ear and the feeling that somewhere along the way our position is eroding. Neptune changes us just as much as Uranus does, but it is a quiet type of change, like water dissolving rock. We cannot resist it, any more than we could push on a cloud. We can work with it by flowing with it, by surrendering to its truth.

The more we learn about Neptune's world, the better we will be at navigating it. It is the world of spirit, of psychic energy, which to most people is illusion because they are not taught to sense it in any way. Although most of us have some way of perceiving it when we are children, we are taught to disregard our perceptions, and soon they become part of our unconscious impressions of the world. However, we can bring them back into consciousness by paying closer attention to what we are really feeling, what we really know. It takes time and practice to learn to separate Neptune's truth from another aspect of Neptune, our imagination. There is a truth in imagination, but when we are trying to make sense of our interactions with our partner or boss, for instance, the application of imagination may be out of place. However, it may be helpful in opening up possibilities or creating solutions once truth is discerned.

One of the things that makes Neptune's world so hard to understand is that it is not constrained by the rules and realities we know so well in the physical, Saturnine world. It is, in fact, the world of space, the great "ocean of energy" that fills our entire universe. Energy is transmitted across the great expanses of our cosmos effortlessly; nonphysical energies are unbounded by time and space.

Once we become attuned to these subtle realms, we can see things such as the reality of energy exchange between ourselves and others. We can experience emotions as they come and go in a person's aura. We can see the effects that someone else's energy impulses have on us, and vice versa.

Attuning to the Reality of Neptune

If Neptune is prominent in our chart, we will work throughout our life on the process of uniting spirit and matter. Since Neptune represents spiritual things, and we live in a physical, material world, we will have to blend them in order to befriend Neptune. We can do so by finding a way to incorporate a spiritual reality into our life, perhaps in an unspoken way. We may find time to meditate daily, practice yoga, define a spiritual path for ourselves, or make religion and church a part of our life. If we truly endeavor to live from the soul level of consciousness, we are bringing Neptune into our understanding of reality.

Neptune in Our Partner's Chart

If we have a strong contact with our partner's Neptune, we will notice it more in their nature. We may think of them as being spiritual, even ideal. They may be more sensitive than others we know. Their imagination and creativity may run very high; they may even be an artist or musician, or just enjoy the arts. If we find it hard to "pin them down," it is probably because reality for them is creative, changing from moment to moment. They are interested in the big picture, and therefore what seems to them to be details aren't that important. As they come to distinguish between inner truth and their imagination, their reality will become more consistent and grounded.

Unless we remain mindful of Neptune's true nature, we can misinterpret our partner's Neptunian behavior. We may feel as though they are aloof or care more for their dream world than for us. They may appear to take us for granted or neglect us. Being open and respectful of their unseen reality will help our partner come into balance. To assist our partner in grounding

Neptune into the "reality" of life on Earth, we can use harmonic induction with their permission. Ask them to open to you. Bring your energy field into the high realms where your beloved dwells. When you have matched their energy, then slowly bring yours down into the earth, grounding it and your partner into the here and now. We can also suggest gentle physical activity such as yoga or walking. If we do not have their openness, we can set an example for them to observe. We can hold a vision of their perfection—a grounded, balanced spiritual being—to assist their growth and keep our faith and trust in them intact.

Pluto, Vehicle of Ensoulment

Pluto represents the process of ego-destruction, or more correctly, the process of dis-identifying with the ego and identifying with the True Self. This comes to us most profoundly through intense experiences where we feel as though we are dying, until we understand that the real part of our self is very much alive. Plutonian processes are those involved in deep, long-term changes, such as divorce or the death of a loved one, or more happily, a marriage or the birth of a child. These are things that irrevocably change our life in profound and far-reaching ways. This is Pluto's specialty.

Changes, large and small, are constantly occurring in our life, so when Pluto grabs our attention, we realize that what he brings is not new. His changes have been brewing for a long time. They are things we have thought about, possibly transformations we have wanted for a long time. Sometimes we have long desired the end result of these changes, but the means of getting there was distasteful. Often, if we had not balked at the possible discomfort and inconvenience, we would have made many more changes than we did.

Pluto puts our priorities in the right place. Though associated with death experiences, it is actually rejuvenating, because no living thing ever dies. When we have changed to a new form, we are reborn, like a babe in the area where the change has occurred. We no longer feel stagnant or dying. Pluto is as necessary to life—to truly living—as it is to death.

At its deepest level, Pluto brings to us the awareness that life resides in our soul, not in our physical embodiment. As long as we identify with our body—what we see—we will have difficulty with Pluto and its transformative processes. We will tend to hang on to the old, because it is familiar and comfortable and feels like life, but isn't. Life is vigorous and self-renewing, not old and comfortable.

Pluto's changes require time and energy; it is better to put our energy into embracing and fulfilling the changes rather than resisting them. When we offer resistance to what must happen, we are weakened, not helped. Resistance blocks the flow of energy and results in a buildup of force like flood waters behind a dam. The buildup can be poisonous due to the stagnation of energies in the situation. Eventually the flood waters break the dam, and we have less control over the results.

If we pay attention to Pluto, we can engineer the changes to suit our needs. The earlier we embrace them, the more choices we have. The best way to work with Pluto is to look at change from the soul perspective. The soul is here to grow, so it sees change positively. It is willing to withstand pain and suffering to achieve its aim of evolving; evolution is much more important than the temporary discomfort that may accompany it. What's more, once we are identified with the soul (True Self), we feel less pain, perhaps none at all, when experiencing transformation.

Pluto is renowned for its association with spiritual transformation. In fact, all real change *is* spiritual transformation.

Harnessing the Power of Pluto

To deal with Pluto's might, we must let go of all resistance. This does not mean to accept everything that happens, or to stop discerning what our experience is, but to *be open to newness*. By being open, we see new things and are inspired by new ideas. We can hear our inner guidance. We don't have to accept all new things; however, we don't want to close ourselves off from valuable options either.

Pluto is always there, preparing our next transformation, even if we don't feel these forces. It is helpful to be aware of all the messages we send with our mind—all the things we say, like "if only . . . , then I would . . . ," or "I wish I could. . . ." We also send messages with our behavior. Let's say, for instance, that we don't like a job, but we are unwilling to leave. We will send subtle signals—lack of interest in doing well, arriving a few minutes late, or showing a slight reluctance to fulfill our responsibilities. These messages are read by those around us, and eventually we will get what we unconsciously wanted. Pluto responds to our unconscious messages much more than it does to what, in our conscious mind, we think we want.

If Pluto is emphasized in our chart, we will engage in life on a deeper level, where the unconscious is found. We will see and feel things that are beyond the grasp of many others. We will have difficulty accepting shallower interpretations and may show or experience a great deal of power in that area, especially when we are challenged. We may be an agent of change for those around us as well as ourselves.

Pluto in Our Partner's Chart

If there is a critical connection between a planet in our chart and our partner's Pluto, then they will be instrumental in bringing about changes in our life. We will feel their power and intensity. We will learn to see into the depths that they know. When we challenge them (if we dare to), they may say or do little at first, but over time, pressure may build. They may release it in an explosion of energy that may be hard to cope with or understand. We may feel attacked or victimized when this occurs.

We have to remember that it is probably not their intent to harm or overwhelm us with their energetic release. However, it is important to keep ourselves safe if this happens. Sometimes it is enough to turn away, rather than directly face our partner, when they are releasing so much power. Other times we may need to leave in order to maintain our integrity.

The issue that provoked the explosion should be explored in a calmer moment and in safety. Often someone else's guidance will get better results, like a counselor or mediator. It is not helpful to "fight fire with fire," since much of the force being exerted is pent-up emotion that probably has more to do with the past than the present.

Until our partner is ready to open to us in a safe and sensitive way, we can hold ourselves in reserve. Seeing them in our mind's eye as open and loving, and setting a self-responsible example, will assist them in moving with Pluto's energy more harmoniously. Explosiveness is not a natural part of Pluto's nature, but only of us humans who don't always know how to handle transformation well.

If our partner does well with Pluto, they will have power, but use it only with prudence and compassion, to support and help others. Their Pluto will be seen in their drive to accomplish great things, and in their depth of understanding and feeling.

Chiron, the Wounded Healer

Chiron is the "wounded healer." It has qualities of both the transpersonal (Uranus, Neptune, Pluto) and the impersonal (Jupiter and Saturn) planets. It seems to bridge the gap between the visible (the planets through Saturn) and invisible (those beyond Saturn), easing our way in understanding the transpersonal forces and in integrating them into our life. Chiron is the flagship that points out where we need to work on ourselves. It opens the door for the outer planets to be felt. With our intent and focus, we heal the area that is triggered.

Chiron enables us to go through healing, which can come to us in many forms. It can be a response to what we normally think of as illness, or it can be a healing of the more subtle levels of our nature. Each wound that we carry, detected on whatever level of our energy field, can be spotlighted by Chiron. No matter where Chiron puts its focus, it will bring out an aspect of our *core wound*, the wound that lies at the heart of all our pain and suffering. Ultimately, it is here to help us heal that core wound; since it focuses on both the wound itself and the way to heal it, Chiron symbolizes both the wound and the healer. While some astrologers feel that the core wound cannot be healed, I have seen that it can.

In chapter 2, we looked at the creation of the ego mask or false self. Our false self contrives the "not me" pattern of orchestrated responses, strategies, and formulae for success. We use them to cover up our real reactions to our experiences and to our True Self. When we wall off our unpleasant emotions from our awareness, we create a "not me" block in the body and energy field (aura). This block becomes the core wound.

The core wound can spread to other parts of the body and energy field.

It grows with each experience that we interpret as unpleasant, and that we associate with the things we were taught to separate from ourselves. As the core wound grows, we develop methods of hiding it and protecting it from the notice of others, because to let others in is to experience pain. The protection is our ego mask. This is how and why the ego is created.

In healing the core wound, Chiron leads us to know and identify with our Soul (Higher or True Self) and Spirit (God Self). Since the God Self is already perfect and unflawed, it carries the forms, the blueprints, that will heal the lower parts of our energy field, including the physical. Since the True Self has access to the God Self, it already knows how to heal the lower bodies; we merely need to acknowledge it, and allow it to assume the throne of the Self. Illness may originate on any level but the God Self, so we always have the capacity to heal what is imbalanced.

When Chiron touches a part of our chart, we can heal that part. Chiron is not the wounder: it is the wound that already existed, but that we were unaware of. Every pain or wound we experience ultimately ties back into the core wound.

Occasionally, the healing of the wound means the death of the physical body. We have all known people who have chosen to heal their soul by taking on a terminal illness. Since the soul lives eternally, it is willing to make this sacrifice. The more we identify with the Soul-Spirit complex, the less this will concern us. However, leaving behind the life of the physical is difficult for all of us, and something that is never taken lightly, here or in the world of Spirit.

Chiron's place in our chart shows us where and how we can fulfill the purpose of Chiron's lesson. It gives us one way that we can see the nature of the core wound, although the core wound will be shown elsewhere in our chart as well. Chiron teaches us this: *It is where we are wounded that we become most able to serve.* Once we have survived and healed a wound, or are in the process of healing it, then we can serve others who are healing the same type of wound. This is why, for example, survivors of incest are often the best therapists for other survivors, provided they are properly trained and have truly explored, come to understand, and substantially released their core wound.

Chiron in Our Partner's Chart

Chiron's place in our partner's chart can help us see their wound. It will show where our partner seems to be flawed. A connection between Chiron in their chart and a planet in ours signifies where we can choose to heal ourselves as a result of contact with our partner. We will become acutely aware of a part of ourselves that can be strengthened, may carry pain, or is not being expressed as it could be. It may be painful to go to that part of our nature, and the planet highlighted in our chart may be a part of our nature that we seek to avoid, until we recognize the power and rewards of healing.

Often, we experience our partner's Chiron as a journey into our dark side. It may make that part of our nature seem especially difficult. Trying to make progress there may feel like swimming through molasses!

The core wound is inevitably what we encounter through our relationships, because nothing can take us deeper into our self than love. If we are willing to face ourselves, our mutual Chiron contacts give us an opportunity to look at what in our nature we can heal together. Chances are very good that, if the relationship is significant, the Chiron contact will cut to the very heart of our need to heal. This means that it may feel wounding when we first realize all that the relationship holds for us. We can mistake the pain we feel for something coming from our partner. Even if our partner does something palpable to bring on our pain (as in abuse), we have contributed something to the experience (at least, being there to receive the abuse). By going inside ourselves, we can discover what is wounded. By seeking the help we need (if necessary), we can release the pain of our core wound.

Significant Chiron connections also show where our partner can heal; however, we cannot force them to heal. We may see the pain and suffering they experience there, but we cannot rescue them. They must rescue themselves. As free, sovereign beings, they must choose. We can only set an example and be open to the development of their higher potential without forgetting who they are in the now.

C H A P T E R　　S E V E N

THE PLAYERS ON STAGE
Relating the Planets to Each Other

Now that we have looked at each planet in our chart, we can look at what they mean for our relationships. We have explored their meanings in pairs (chapter 6), but we don't yet know how to relate them to our charts. Now it's time to see how each pair works together. When we look at a pair of planets in two charts, we have four combinations. For instance:

> my sun ~ my partner's sun
> my sun ~ my partner's moon
> my moon ~ my partner's sun
> my moon ~ my partner's moon

We will be addressing each planetary pair in all four of its combinations. There are instructions throughout this chapter to assist you in figuring out each planetary pair. These are repeated in a set of worksheets found in the appendix on pages 306-310. Once you have completed the worksheet for each set of planets, you can look back at the interpretations for each combination—how the planets blend by polarity, resonance, approach type, response type, companionship, or none of the above.

First, let's review what each planetary pair represents:

Sun–Moon	basic compatibility
Venus–Mars	how you have fun together; sex
Jupiter–Saturn	how you blend with the world

The planets that are not paired symbolize:

Mercury	the mixer and communicator
Uranus	the awakener; brings shocking events and experiences
Neptune	the dissolver; melts our illusions so we can see the inner truth
Pluto	the transformer; brings deep change so we learn to identify with the Soul instead of the personality
Chiron	the wounded healer; focuses on our wounds so we can heal them

In this chapter, we will explore the paired planets and Mercury. We will discover more about the roles of the other singleton planets in chapter 8.

How to Interpret Their Interaction: General Rules

Before we explore the nature of each planetary pair in more detail, let's also review the concepts related to the signs that we have explored. For further clarification on how the signs are interrelated, refer to the chart in the appendix on pages 299-300.

If the planets are found:	They share:	What it means:
in the same sign	resonance	blending, natural unity of the planets
two signs apart (one sign in between) or any multiple thereof	companionship	natural friendship, mutual understanding
three signs apart	response type (modality—cardinal, fixed, or mutable)	natural challenge; response can become reaction
four signs apart	approach type (element—fire, earth, air, water)	natural harmony, similar approach to life
opposite each other (six signs apart)	polarity, response type, and companionship	natural challenge to balance (complementarity) or split (opposition); response can become either reaction or mutual understanding
five signs apart, or in signs that are next to each other	dissimilarity	naturally unfamiliar to each other, but can find common qualities

Even with the interrelationships that are difficult, it is possible to develop harmony—in fact, this is the work of our partnership. At the soul level, all interrelationships are harmonious.

We expect relationships to be harmonious without any work if we have the right partner. If they aren't, we often think that we must have chosen the wrong person, and that there's another person out there who is right for us. Even if we recognize that our impasses can be worked out, we are often at a loss because we don't know how to sort them out and create harmony in the relationship.

It may actually seem as though our partner is deadly accurate in finding our weakest points. This is because, in choosing a partner, we are moved by our soul's unconscious desire to grow. Our partner will have the same experience! When both people are hurting, it is hard to reach beyond the pain and find higher ground, yet we can do it. Even if we have a great many areas of potential conflict, we can still learn to create harmony. Learned harmony is often better than natural harmony, because it is born of wisdom rather than innocent "luck," and represents growth. Although we need some natural harmony in all of our relationships—we can't work on everything at once—in a soul-level relationship, areas of conflict need only be temporary. We can change conflict to learned harmony by applying an understanding of our astrological charts to our lives.

Dissimilarity

In the chapters and tables above, we have already discussed each type of planetary interrelationship, except dissimilarity. Dissimilar signs have nothing natural or apparent in common, but like the other inharmonious sign interrelationships, harmony can be cultivated. The technique with these signs is different. Because there is nothing evidently in common between them, we can take two approaches:

- Find what is common between the planets involved and increase the resonance of those qualities with our focus. For example, if the sun and moon are involved, open up to their natural way of expressing with each other. The moon wants to be receptive to the sun, even if it seems to behave "oddly." The sun will want to shine, and if it is appreciated by the moon, no matter how strangely, it will accept that attention.

- Creatively explore the nature of the signs involved and look for commonality between them. While the common areas will not be the predominant characteristics of the signs, we can find such areas. Harmony can be cultivated by focusing on these

---

areas. For instance, Virgo and Aquarius are dissimilar signs. However, both are technologically oriented. Although this is not the most dominant quality of either sign, their harmony with each other can be enhanced by focusing on this, and on related qualities.

Dissimilar signs that are next to each other express an evolutionary step in the progression of the zodiac. This evolutionary common ground can be capitalized on as well. Since Aries has the function of expressing the Self without filter or barrier, and Taurus's function is to manifest the Self through physical form, we can use this mutual focus to bring them into cooperation and mutual appreciation. With dissimilarities, we tend to change part of our nature to be like the sign of our partner, or to force our partner to change into our own image in this area. This is the danger with all dissimilar signs, because what we don't understand we try to change; or we try to change ourselves. If we can find common ground and enlarge upon it without changing, we will be able to achieve harmony within these sign combinations.

Interpreting the Planetary Pairs

We will be interpreting the meanings of each planetary pair based on all four possible combinations using a step-by-step process. We will be relating them by one of the relationships between signs shown in the chart above. Once you know the relationship that exists between two planets, you can look up more specific information about their qualities. For instance, if your sun and your partner's moon are in the same response type, then in the following section, you can learn more about how this planetary pair behaves when they are in this interrelationship. Then you can read more about that specific response type to find out even more about how you will relate to each other when you are expressing the two parts of your nature represented by these planets.

This way of combining the planets is how astrologers interpret our charts. Although in this book we won't be looking at every planetary combination, as an astrologer would, we will be relating the planets in various ways to get to the real heart of our relationships and how they tick. We will analyze the potential for growth of the individuals. Also, we will see where and how we can revise our understanding of ourselves and our partner; then, if we are having difficulties, we can improve our way of relating to each other.

Interpreting Our Chart Combination Step-by-Step

The planets in a pair are like two actors on stage, in dialogue with each other. Even though each planet relates to every other planet with greater or lesser intensity, the planetary pairs we have explored talk to each other more because of a natural affinity between them. They are highlighted when we interact with other people, particularly those who are close to us.

Here are the steps to putting together all of the factors we have considered so far:

Use the table entitled "Sign Interrelationships" in the appendix (pages 299-300). This way, you can determine what type of combination exists between each planetary combination as you follow the instructions below.

- Using your chart or chart report, fill in "My Astrological Profile" in the appendix starting on page 301.

- Do the same for your partner, filling out "My Partner's Astrological Profile" beginning on page 304.

- Complete "Our Sun–Moon Combinations" using the planetary profiles, found either in this chapter or in the appendix (page 306).

- Interpret the four Sun–Moon combinations following the guidelines given below.

- Do the same for the other planetary pairs, Venus-Mars and Jupiter-Saturn.

- Regardless of the type of interrelationship, read the entire section related to the planetary combination you are investigating to get a feel for the many ways the planets can express together.

- Remember to place the information on the planetary pairs in the context of the main information you have gathered on your and your partner's charts from chapters 3–5.

If you don't have your charts to work with yet, just read on and see what fits. Since the sun and moon are the most important pair, let's start with them.

The Sun and Moon

The sun and moon tell us a tremendous amount about ourselves and our partner. In looking at our relationship, the sun-moon combinations are a treasure trove for understanding how our partnership works. Remember to organize the information about your and your partner's sun–moon combinations according to the instructions shown above first.

My sun ($\odot$) is in _____.
My partner's sun ($\odot$) is in _____.

My moon ($\mathcal{D}$) is in _____.
My partner's moon ($\mathcal{D}$) is in _____.

Between our charts, my sun to my partner's moon is in:
_____ resonance (the same sign),
_____ companionship (two signs apart),
_____ the same response type (modality),
[response type: _____]
_____ the same approach type (element),
[approach type: _____]
_____ the same polarity, [polarity: _____] or
_____ dissimilarity (none of the above).

Between our charts, my moon to my partner's sun is in:
_____ resonance (the same sign),
_____ companionship (two signs apart),
_____ the same response type (modality),
[response type: _____]
_____ the same approach type (element),
[approach type: _____]
_____ the same polarity, [polarity: _____] or
_____ dissimilarity (none of the above).

Between our charts, my sun to my partner's sun is in:
_____ resonance (the same sign),
_____ companionship (two signs apart),
_____ the same response type (modality),
[response type: _____]
_____ the same approach type (element),
[approach type: _____]
_____ the same polarity, [polarity: _____] or
_____ dissimilarity (none of the above).

Between our charts, my moon to my partner's moon is in:
_____ resonance (the same sign),
_____ companionship (two signs apart),
_____ the same response type (modality),
[response type: _____]
_____ the same approach type (element),
[approach type: _____]
_____ the same polarity, [polarity: _____] or
_____ dissimilarity (none of the above).

The sun and moon are fundamentally important to our interaction; we use them and blend them in our own nature without thinking. They are the cornerstones of relationships. They show how we use our past experiences to inform our current decisions. Our best abilities to express our True Self come through the sun; our emotional patterns enter into the mix through the moon. We are always relying on what we know from the past, making analogies between new experiences and similar experiences of the past.

By combining our placements of these planets with those of our partner, we find how our conditioning fits with our partner's self-expression. We find out how our past meshes with theirs. We can see if we will have difficulties with family loyalties, if our ways of expressing our emotions and our purpose are intrinsically understandable or difficult for our partner. While a certain amount of challenge is workable, we generally want to achieve comfort between the suns and moons in the charts. We unconsciously strive to bring these four cornerstones of the relationship into harmony. Without some kind of natural harmony among these planets, it is unlikely that a stable, long-term relationship will form, although other planets can compensate for a lack here.

These planets are the foundation of trust and reciprocity in the relationship. In relationships based on traditional roles, it is customary for men to express their sun and women to express their moon. The woman would project her sun (her interests and sense of purpose) onto her partner or male child, and the man would project his moon (his emotions and other feelings) onto his partner or female child. In more modern, reciprocal relationships, each partner tends to and should strive to express both planets themselves. Therefore, both sun-moon combinations are important. Sometimes, where a woman's sun and a man's moon blend together well, this combination may take precedence, and a "role reversal" may occur. In reciprocal relationships, roles are flexible and shift back and forth depending on our needs in the partnership. If we become stuck in one role or the other, it is a sign that reciprocity has been weakened. A focus on the other of our planets in the pair will help us re-establish it on firmer footing.

The four combinations that follow give us much information:

1. *My sun–my partner's moon* tells how my desire and ability to shine and to fulfill my purpose is supported by my partner. When I express myself, my partner's favorable feelings toward that expression are the most basic element of the relationship. Our way of seeing life and pursuing our purpose goes deeply within our soul. We want nothing more than for our expression, the way we want to change the world, to be received sympathetically by our partner. The sun shows our conscious efforts at living; the moon our unconscious ones. The conscious and unconscious communicate with each other all the time, both within us and between ourselves and our partner. My sun's interrelationship with my partner's moon shows how well that communication takes place—whether my partner really understands me, and whether they feel comfortable responding to me based on the signals I send, consciously and unconsciously. It shows how empowered I feel by my partner's support. This planetary combination shows how easy it is for my partner to shift their primary loyalty from their family to our partnership. It shows how able they are to give me feedback, emotional and

otherwise, that I can accept. It also expresses how easy it is for my partner to go along with the ways I want to follow my bliss.

If these two planets are found in similarity (resonance, companionship, or approach type), they will be naturally harmonious. I will tend to find that my basic way of being is received well by my partner. I feel understood; I know there's someone there for me, and trust builds more easily because there's a sense that we look on the world with the same eyes. They will look to me for inspiration and direction, and allow me to take the lead, even if this involves an apparent role reversal. We won't have to work on the harmony between the way I want to change the world, and the world my partner lives in. We will find our relationship easy and comfortable. Our partnership will feel secure when we are expressing this particular combination. I will get along with their family and feel that I can be myself with them, by and large. I may feel a sense of kinship with them. However, we may have to take care not to get stuck in a rut. Ruts may feel comfortable to us in the short run, but sooner or later they will catch up with us; we will be unable to respond to newness, and eventually my partner's solar expression will dim.

If they are in polarity, they will easily tend to express complementarity (harmony) instead of opposition, because the sun and moon are naturally complementary. The moon easily receives the impulse of the sun and reflects it back. The sun duly appreciates the audience! It's hard not to appreciate the other when they are doing what we want them to, even if we don't see everything the same way. However, at times, I may not get the sympathetic response that I want from my partner. They may have a hard time focusing on my goals and seeing things from my perspective. They may become wrapped up in their own situations and experiences. I may not be able to connect with their emotional needs. They may have a hard time letting go of their family and giving their primary loyalty to me because the necessary trust is not there. We may find ourselves bringing our relationship to a crisis point periodically to try to reaffirm our love. This is where the need to develop complementarity comes in. Once we gain the soul's perspective, we can see the common bond that the opposing signs share. We can develop a common view of the world that builds trust. We become a team.

With the sun and moon in the same response type, harmony between the two planets will need to be learned. We will spontaneously trigger each other's "reaction mode" every time we try to get closer until we can learn to do otherwise. It may seem as if what I do is designed to irritate my partner and vice versa. What's more, we will both tend to be challenged in life at the same time, so we won't have a reserve to lend support to each other. When both of us react the same way, we may have difficulty breaking the pattern because we will both be triggered at the same time. My partner's way of being may hit me right in my biggest blind spot. They may feel confronted and self-protective when this circumstance is triggered. I may react by becoming proud, even arrogant, because I feel let down or betrayed. My partner may seem to want to mother me, or may perceive that I try to exert an unwelcome influence on them. We may have difficulty living together. My partner's past may seem to hinder me in what I want to accomplish. I may not feel comfortable expressing myself with their family. There may be an unconscious use of force that interferes with the willing exchange of energies between us. My way of being myself may create friction with my partner's habits, or how they were taught to behave, until we learn to understand and accept each other more fully. On the soul level, there can be no conflict. Once we come to recognize that each of us reacts to the other in the same way, and learn to put ourselves in each other's shoes, we will be able to empathize with each other. This lays the foundation for learned harmony.

If my sun and my partner's moon are found in dissimilarity (no interrelationship with each other), I may have difficulty bonding with my partner's emotional nature and habit patterns. They may feel as if I am indifferent to them because I don't know how to accept their emotional responses. It may seem as if they are from a different world. I may express myself in ways they simply cannot fathom. We may have difficulty understanding each other. It may seem as though my partner's family expects me to be entirely different from who I am. When we learn to see life through the other's eyes, we will no longer consider each other to be mysterious and incomprehensible. We will know the comfort and safety that comes of any good sun-moon combination. Our way of expressing our energies together may end up being unique, and bring out a creativity in our relationship that was not present before.

2. ***My moon–my partner's sun*** tells how I support my partner's desire and ability to shine. It shows how I am able to receive, interpret, and respond to my partner's spontaneous self-expression and sense of purpose. This combination represents how my partner makes sense of my unconscious communications— whether they feel supported, acknowledged, and empowered by the way I express my feelings. It also shows how well we really understand each other and whether we relate to life in similar ways. This combination shows whether my partner and my family get along well; it represents how well we can build trust, and how safe I feel with them. It also expresses whether, when we look at my partner's dreams for the future, we can do so as a team.

If my moon and my partner's sun are found in similarity (resonance, companionship, or approach type), their blend will be easy and comfortable. I will appreciate the way that my partner takes the lead, shines their light into the world. I will feel comfortable most of the time in following their example and have a natural understanding and appreciation of their approach to life, and the purpose they find in it. Our partnership will feel secure when we express through these planets. My personal background—my family upbringing and habits—will seem familiar to my partner. They will feel more confident in their ability to shine because I am comfortable being supportive. They can feel my support; we trust each other. However, we may tend to "overexpress" these planets and ignore other necessary parts of our nature. While comfort is an important factor in all relationships, we need to balance it with all aspects of our nature to create a robust union.

If they are in polarity, complementarity (harmony) will be their natural inclination, but it may take some cultivation. They will not split into opposition easily, since the sun and moon complement each other by their nature. If they do split, it may be because my past—family ties, old friends, old habits, or leftover emotional baggage—may interfere with our relationship. My partner may be impatient to get beyond or overlook things that I find important and feel a need to include in my life. I may look like the "emotional bad guy" if all the emotions are projected onto me. Emotional climaxes may occur regularly, rather than balanced, ongoing emotional expression. When a split occurs, it helps to look to the polarity in question to find what the signs have in common. At the soul level, the sun and moon will easily find their complementarity and work as a team toward their common needs and purposes. We can reaffirm the importance of our bond and return to the mutual empathy and support needed to work through issues from the past.

With the sun and moon in the same response type, we can foster harmony between the two planets, but it may not be there spontaneously at the start. I may have difficulty responding to my partner's way of pursuing their goals. I may misunderstand them or unconsciously trigger defensive action from them until we have learned to break through our mutual blind spot. This may cause difficulty in the constant contact of living together. We may both seem to get hit with difficult circumstances at the same time, so we could be too distracted to truly support each other. They may feel let down and betrayed when this way of relating is triggered. We may feel sensitive and want to retreat. My past may seem to get in the way of our union. By exploring how we trigger each other, we can discover the nature of our blind spots. Then we can begin to see how we really have deep similarities and can work toward common goals—the ones that initially drew us together.

If they are in dissimilarity (no interrelationship with each other), I may have difficulty understanding why my partner acts the way they do. They may not see the value in the way I respond to them. We may not know how to keep from stepping on each other's toes, and trust may build more slowly than we like—it may seem as if there's none there at times. My partner may seem a world apart from my family and the background I share with them. I may have difficulty understanding our emotional and cultural differences. Taking the relationship to the soul level will bring out the natural commonality that can be found between the sun and moon. At that level, we can find common ground between the signs they are found in, as well.

3. *My sun–my partner's sun* tells how well our senses of purpose and life direction mesh. It shows how well we can work together to express the truest, most genuine, most unique part of who we are. When the two suns connect, our True Selves beam to each other. We can share a childlike innocence or a fiery intent when the two suns work together well. Less naturally harmonious planetary interrelationships sometimes bring out competitiveness or power struggles, until harmony and balance are learned and trust is built. A good sun-to-sun connection, whether learned or intrinsic, gives us a deeper union based on a sense of common purpose and a union of the True Selves.

In a similarity interrelationship (resonance, companionship, or approach type), we will find that we work and play together with a feeling of common purpose and direction. We can shine on each other and bask in the mutual glow. We may feel as if we share a special destiny, and our True Selves may be stimulated to express more fully in our lives. This type of solar connection is very powerful, as if two suns were shining in the same sky. We feel strengthened and empowered by each other and can accomplish many lofty goals, together and individually.

A polarity relationship between the two suns can have aspects of both harmonious and challenging interrelationships—some feeling of commonality and some competitive drive. The combination may feel threatening in an ego-centered relationship, but once trust is built and the souls consistently sit at the throne of the self, the best qualities of complementarity can be fulfilled. When at the Soul (complementarity) level, our suns lead us to find our true purpose, and we can work as a team to accomplish the highest goals within the framework of their polarity.

With the two suns in the same response type, we may have difficulty until we learn to let go of pride, and not fear being upstaged by each other. We need to learn to appreciate the way each of us wants to shine. If my partner's direction feels different from my own, we may begin to pull away from each other. We may feel competitive toward each other. Looking at what they do that triggers me will help me to learn about my own shadow side, the part of myself that I don't want to know about. Friction can be turned into a powerhouse of common purpose once we learn to understand and appreciate the ways we react alike.

If our two suns are found in no interrelationship with each other (dissimilarity), I may not understand the way my partner acts or how they make sense of their world. My partner may have some ways of behaving and responding to challenges that seem foreign to me. Those ways can be irritating or painful if we judge each other's behaviors on our own terms. Until we learn to see each other's patterns through our partner's eyes, we might each consider the other to be unfeeling and unappreciative of who the other is. Once we develop new pathways of union between us, we will find a gift in the uniqueness of our union.

4. *My moon–my partner's moon* tells how comfortable we will be with each other. We find out if our emotional rhythms flow in the same or different patterns, and if we see our experiences in the same way. This tells a great deal about the similarity of our family and cultural backgrounds, and generally whether

our individual pasts will give our union any trouble. As a rule, similarity interrelationships between the two moons suggest an easier time living in the same household with our partner. We may feel as though we share common backgrounds, outlooks on life, political views, and attitudes toward family and personal conduct. With any other interrelationships, harmony may be more difficult but can be developed.

If the two moons are found in similarity (resonance, companionship, or approach type), we will find mutual receptivity and sympathy. We will tend to find that our backgrounds, emotions, and habit patterns flow well between us. We will see the world's behaviors toward us in similar ways, and even where we are different from each other, we will feel as if there is an emotional support between us that cannot be shattered. We will more likely be comfortable with opening our feelings to each other, and we will feel mutually accepted. It is also likely that we will be able to live in the same household together, without having to make accommodations for each other. We will blend our habits easily—we will tend to like the same foods, for example. Since the moon induces us toward the formation of habits, we must take care that we "come out of our moons" to explore and develop other aspects of our relationship. Even good qualities can become weaknesses when they are carried to extremes. We could feel that our similarity to each other gives us license to indulge in our lunar nature. We could become too comfortable, never take a risk. While it is good to share and open to this part of ourselves, we must balance it with other parts of who we are.

If the two moons are in polarity, we can easily learn to express complementarity instead of opposition with each other, because moons are naturally receptive. However, two receptive beings do not necessarily connect, so we will have to learn to take the initiative with each other, or a split can occur. Through our moons, we can tend to be self-involved, and it may seem to us as if we don't need each other or want each other's input. A split will usually be created when one or both of us indulge in our moon's worst habits. Since the moon is where we store our accustomed ways of doing things, "good" and "bad," the habits that we find unpleasant may be difficult to break. Either partner may cling to them for reasons related to our past experiences, not to what we are encountering now in our life. We may retreat into the old habits out of sensitivity. If so, we may tend to guard them overvigilantly since, at the heart, we know that our old habits should be replaced by new, healthier patterns. With our moons, we may tend to feel that our "space" is being invaded, when that is not the intent of our partner. When we retreat from each other's suggestions, it is a sign that this is happening. But if we remember that we're each just waiting for the other to reach over to us—to take the first step—then this tendency can be overcome, and we can bridge the gap. As long as we are willing to appreciate each other's differences in background and response style, polarity can be fostered into complementarity.

If the two moons are found in any other interrelationship (response type or dissimilarity), harmony between the two planets will probably need to be cultivated. The same difficulties discussed above for moons in polarity can also be encountered for moons in the same response type or in dissimilar signs. *With the moons in the same response type,* there is an especially strong tendency to trigger each other's defensive reactions, since the moon is so strongly receptive and patterned. Since our moons try to respond to the impact of others, more than trying have a unique impact, we may feel more easily overrun by each other's habits or emotions. This friction can be dispersed by letting go of our emotions, perhaps by expressing them with the purpose of moving from reaction to response. When we let go of our emotional states, we can move out of the self-protective pattern so often invoked when we are in lunar mode. *If my and my partner's moons are found in no interrelationship with each other (dissimilarity),* we will have difficulty connecting with each other's emotional nature and habit patterns. My partner will express their feelings in ways that I may consistently misinterpret, and they will be at as a great a loss to understand me. By exploring our backgrounds together, discovering what is meant by each behavior pattern, and making an effort to disperse unhelpful responses, we can learn to be at peace with each other's emotional and habit-related patterns and ways of reflecting the world.

Venus and Mars

My Venus (♀) is in _____.
My partner's Venus (♀) is in _____.

My Mars (♂) is in _____.
My partner's Mars (♂) is in _____.
Between our charts, my Venus to my partner's Mars is in:
_____ resonance (the same sign),
_____ companionship (two signs apart),
_____ the same response type (modality),
       [response type: _____]
_____ the same approach type (element),
       [approach type: _____]
_____ the same polarity [polarity: _____] or
_____ dissimilarity (none of the above).

Between our charts, my Mars to my partner's Venus is in:
_____ resonance (the same sign),
_____ companionship (two signs apart),
_____ the same response type (modality),
       [response type: _____]
_____ the same approach type (element),
       [approach type: _____]
_____ the same polarity [polarity: _____] or
_____ dissimilarity (none of the above).

Between our charts, my Venus to my partner's Venus is in:
_____ resonance (the same sign),

_____ companionship (two signs apart),

_____ the same response type (modality),

[response type: _____]

_____ the same approach type (element),

[approach type: _____]

_____ the same polarity, [polarity: _____] or

_____ dissimilarity (none of the above).

Between our charts, my Mars to my partner's Mars is in:

_____ resonance (the same sign),

_____ companionship (two signs apart),

_____ the same response type (modality),

[response type: _____]

_____ the same approach type (element),

[approach type: _____]

_____ the same polarity, [polarity: _____] or

_____ dissimilarity (none of the above).

The four combinations of Venus and Mars can be interpreted differently, depending on the sex of the partners and whether we accept our own shadow side, the "opposite-sex" side of our nature. Same-sex partners must evaluate what role each other seems to play most of the time, or if they shift back and forth. Regardless of our sex, our Venus is how we want to be loved, and since we love others the way we want to be loved, it is also how we love. Our Mars is how we pursue what we desire—and the desire itself.

Remember that there are two Venus-Mars combinations (disregarding Venus-Venus and Mars-Mars for the moment) between our charts, just like sun-moon. Venus and Mars combinations can be confusing, because we project these "cross-"qualities on each other. Use the following guidelines in interpreting your Venus-Mars combinations:

- Each of us has the ability to act out both our Venus and our Mars, although we will tend to favor one of the Venus-Mars combinations over the other. In a relationship with balanced reciprocity, the roles will be flexible.
- The type of combination that exists between them doesn't matter so much, as long as there is one. Dissimilarity is the only

"combination" that doesn't work rather easily at first contact, because the planets have a hard time finding something in common without our thoughtful attention.

- If both Venus-Mars combinations are significant or highlighted in our chart, we will tend to favor the one with the male partner's Mars and the female partner's Venus in a heterosexual relationship, as a rule. We may shift back and forth between them as our mood suits us.

- If one Venus-Mars combination is dissimilar, we will rely on the other combination, regardless of whose Venus and Mars are involved.

- If neither Venus-Mars combination is well-connected, we may substitute another planet to generate fun and sexual interest. We may, for instance, use a Venus-Sun combination.

- In same-sex partnerships, we will usually let the easiest Venus-Mars combination dictate who plays what role. If both combinations are solid, role-switching may be common.

For these reasons, I will use the same interpretations for the first two combinations (my Venus to my partner's Mars and my Mars to their Venus) to avoid repetition. The Venus-Mars combinations can be understood as follows.

1. *My Venus–my partner's Mars:* This is how I receive my partner's advances on all levels, but particularly in fun, romance, and sex. *If I am female and my partner is male,* this combination tells how the classic interaction between the two of us will flow. Mars and Venus have to do with the playful, flirtatious, and sexual side of our nature. Here, my partner gets to play out his masculine side, while I get to enact my feminine side. I will be feminine according to what I think is feminine; this may involve culturally and socially imposed ideals or those that come from my own inner sense of femininity. My partner will

be acting out his masculine side according to his own ideals, whether internally or externally motivated. Our experience will depend on the way they combine. *If I am male and my partner is female,* we will play this combination out in two ways. First is the way that I express my feminine side as a male, and my partner expresses her masculine side as a female: my female partner's role as the initiator in sex and play, to my male role as the receptive and attracting partner. Second, my Venus is how I envision my ideal partner, as well as what I perceive in my partner. *In a same-sex relationship,* we will have to observe who plays what role and interpret the roles accordingly. When I change roles with my same-sex partner, the interpretation will vary with those changes. Regardless of which roles we tend to play, our Mars is always our assertive-desiring side, and our Venus is our receptive-attracting side.

2. ***My Mars–my partner's Venus*** shows how I assert myself with my partner and how my partner receives my advances. *If I am female and my partner is male,* my Mars also shows how I find him appealing; his Venus indicates how he would prefer to receive me and what type of woman he prefers. *If I am male and my partner is female,* this is the one combination that will tend to express the most in our relationship (if the planets are connected), since most people tend to play the masculine role if male, and the feminine role if female. Unless this combination is very difficult or based in dissimilarity, we will rely on this most in our romantic and sexual interactions with each other.

No matter whose they are, *if these two planets are found in similarity* (resonance, companionship, or approach type), our Venus-Mars combination will flow easily. There will be few obstacles between me and my partner, and we will understand each other's sexual style. Our sexual rhythms will be similar. We will enjoy spending time together, going out on the town, or spending a quiet evening at home. In fact, this is likely to be an important part of the relationship. With harmony between Venus and Mars, we can rely on continuing courtship in our relationship to improve its stability. The Venus person will enjoy being the object of the Mars person's desire—receiving their advances. The Mars person will be encouraged by the Venus person's receptivity. We will both function in somewhat the same way, and so understand each other's needs in romance and sex. We may fulfill each other's notion of the ideal partner.

If these planets are in polarity, then at the outset there can be the attraction of the unattainable in our bond. There is something mysterious about our partner, and it keeps bringing us back for more. However, as the relationship matures, we will need to deepen our understanding of this sign polarity. Otherwise, the challenge of the hunt may fade, leaving us wondering what we ever saw in each other. We may have a hard time reconciling our image of what we want a partner to be with what the other actually is! By deepening our understanding of the polarity, we can see more clearly what each of us brings to the relationship. Once we see how we each supports the other, this combination can be very exciting as well as comfortable. It may seem strange, but it works, especially once we work out our polarity issues.

The other interrelationships between these planets (response type and dissimilarity) do not have to be difficult. However, with dissimilarity, we will need to develop harmonic resonance. *With Venus and Mars in the same response type,* there may be times when we will trigger each other's "defensive mode." At those times, it may be difficult to connect, and irritation may result. However, quite frequently, we are simply excited by each other's presence and way of being, especially if trust has been established and our tendency to react to our partner is reduced. The Mars person will tend to initiate the action, and the Venus person will tend to respond. In dating or going out together, we may be at odds with each other. One may want to stay home when the other wants to go out, but our interests should generally coincide. If we can work through our common mode of responding (that is, enjoying the familiar, taking the lead, or being flexible), we can overcome the obstacles that differing rhythms throw up in our path to enjoying each other. *If no inter-relationship between one's Venus and the other's Mars is found,* we will probably rely on the other Venus-Mars combination in our charts, or substitute another planetary combination (Venus-Sun, Mars-Mercury) to compensate. However, in a long-term relationship, it is wise to cultivate the connection between dissimilar Venus-Mars through conscious effort. It can produce some surprising and rewarding results.

3. *My Venus–my partner's Venus* has two facets: how our styles of loving blend with each other, and how closely the more feminine partner matches the image of the more masculine partner. It will also show our capacity to be good, loving friends. *If I am female,* this connection will tell me how supported in my femaleness I am likely to feel with my partner. *If I am male,* this combination shows whether my image of the feminine matches or clashes with my partner's feminine expression. *In a same-sex relationship,* particularly between women, this combination is important. It shows how they harmonize their same-sex/feminine energies. Men in same-sex relationships with a harmonious Venus-Venus aspect may find it easier to balance their internal feminine nature, their interpersonal expression of their female side, and their capacity for loving friendship.

If these two planets are found in similarity interrelationships (resonance, companionship, or approach type), good feelings abound! We will be able to commune deeply in our shared moments. We are likely to feel loved and loving—these partners can truthfully say, "No matter what happens, we'll always be friends." This combination will go far toward mending many a misunderstanding—or preventing its very occurrence. This combination tends to reduce the competitive drive of the relationship. Its effects can spill over onto other parts of their combination that might be more contentious. Venus-Venus similarity can also abate the power struggle that every partnership must come to terms with. It can heal many wounds and overcome many obstacles.

If they are in polarity, in spite of somewhat different styles, we may find that we enjoy the benefits of similarity anyway. Chances are, if our Venuses are in polarity to each other, our Mercuries and suns are, also. Venus-Venus may do much to assuage the challenge and mend the split that may arise with the other combinations. Although each of us may acknowledge that the other is different—we like to go out on the town while our partner likes a mountain hike—we are likely to be tolerant, even accommodating of each other's preferences. The most important thing is to be together and to enjoy what we came together for to see how the "other half" (of the polarity) lives.

If they are found in any of the other interrelationships, the two planets' natural inclination will be more challenging or disconnected, but since Venus's basic drive is to cooperate and harmonize, even these can be turned to our mutual benefit. *With both Venuses in the same response type,* we may find that our social style clashes with that of our partner. We may be embarrassed by the way they dress or act in public, or vice versa. More important, our styles of loving may seem to be at odds. In the same response type, each partner may act distrustfully, competitively, or indiscriminately toward the other, hitting the other's blind spot. However, a thorough airing of each partner's concerns—which the Venuses desperately want—will clear the misunderstanding; vigilance will keep each attuned to the other's needs in love. It also helps to "switch Venuses" for a while and feel what it's like to be loved and loving in the other person's way. This is Venus's ideal recipe for success in love. *If my Venus and my partner's Venus are found in no interrelationship with each other,* we will probably be able to build our friendship interaction with little difficulty. Since Venus is highly oriented toward finding a way to bond, with some effort we will be able to do so. However, this combination not likely to be strong enough to compensate for other weak connections. More likely, we will find other ways to relate mental companionship through our Mercuries, athletic competitiveness through our Marses, and the wide variety of other combinations that can occur between our charts. Since Venuses in dissimilarity will probably not conflict in any way, they merely get out of the way for other harmonies to operate.

4. *My Mars–my partner's Mars:* In combination, this shows, first, how our competitive, desiring, and assertive sides blend with each other; and second, how similar to the female partner's image the male partner is. *If I am female* this combination shows how I am likely to respond to my partner's maleness. *If I am male,* this connection will tell me how supported in my maleness I feel by my partner. *In a same-sex relationship,* particularly between men, this combination is important. It shows how men harmonize their same-sex/masculine energies. Women in same-sex relationships with a harmonious Mars-Mars aspect may find it easier both to balance their own internal masculine and feminine natures, and to express their male sides interpersonally.

If these two planets are in similarity (resonance, companionship, or approach type), everything active and assertive in our relationship connects! We feel stimulated, supported, and challenged by each other in a good way. Our ways of projecting our energies into the world are similar; we play and fight the same way. We are less likely to fight with each other, and more likely to team against an outside force. Where sports and athletics are concerned, we may share the same interests and pursuits. Our energy levels will be similar. With this type of connection, we are more likely to enjoy sharing our energetic expressions, and we may spend a lot of time "chumming." People with this connection are often great buddies.

If they are in polarity, the balancing act—the expression as complementarity—may not be easy. They will have a natural tendency to compete, even to argue or conflict. Mars's singular focus on its own survival makes it hard for it to have any interest in a perspective other than its own. Sharing and opening to another's perspective is essential in working from opposition to complementarity. If each partner expresses their own Mars well, this need not be a difficult aspect. Quite often, this combination indicates an interest in common projects and a mutual inclination toward the same sports or athletic pursuits. There is usually a competitive edge to the activities, but we can express it playfully rather than conflictually. If other, less self-oriented planets can be brought to bear, we may be able to feel the polarity from another angle and get in touch with it. Once we discipline our Mars nature, and develop inner independence rather than selfishness, complementarity will flow more easily from this combination.

If any of the remaining interrelationships is found (response type or dissimilarity), the two planets' natural inclination are more likely to be strident and confrontative. *With both Mars in the same response type,* a direct sense of challenge and dispute emerges. Conflict may be difficult to avoid and can be a major stumbling block in the relationship. Since Mars's disposition is to probe and attack, or react and defend, this combination can be difficult to bring into harmony. Generally, other planets that connect with each Mars can be brought in to help build harmony. A context for the release of tension between the two planets is important, such as a competitive sport or debate. In this combination, each partner must learn to express their own Mars energy well. Often, people with this Mars-Mars interrelationship are drawn to each other through a context where the Mars-Mars interaction is already being expressed, such as between athletes. Regardless of how we decide to do so, it is possible to blend the energies well. *If my Mars and my partner's Mars have no interrelationship,* we will probably rely on other chart interrelationships to sustain our interaction. Since Mars is usually highly individualistic anyway, it doesn't mind if someone else is as well, as long as they don't get in its way. A relationship with Mars-to-Mars dissimilarity is likely to be low in competitiveness unless the suns are in challenging placements to each other. There may be little drive to try to get them to work together, and the relationship will probably work quite well without it.

However, eventually it will be good to explore their similarities to add a unique flavor to the overall relationship mix.

Jupiter and Saturn

My Jupiter (♃) is in _____.
My partner's Jupiter (♃) is in _____.

My Saturn (♄) is in _____.
My partner's Saturn (♄) is in _____.

Between our charts, my Jupiter to my partner's Saturn is in:

_____ resonance (the same sign),
_____ companionship (two signs apart),
_____ the same response type (modality),
[response type: _____]
_____ the same approach type (element),
[approach type: _____]
_____ the same polarity, [polarity: _____] or
_____ dissimilarity (none of the above).

Between our charts, my Saturn to my partner's Jupiter is in:

_____ resonance (the same sign),
_____ companionship (two signs apart),
_____ the same response type (modality),
[response type: _____]
_____ the same approach type (element),
[approach type: _____]
_____ the same polarity, [polarity: _____] or
_____ dissimilarity (none of the above).

Between our charts, my Jupiter to my partner's Jupiter is in:

_____ resonance (the same sign),
_____ companionship (two signs apart),
_____ the same response type (modality),
[response type: _____]

_____ the same approach type (element),
[approach type: _____]
_____ the same polarity, [polarity: _____] or
_____ dissimilarity (none of the above).
Between our charts, my Saturn to my partner's Saturn is in:
_____ resonance (the same sign),
_____ companionship (two signs apart),
_____ the same response type (modality),
[response type: _____]
_____ the same approach type (element),
[approach type: _____]
_____ the same polarity, [polarity: _____ or
_____ dissimilarity (none of the above).

Jupiter and Saturn combine to give us the framework for our relationship. They connect us to society and the world, at large through religion, philosophy, spiritual path, custom, law, and societal role (everything from job title to income bracket to social class). In all areas of life, Jupiter is how we make sense of the world and Saturn is how we apply that sense in our lives. Both involve integrating our major life lessons into our understanding, and implementing them in order to be a more successful human being. Jupiter and Saturn in combination also show how we handle growth in our relationship. They have to do with business and enterprise as well. Although not every intimate relationship branches into the business world, committed relationships do have a business side to them, including things like the legalities of marriage, from prenuptial agreements to divorce decrees; filing joint (or separate) taxes; owning property; and handling finances. These are all important aspects of our partnerships. Finally, Jupiter and Saturn show how we deal with commitment—do we want it in this partnership, will we stick with it, does it feel good to us? With Jupiter and Saturn, as much depends on how well we express the planets as on how well they mesh between us. Even a wonderful interrelationship can be a burden if we or our partner do not express our own planets well. For example, if we refuse to take responsibility in our life, no amount of harmony with our partner's planets will make ours work better. What we may find is that our partner compensates well for our weakness, but unless we are willing to grow into responsible expression, we will weaken even the strongest tie.

The four combinations give us information as follows.

1. *My Jupiter–my partner's Saturn* shows how my expansion filters work with my partner's limitation filters. Do my risk-taking ventures feel safe to my partner? Do my partner's limitations and structures seem reasonable to me? Are we balancing responsibility with risk in our relationship? Is my partner supportive of my spiritual path, or cynical? My philosophy and beliefs must find a way to harmonize with those of my partner. As our lives blend, our individual philosophies and our application of them have an increasing effect on each other. My goals and ideals, my sense of what is socially correct, my level of optimism, and my way of approaching life to make it work all have an impact on my partner. This particular combination shows whether my beloved's way of attempting to fit into the world will work with my attempts to mold the world to my liking. It also indicates how my desire to venture into commitment, and to grow through our relationship, will be received by my partner's responsible, conservative side.

If these two planets are in similarity (resonance, companionship, or approach type), my beliefs, ventures, and ways of growing will be harmonious with my partner's natural way of structuring their life. This is a very powerful interrelationship with lots of potential—one that suggests a common approach to building a relationship, even a life, together. Although much depends on how well we express these planets, the similarity interrelationship bodes well for getting us off on the right foot and keeping us there. If this bond is strong, we may come to rely on it a great deal: My partner may look to me for fresh ideas, while I may look to them for the wisdom and natural caution to make sure things will work. With harmonious ties, I will come to trust my partner's ability to provide structure and practicality, and they will place their confidence in me to lead the way into new adventures. Commitment will not be an issue—it will just seem to happen in the right way when we are expressing this Jupiter-Saturn combination.

If my Jupiter and my partner's Saturn are in polarity, we may have difficulty agreeing on where we're headed as partners. We may not value each other's approach to the structures and opportunities of life—at least at first. However, through my Jupiter, I will look for a way to make things work, and my partner, through their Saturn, will work through their fears and face what is before them. Together, we will be able to find the common bond of the signs in polarity and lift their expression to complementarity. This may not be easy—it may take time, but it will be well worth the effort, because together, Jupiter and Saturn in complementarity can achieve the greatest of goals, from personal growth to world service. Eventually, we will come to see how we have helped each other grow. In spite of its difficulties, this aspect suggests that the relationship will be long-term because there is something important to be learned through it.

With my Jupiter and my partner's Saturn in any of the other interrelationships (response type, dissimilarity), it will take willingness to grow and learn over the long term to bring Jupiter and Saturn into harmony. However, it can be done. With my Jupiter and my partner's Saturn in the same response type, we may seem to bring out the worst in each other. My Jupiter might bring me to express exactly what seems to threaten my partner the most—I may unwittingly trigger my partner's "fear reaction." To me, they may seem overly conservative about taking risks; to them, I may seem cavalier about life. I may be leery of committing to a person who seems so limiting to me, while they may want more stability from me than I am comfortable giving. At times, we may seem to bring out the worst in each other, or to make growth harder for each other. However, by each learning to understand what makes the other tick—and since we share a response type, this shouldn't be too hard—we can begin to soften our mutually irritating patterns. We will begin to adjust harmonically to what we really need to learn from our partner. In this way, we can create resonance out of the challenge of sharing the same blind spot, and make ourselves into a dynamic team ready to face the world together. *If my Jupiter and my partner's Saturn are found in dissimilarity to each other,* the planets simply will not connect. As with similarity, bringing them into long-term harmony will be challenging. We will probably try to rely on the other combination—my Saturn and my partner's Jupiter—but it is worth trying to cultivate this Jupiter-Saturn connection as well. Sometimes it is difficult to recognize that Jupiter (expansion) and Saturn (limitation) must work together. When they are in dissimilar signs, we may feel as though they are completely unrelated, even inimical to each other. I can assist my partner's development by balancing the Jupiter and Saturn in my own nature. When we are at peace with these two balancing forces in ourselves, we can be at peace with each other's way of using them, even if the other's technique is difficult to understand.

2. *My Saturn–my partner's Jupiter* tells how my way of structuring my life and dealing with the rules, laws, and customs of culture, civilization, and cosmos works with my partner's way of making the world serve their needs. Do I feel safe with the risks my partner takes? How much does my partner accommodate my concerns? Can we plan and grow together, if I provide the checks and balances? By its nature, of course, this is the same as the first Jupiter-Saturn combination, but the roles are switched.

If these two planets are in similarity (resonance, companionship, or approach type), my partner will be likely to understand and heed the ways I want them to temper their expansive plans and gambles in life. I will feel comfortable with the type of adventure they suggest; the risks are ones I can live with. My partner will more easily appreciate my fears and caution in exploring new things and expanding in new ways. We will find it easier to cooperate on putting our relationship into concrete form, and we may even want to go into business together or take on other tasks of social significance. We will more easily agree on what level of commitment will work in our relationship, and what type of structure will work best. We will both tend to take the same approach to growth in our partnership, at least through this Jupiter-Saturn link.

If my Saturn and my partner's Jupiter are in polarity, we will have to work to understand each other's approach to making life work. However, because the planets in polarity are intrinsically related by a deeper common cause, this can be accomplished with patience and the right focus. When we come to understand our Jupiter-Saturn polarity, we can bring it into harmony and complementarity. Since Jupiter and Saturn move more slowly and have to do with concepts and experiences outside the self, change related to them is usually slow. They are grist for the mill of life, and most of our lessons involve the functions of these planets, at least indirectly. This combination, once brought into balance, can move mountains. Through these planets, great works on earth are performed, and a reconciled polarity is one of the most powerful energetic interrelationships to bring this about.

If they are found in the remaining interrelationships (response type, dissimilarity), harmony is not likely to occur naturally, though it can be cultivated. With their Jupiter and my Saturn in the same response type, we are likely to unconsciously trigger each other's "reaction mode." I may react by becoming fearful and overly cautious. My partner may react by becoming more adventurous, even reckless, as a way to assert their freedom. We may each feel threatened by the other's behavior, and we may feel as though we will suffer for it in the world at large. I may fear that our disharmony could become public or have repercussions in our level of success in the world. To work with this, we can use our other Jupiter-Saturn combination, and we can learn to be more at peace with our own individual Jupiter-Saturn functions. If we are willing to take self-responsibility, we will do better with this or any other interrelationship between Jupiter and Saturn. *If my Saturn and my partner's Jupiter are in dissimilarity,* I will probably have difficulty connecting with my partner's way of expanding their world, although with effort we can create affinity. Their philosophy of life may be a mystery to me, while my sense of what the rules are and how to deal with them may seem unfathomable to my partner. The planets can be brought into accord and into awareness of each other, if we each develop our own Jupiter-Saturn balance and then bring this self-responsibility to our partnership. Though we could rely on our other Jupiter-Saturn combination to increase harmony, it is good to develop this one as well.

3. *My Jupiter–my partner's Jupiter* shows how well our education, beliefs, philosophy, and goals work with each other. Since Jupiter is also our social environment, their blend will show whether our social backgrounds are harmonious. When we want to grow, we rely on our Jupiter to make sense of all new information. This interrelationship shows whether we both want the same things out of life and whether we understand things in similar ways, including our relationship.

   If the two Jupiters are in similarity (resonance, companionship, or approach type), we will want to grow together. We will tend to both want the same things in life, and we will want to grow in similar ways. Our approaches to growth will blend well. We won't have to adjust to each other's philosophy or social group—we may actually come from the same background. Even if our cultures or religions are different, we will be able to work out how to balance them. We will share optimism and ideals, and the rhythm of our lives' paths—job changes, career goals, spiritual goals, social interests—will be harmonious as well. The only danger here is to be too cavalier or to expect life, growth, and goals to take care of themselves.

   If they are in polarity, they can be brought to express complementarity with relatively little effort, since Jupiter is by nature magnanimous and open-minded. Even if our philosophies or religions are different, we can choose to engage in healthy debate and find the common threads in each of them, perhaps blending them into something of our own making. If our social backgrounds are different, we may decide that social class and the "shoulds" of society matter less than the love we share. We may use the polarity to unite instead of separate us. This pattern can be stimulating in the best way.

If they are in the same response type or in dissimilarity, they can still be basically harmonious. Since Jupiter has to do with the higher mind, these interrelationships often stimulate new mental growth and understanding, unless we have learned to be narrow in our tolerance of others' ideas and opinions. *With the Jupiters in the same response type,* we may want to debate each other, but we are not likely to have strong, serious reactions to each other. When rigidity enters the scene, it is not coming from Jupiter, but from Saturn (the "rules"), Mars (self-preservation and pride), or the moon (our past conditioning). Jupiter will want to understand more, even about ideas foreign to itself. The main difficulty can be intolerance of our partner's ideas and beliefs because our enthusiasm for our own is so strong. There may be religious or philosophical differences that will urge us toward introspection, personal growth, and openness with each other. We may also egg each other into unreasonable levels of risk, competing to be the biggest and the best. By cultivating sensitivity between partners, such impasses can be overcome. *If they are in dissimilarity,* we may have difficulty connecting with each other's philosophy, religion, spiritual path, or way of blending with society. However, we may not notice it. We may be more like "ships passing in the night"— either tolerant of each other's beliefs and knowledge, or not really aware of them at all. We may be curious, but not interested in adopting each other's way of expressing Jupiter. Our relationship simply may not be oriented toward an interest in beliefs and philosophy. While it is good to at least understand how we each express our Jupiter, it is not necessary for every relationship to achieve harmony in this area.

4. *My Saturn–my partner's Saturn* shows how our ways of structuring our lives and taking responsibility for ourselves mesh with each other. Our Saturns also show one part of our life lesson. The harmony between them indicates whether our long-term lesson-learning processes are like two horses pulling as a team, pulling against each other, or pulling in separate harnesses. They also show how well we support and feel supported by our partner's structured side. Saturn must be expressed well by each partner individually for them to work well in partnership, regardless of interconnection. Otherwise, partners with well-connected Saturns could, for example, agree to be irresponsible together.

If these two planets are in similarity (resonance, companionship, or approach type), they will work well together. Our relationship will be naturally constructive, and we will see eye-to-eye on many of the big issues that confront us throughout our relationship. We will tend to feel supported by each other in the long-term issues that we face, both individually and as a couple. We will both have the same approach to our responsibilities. However, much relies on how well we each individually deal with our Saturn processes. A poorly used or understood Saturn cannot be compensated for by a good interrelationship with our partner's Saturn. One partner may take on too much responsibility, so that reciprocity in the relationship is lost. For this combination to work well, even in the most harmonious interrelationship, we must be willing to do our own work on ourselves. Part of Saturn's lesson for us is to learn to stand on our own.

If the two Saturns are in polarity, they may stagnate into an oppositional split. Since Saturn by its nature requires us to work on our own, Saturns in polarity can lead us into isolation. However, at the highest levels, these Saturns are likely to cooperate, since Saturn also wants to lead us to the highest, most soul-oriented way of perceiving our lives. Therefore, although we may feel less supported by our partner, we are unlikely to feel undermined, either. What's more, since we are really working on the same issue at a deeper level, we may come to recognize this as a common bond, especially if we apply conscious care and focus. It is possible that a difference in age is a factor, since we are probably about 15 years apart in age.

When both Saturns share the same response type, harmony between the two Saturns will need to be learned. We are more likely to feel unsupported or undermined by each other's way of pursuing our own life lessons. We may react with fear in the same way and to the same things, since Saturn is where we store our fear. We are likely to have less insight into each other's reaction pattern because it is so like our own. We may not be able to reach out to help each other in the way that we would like, so we may feel as though we don't meet each other's needs. We may also find that one of us wants a different level of commitment to the relationship than the other, or that once formed, a commitment does not mean the same thing to each of us; also, we may feel that our individual paths pull us apart. This is not an insurmountable difficulty, but overcoming it may be easier with the help of another person who does not have the same blind spot in their nature.

If our Saturns are dissimilar to each other, we will have difficulty connecting our senses of structure and responsibility. Our way of approaching life's big tasks and responsibilities may seem unrealistic to our partner. Our partner's way of being responsible and dealing with rules and laws may feel strange or threatening to us. Commitment may mean something different to each of us, and we may have difficulty reconciling the two approaches. We can compensate for this by relying on other parts of our chart combination to assist us in building the relationship. If we become responsible for understanding and applying Saturn's wisdom as individuals, this interrelationship will be of less concern.

What about Mercury?

Since Mercury blends with anything, we can look to the Mercury contacts in each other's charts to reveal what we like to talk about, and what parts of our natures affect our ways of communicating. To see how we think and communicate verbally in common, we can look at our Mercury-to-Mercury combination. This blend will show whether we really can understand each other's way of expressing things through language. Do we each use words in the same way? Do we choose the same times and circumstances to communicate? Do we like to communicate about the same things? Do we both like to talk the same amount? Do we have the same communicative needs? Do we think alike?

If my Mercury and my partner's Mercury share signs of similarity (resonance, companionship, or approach type), we will find that the answers to all these questions are likely to be "yes!" We will find verbal communication so soothing that we may spend a great deal of time exploring our connectedness through speech. We may talk late into the night and thrill to each other's ways of articulating our thoughts. We will tend to know when the other is receptive to verbal interaction. We will speak "each other's language" and understand things on the same level. The way we perceive the world will be similar, or at least we will be able to see where the other is coming from. We will also tend to place the same value on communication, and want to give it the same level of importance in our relationship.

If our Mercuries are in polarity with each other, we will have a harder time seeing things the same way. I may feel as though my partner's way of communicating is difficult to understand, or even misleading. They may feel the same way about me. We will have different ways of seeing the same things. Each of us will communicate a little differently and at a different level of depth. However, this can be overcome. The biggest problems arise when we expect our partner to agree with us. If I am willing to accept that my partner's viewpoint is not an attack but only distinct, I can be more open to their uniqueness. I can begin to see how my partner's viewpoint is really the shadow side of my own—not so different, just complementary. I may come to recognize the common bond that exists between our perspectives at the deeper polarity level.

When our Mercuries are in less harmonious interrelationships (response type or dissimilarity), we can achieve the same level of camaraderie, but it may take some focus and application on our part. By calling upon what our Mercuries do have in common, we can learn to harmonize our communicative styles. *When my and my partner's Mercuries are in the same response type*, our ways of communicating may rub each other the wrong way. I may find many ways that my partner's words irritate me. They may not seem to know when I am open to talking and when I prefer silence. They may not have the same need for speech or writing. Communicating may mean different things to each of us: It may be a solution for one of us and a problem for the other. We will tend to have different interests and verbal styles. We can overcome this by being patient with each other and getting to know each other's ways. We can find other ways to interact and let each other know how we feel. Sometimes writing to each other can break a difficult verbal pattern. By becoming more aware of our own communicative strengths and weakness, we can overcome our mutual tendency to trigger a reaction in each other. *Even when the Mercuries are in dissimilar signs*, we can find something unusual to bind us in words. We may not tread the conventional path in the way we communicate, but we can find a cord to trace into each other's heart. With an open heart, any Mercury combination can work, and even the most dissimilar techniques can be reconciled.

Some Final Thoughts

We have just explored many ways that our chart blends with that of our partner. Even though there is a lot to consider here, we have only tapped the surface of the gold mine that lies within our charts. Every planet can be combined with every other planet. Each combination means something different and gives more insight into how we get along with each other and how we can build our relationship. Following are some other ideas to keep in mind as we contemplate what we have just learned:

- Remember that we aren't going to have every planetary pair linked in our chart combination. The ones that aren't strong are put in the background, but we still have the option to cultivate them. However, as is natural to us as humans, we will pay attention to what *is* combined, for those links will grab our attention. Other planetary pairs just won't be as important, and your relationship will grow in a direction that reflects those combinations.

- What we learn about our chart, and its combination with our partner's chart, is meant to be a launching pad for growth, not a dead-end street. Every combination can be an asset or a liability to a relationship—it depends on how we handle it. I hope that you will use what you have learned to stimulate you to new heights of loving each other; that is the highest use of astrology.

- If you seem to have a large number of discordant combinations in your relationship, don't be distressed. There is no right or wrong number—there is no bad amount of challenging interrelationships. Some people thrive on challenge! Chances are good that you have worked things out, or will be able to once you make the effort together. Give yourself this opportunity to see what is there without judging it good or bad.

- Any planetary combination, even a harmonious one, can be difficult if we do not use the planets in the combination well. It is up to us to do our own work, and to nurture the relationship in our own way, for each combination to be at its best.

- Where a planetary combination does not seem harmonious, or is dissimilar, we often involve another planet or planetary combination and "work around" the difficult combination. This simply means we are using other parts of our nature—sometimes developing new ways of using them—to provide more support for our partnership.

- We will also tend to put inharmonious or dissimilar combinations in the background of our relationship, relying on the more pleasant ones, especially at the beginning. For instance, if one sun-moon combination is easy and the other more difficult, we may rely on the easy one and ignore the other. This may mean that one partner's emotional responses and needs are swept under the carpet. The key to a solid, growing relationship is to explore and develop harmony even with difficult but important combinations—but we do not have to take them all on at once. If they are ignored, the pressure can build up and cause more difficulties than necessary.

- Once we take on the cultivation of a difficult combination, we should not expect progress to proceed in a straight line. All improvement follows an up-and-down, zig-zag course. This is actually the quickest way to our goal. Do not expect yourself or your partner to change without making some mistakes as you both learn; we all need time and space to learn and grow.

- Humans are endlessly creative, and we can always come up with our own unique ways of making things work. Because of this, we may not follow the standard pattern with all combinations. Do not read this book as if it is cast in stone.

It is important to remember that, when we apply our understanding of love at the soul level to the insights that astrology provides, we are doubly equipped to meet the challenge of creating a loving bond. Any planetary interrelationship can be used to unite us in love. Truly, love conquers all.

What's Next?

In the next chapter, we will be bringing the transpersonal planets into the mix, and looking at Chiron in our partnership. These planets lead us into the depths of our partnerships—the hidden, mysterious side. They will show us where the treasure of our relationships lies, as we explore what's really going on.

★★★ ★★★

C H A P T E R   E I G H T

WHAT'S REALLY GOING ON?
Our Wounds and Our Relationships

Relationships are not just about sharing our personalities—they are about growing and changing together. Something deeper happens, as every couple will attest, whether they wanted it or knew about it in advance when we enter a relationship. As soon as we form a partnership with someone, ghosts start coming out of the woodwork.

In chapters 1 and 2, I mentioned some of the reasons this happens and some of the factors that influence the experience of our partnerships. In this chapter, we will explore this in more depth, from an astrological perspective. Now that we have our astrological tools available, we can look at the phenomena surrounding the growth in our relationships to see what's really going on.

In chapter 6, we looked at the wild-card planets—Uranus, Neptune, and Pluto—and at Chiron, but we didn't apply them directly to our charts. In this chapter, we will learn how to do so. These planets show us where we plan to grow through our relationships. They show us our karma, in terms of the lessons we can learn, and they speak to the soul agreement that we made with each other. These planets tell us that there *is* purpose in our experiences, in our coming together—and they tell us *what* that purpose is. Through the magic of astrology, we can apply our understanding of these planets and how they work to help us fulfill our purpose together more profoundly. We can learn more about ourselves, our partners, and our world.

This is the deepest and most complex part of astrology, and there are many more factors than we can take into account here. To do so would be to teach the whole of astrology! What I want to do is to give you a somewhat simplified look at your relationship and what issues lie at its heart. To really see into its core with astrology, additional techniques must be applied. If you want more after this chapter, it's time to gain the advice of an astrologer or learn astrology yourself.

As you read on, you may come across patterns of behavior that you recognize, but they don't seem to show up in your chart combination. If the pattern fits, accept what it has to teach you. A skilled astrologer would be able to identify a planetary interconnection other than those covered here which can be related to what you have found.

Our Relationship's Purpose and the Wild-Card Planets

Uranus, Neptune, and Pluto represent powerful forces that have a profound effect on our lives, especially our relationships. These forces move through our lives slowly. They change everything they touch, like a tidal wave, but the tidal wave can be a friendly influence, even if challenging. In everything we experience through them in our lives, we can always enjoy a positive benefit, even if in the short run that benefit is not obvious. They always bring about necessary growth in the areas where we are most deeply flawed, where we perhaps feel we could never change.

When we have a personal planet that contacts our partner's wild-card planet, the slow-moving nature of the wild cards means that everyone born within three or four years of our partner will reflect that same interrelationship. However, for our partner, this contact is unique. They will find that their spiritualization process is "lit up" uniquely through interaction with us. There will be other people with personal planets in that area, but the link will not be "global" in the same sense, where many people in a single group touch into it. Even though these contacts show the real work of the relationship, it takes the personal-to-personal planetary contacts described in chapter 7 to bring a relationship together.

It also follows that, if our partner is born within three or four years of us, they will have many contacts in common with us. For instance, our Plutos will be in roughly the same location. These contacts are significant, but because they are "age-group" contacts, they are not as personally important.

When we meet someone with whom we connect on the deep, soul level, someone with whom the inner connection is strong, we can expect contacts between the wild card planets in that person's chart and the personal planets—sun, moon, Mercury, Venus, Mars—in our own. This tells us that we have *personal issues*—we could say karma and soul agreements—which we can work out with this person. These planets are where all the action and excitement are, as well as where we find our woundedness.

By exploring the possible meanings of each wild-card planet–personal planet contact, we can discover how our lives may be impacted. Although we can connect each of the wild cards to each of the other planets, the most significant effects will be felt when they contact the most personal parts of us. We will also simply ignore some kinds of interrelationships between the wild cards and the other planets. The most powerful ones are resonance, polarity, and response type. We will say "yes" to looking at these. The other ones will not draw our attention like these will, so we will say "no" to exploring them here.

To find out what to look for with the wild-card planets, use the following guidelines.

---

1. Use the form found in the appendix (starting on page 311) or at the beginning of each section to determine which combinations of personal planets to wild-card planets are found between the charts of you and your partner.

2. There are two combinations for each personal planet to each wild-card planet, e.g., my Uranus to my partner's sun and my partner's Uranus to my sun. Check each one for contact.

3. Contact is made if you find the two planets related by resonance, response type, or polarity interrelationships. If you find one of these, check the line related to that combination. If any other interrelationship is found, go on to the next combination.

---

4. If two planets are found to connect, read all the descriptions for that combination. You will be able to look at it from the soul level, your viewpoint, and your partner's perspective, and as well.

5. (Optional) Read the descriptions related to the sign(s), polarity, or response type that are involved in each combination. The sign(s) or other qualities involved suggest the issue that needs to be transformed or healed.

Since all of the combinations with the wild-card planets and Chiron are "working" combinations, they require our focus and long-term efforts in order to get the best out of them. They will give us meaningless pain unless we look for the meaning in what we feel. Pain is one of the earmarks that one of them is being triggered. By looking at our pain as a signal that something is ready to be healed, we can get the most out of each painful experience. We can improve our relationships and our self-knowledge. Once we recognize the opportunity for healing, we can further the healing process by going inside and seeing what's there. If we are in a trusting relationship with our partner, we can explore our wounds together. By gaining the insight of someone with whom we feel safe, we can fulfill the healing purpose of the relationship and step fully into the love that we were meant to share.

By looking at our pain as a signal that something is ready to be healed, we can get the most out of each painful experience.

Although everyone has their own unique story and way of expressing themselves, there are five different fears that influence the way we act out our wound: the fear of death, the fear of abandonment, the fear of betrayal, the fear of invasion and control, and the fear of being basically flawed. Although we usually have one predominant way that we express our wound, we have all five fears and modes of expression in our nature. No matter which of these fears shows up on the surface, the core issue is always the fear of separation, the original misunderstanding that we took on when we were born. We can't tell from looking at a person's chart alone which fear will emerge most in their behavior. It is best to be aware that there are several different ways that a wound can appear, and to be open to whatever form it takes in ourselves and our partner. Even if we can identify the underlying fear one time, it may come out in a different form the next time, although one theme will tend to surface more often for each of us throughout the healing of our relationship.

Uranus: Awakening to Love

Uranus awakens us to another world of existence. It peels off the layers of expectation and conditioning, replacing them with the openness born of an encounter with chaos. Uranus reveals a truer, less certain reality, but in that chaos is the seed of creativity. Creativity is born in this realm. It is as if, when we meet Uranus, the shell of the world we live in is cracked open to reveal something strange and exciting. In relationships, we often encounter it through love at first sight, or a relationship that is socially out of bounds. When our partner's Uranus contacts our chart, we know that we have been star-struck. However, the planet it contacts will determine in what way we feel its awakening forces. Like the bolt of lightning it symbolizes, we do not usually feel Uranus for long, but its aftermath may reverberate through our soul for eternity, leaving a memory of what touching the soul feels like. Once hit by lightning, we don't ever forget it!

If our chart has planets significantly connected to Uranus, we may have had difficult experiences in childhood that seemed to us unsafe. Some of us grew up in a world that was unpredictable. Maybe our family moved a lot. Maybe our mother was ill and unable to fulfill her responsibilities. Perhaps our father was in the military and was seldom home. Maybe one of them abused drugs or alcohol. Maybe they just didn't get along well and fought frequently. Children need rhythms and patterns in their lives to feel safe and secure, to remain healthy, and to develop the skills they need for adulthood.

If we did not have an orderly environment during childhood, we may unwittingly recreate our childhood confusion and chaos in our adult relationships. We may expect our partner to be unreliable or unavailable to us, to behave as our parent(s) did. We may unconsciously push them to act that way, or they may already act out those characteristics; alternately, we may unwittingly disrupt the partnership ourselves by repeating the behaviors of our parents in our own way.

When we have not yet fully developed trust—when we do not yet feel secure in the relationship—Uranus can also trigger experiences of rejection. If our partner does seem unreliable, we may feel rejected. Since this is painful, we may reject our partner before we are rejected first. Uranus shows where we must act as an individual. If we have not yet found our own individuality, we may feel that our partner's efforts to find theirs feels rejecting. Or, if our partner wants to cling to us, and we do not ourselves yet feel whole, we may withdraw abruptly, and our partner may feel rejected. If we need to affirm our individuality, it is better to do so calmly and gently, by retreating and allowing our beloved to grow; in this way, they are less likely to feel as though we are rejecting them.

Our Uranus-Sun Combinations

My Uranus (♅) is in _____.

My partner's sun (☉) is in _____.

My partner's Uranus (♅) is in _____.

My sun (☉) is in _____.

Between our charts, my Uranus and my partner's sun are:

_____ connected* or

_____ not emphasized.**

Between our charts, my partner's Uranus and my sun are:

_____ connected* or

_____ not emphasized.**

*in resonance (the same sign), the same response type (modality), or the same polarity
**any other interrelationship

The soul agreement shown by the sun-Uranus combination suggests that both partners have agreed to be awakened by each other to the deeper meaning of life. In past lives, the individuals may not have developed their individuality in their times together, and so have chosen to focus on that now. They may each feel as though the relationship touches something deep within them, but for the sun person it will feel more personal. Both partners may feel as if life is more vivid, that there is something more to life since they met each other. Since the sun sheds its light on Uranus, it draws focus to the Uranus person's spiritual growth process. They may be newly awakened to the realms of spirituality, or experience a burst of growth and stronger feelings of aliveness once this contact is made. The sun person has agreed to be triggered or awakened to spiritual reality by the Uranus person so that they can express it more in the fulfillment of their purpose. They may look deeper in their nature than before to find out why they are on the path that they have chosen. They may decide to make changes in order to add meaning to their life.

This may bring the first step of spiritual growth for one or both persons. The acceptance of the unseen realms is a big step, and one that we cannot rush another person through. *More than anything, Uranus signifies something that must be engaged in of our own free will.* The Uranus person may react strongly to any type of pressure, implied or direct. The sun person may try to apply force to influence the Uranus person to see things their way. The Uranus person reacts because the sun person hits a sensitive area for them. The reaction can feel like rejection to the sun person. If pushed, the Uranus person may break off the relationship altogether, because their freedom is of paramount importance. The Uranus person will have their warning system on full alert because they have agreed to learn to live free of any coercion in the Uranus area of thier chart.

This combination can challenge both partners to deal with their self-empowerment issues. The Uranus person is likely to introduce what feels like chaos into the relationship. The sun person may feel as though the Uranus person is "messing up" their life. This is what awakening, being at the source of creativity, feels like.

My Uranus to my partner's sun shows that I am likely to be a continual surprise to my partner. No matter what I do, it's as if I speak to a different level of their being than they have felt before. They may feel profoundly affected, sometimes uncomfortable, by who I am. This combination can have an unsettling effect on both of us. It usually indicates that our meeting was unexpected, and our relationship may be unusual in some way, violating social boundaries such as those related to marital status, age, race, religion, or sex. It is important for me to realize that I am having a strong impact on my partner even if they don't show it, because they are being awakened to their True Self, their solar nature. It will certainly awaken them to the world beyond the physical, to the unseen reality beyond what science and culture teach us. I must be patient with my partner since they may be bewildered, unless they have had prior experience with the world of the Spirit and the strange feelings it evokes.

My partner's Uranus to my sun suggests that I will feel intrigued by my partner's nature. There will be something strangely stimulating about them—I will feel lit up, awakened to a deeper part of who I am. I may feel confused or overwhelmed by this heady feeling, and I may enjoy it so much that I try to recapture it after it fades. My partner may seem unpredictable at times, and they may be unusual to me, having experiences that I have always wondered about or that I want to have myself. I may fear that my partner will upset my life, bringing turmoil that will spill over into other areas of my life. If I have any feelings of discontent with the path I am on, I am likely to feel drawn to change it, or I may be inspired anew through our contact. I should realize that I may need change in the very areas I fear. Stagnant energy kills us unless it is changed. If we follow the flow of this relationship by listening to ourselves, we will find our life rejuvenated.

Our Uranus-Moon Combinations

My Uranus (♅) is in _____.

My partner's moon (☽) is in _____.

My partner's Uranus (♅) is in _____.

My moon (☽) is in _____.

Between our charts, my Uranus to my partner's moon are:

_____ connected* or

_____ not emphasized.**

Between our charts, my partner's Uranus and my moon are:

_____ connected* or

_____ not emphasized.**

*in resonance (the same sign), the same response type (modality), or the same polarity
**any other interrelationship

The soul agreement that exists with a moon-Uranus combination will involve opening to a new way of experiencing feeling and emotion on the part of the moon person. Together, the pair will have agreed to assist the moon person in changing their old, outworn patterns, to meet new circumstances in life without relying on past experiences to interpret them. The Uranus person has agreed to go to a new level of their own consciousness in this relationship. In past lives, they may have become overly dependent on those around them. This combination has a way of drawing the moon person to reconsider everything they learned in the past, giving them a completely new perspective on what their experiences mean to them. If they have learned to repress their feelings, this will become less possible. They may find that their partner draws them into a strange new world of feelings that they didn't know they had. They may be shaken out of old beliefs and responses; they will probably be called upon to let go of many ways of seeing themselves and others. Their partner may have ways of being that are shocking to them or their family. This may unexpectedly trigger fear and pain, or excitement and humor, depending on how easy it is for them to deal with disruption and its emotional ripples in their life. It may be painful, or just refreshing.

The Uranus person is learning to experience things at a new level of awareness. They may be intrigued or troubled by their partner's emotional nature. It may trigger their own emotions, or they may be stimulated to study the realm of feelings, family, and conditioning to gain an objective viewpoint. The Uranus person is also likely to find that they get a stronger emotional response from the moon person than they expected. They may find that they must be unusually sensitive to their partner's emotional needs in order to build trust. The moon person's circumstances may place them at an emotional disadvantage, or require them to move away from their familial or cultural comfort zone in order to help them grow. The Uranus person will have the opportunity to develop sensitivity to others' needs through the moon person. They may react to what they perceive as clinginess in their partner. They may feel as though their independence is threatened. The Uranus person may be from a different religious background or social stratum, or they could bring unusual or disruptive family situations to the relationship, such as children from another marriage, lots of pets, or a chaotic lifestyle. This combination will put the spotlight on feelings and family, especially loyalty issues.

If either partner comes from an unsettled background, this contact will be especially challenging to the peace and comfort of the relationship. The challenge is to build trust. Although this may take longer than it seems it should, it is important not to compromise on laying this crucial foundation for the relationship. Patience and sensitivity are the ingredients for success. Ultimately, this contact can help us to open to our spiritual nature by removing the veils of conditioning that keep us from knowing that part of ourselves.

My Uranus to my partner's moon suggests that I may be disruptive of my partner's emotional patterns and ways of interpreting life based on past conditioning. My partner's family background may be difficult to reconcile with the way that I express my true nature. I may express myself in a way that flies directly in the face of the beliefs and structures of my partner's family. For instance, I may insist on a relationship without commitment, while my partner's family may believe strongly that all intimate relationships should involve marriage. Or I may bring unusual situations into the relationship that affect my partner's emotional well-being, family, and home life. I may have children from a previous marriage, or I may need to do something in the home that feels like an unaccustomed intrusion to my partner. I may have behaviors that trigger old wounds and difficult feelings for my partner, so they have a hard time trusting me. They may easily feel threatened by some things I do. I may have to change some of my own ways of being and seeing things in order to help the relationship grow and adjust to my partner's needs. I may be inspired by the depths of my partner's emotions, or I may enjoy shocking my partner because we both enjoy the unexpected results. We may lead each other into transcendent states of aware-ness by opening to each other.

When my partner's Uranus contacts my moon, I may find that my part-ner catches me emotionally off guard. There is just something about them that challenges my old patterns, forcing me to think in new ways about how I respond and react to the world. My partner may awaken me to new depths of emotion, maybe even emotions and feelings I haven't felt before. If this is my first contact with deeper feelings in myself, I may feel very uncom-fortable at times. My partner may introduce new conditions into my home and family life such as pets or stepchildren, or even a move; alternatively, they may just express themselves in a way that surprises me. I may awaken to my emotional nature in a way I hadn't before, or I may feel a need to be more emotionally guarded with them until I learn more about them. My partner may challenge my family loyalties and take me out of the realm of the familiar. We may move away from the place I grew up, or into a foreign culture. I may feel strange and unexpected delights with my partner, if I love the spice of adventure and surprise. I may feel uplifted or spiritually awakened by my partner's energy, and we may share an infectious excite-ment when we are able to open to each other in trust.

Our Uranus-Mercury Combinations

My Uranus (♅) is in _____.
My partner's Mercury (☿) is in _____.

My partner's Uranus (♅) is in _____.
My Mercury (☿) is in _____.

Between our charts, my Uranus and my partner's Mercury are:
____ connected* or
____ not emphasized.**

Between our charts, my partner's Uranus and my Mercury are:
____ connected* or
____ not emphasized.**

*in resonance (the same sign), the same response type (modality), or the same polarity
**any other interrelationship

Uranus and Mercury both operate at the mental level, so they tend to work well together, no matter what their interrelationship. The unexpectedness of Uranus is compatible with Mercury's quick mental nature. They are like electricity (Uranus) traveling down a wire (Mercury).

The soul agreement that is shown by the Uranus-Mercury combination is not usually a central part of the agreement; rather, it suggests a support for the main agreement. It could repeat a mental connection developed in past lives. Often, by improving the mental connection, Mercury-Uranus will be instrumental in dealing with other issues in an objective way. At times, the telepathy that results can support the formation of the relationship and induce a flow of mutual creativity. The Uranus partner may inspire the Mercury partner, while the Mercury partner may feed their partner's intuition and help them tune into their higher nature. Humor, and the excitement of mental stimulation, often abound with this combination.

When my Uranus contacts my partner's Mercury, my partner will find their mind electrified by the things I think, say, and do. We share a telepathic connection that makes communication especially strong through the inner connection. I may awaken my partner to new awareness and understanding. They may come to know the spiritual side of life through me, or they may just be startled by the things I know. Even my actions are likely to intrigue them and lead them to new ways of thinking. I may spark my partner's creativity—they may write or become involved in new mental studies and pursuits. Our intuitional capabilities will be stimulated by each other as well.

My partner's Uranus in contact with my Mercury suggests that my mind will be stimulated by my partner's. I may find myself learning and thinking about new things. I may pick up a new study or begin to communicate in a new way. I may be aware of communicating with my partner telepathically, particularly receiving thoughts from them. We may be able to carry on unspoken conversations with each other. I am likely to be attuned to and benefit by my partner's insight and intuition, and my partner may introduce me to aspects of the spiritual realms that I have not encountered before. We may also be stimulated to express our intuitive side.

Our Uranus-Venus Combinations

My Uranus (♅) is in _____.
My partner's Venus (♀) is in _____.

My partner's Uranus (♅) is in _____.
My Venus (♀) is in _____.

Between our charts, my Uranus and my partner's Venus are:
_____ connected* or
_____ not emphasized.**

Between our charts, my partner's Uranus and my Venus are:
_____ connected* or
_____ not emphasized.**

*in resonance (the same sign), the same response type (modality), or the same polarity
**any other interrelationship

The role of a Venus-Uranus connection in a soul agreement is usually to bring two people together and to awaken them to the impulse of love that can exist between them. It is the primary "love at first sight" connection. In past lives, they may not have awakened to love and spirituality as desired by the souls, so they have chosen a powerful stimulus in this lifetime. Although there are many other contacts that can stimulate mutual interest and awaken love, this one does it with fireworks! It is seldom thought of as a central part of a relationship, but when it comes to awakening to a deeper destiny that is expressed by other planets, there is no equal. This can also stimulate a recognition of the spiritual side of our nature, since love is the main vehicle for that energy. The partners' love may electrify each other. The feeling of rejuvenation and aliveness can be intoxicating by itself. However, it is an experience that we cannot stay in forever, so it must be balanced with other aspects of the combination.

Sometimes the Uranus person may engage in behavior that is shocking to the Venus person. Before trust has been built, the Venus person may feel unsafe with their partner and easily experience rejection. However, the Uranus person may not intend for this to happen. If they are pushing their partner away, it is often because they fear losing their independence in a situation that feels overwhelming to them. Sometimes this contact can make it difficult to agree on level of commitment. It may suggest that another commitment already exists, or that other fears and prohibitions are in the way. Deep distrust is often at the heart of any difficulties that arise. Time, patience, and love are needed to dissolve such an obstacle. Whatever the deeper issues, there is a "come hither" allure that accompanies this combination.

My Uranus to my partner's Venus is an emotionally and sexually stimulating combination. I excite my partner's loving nature, and they are drawn to me. They are easily aroused sexually by my style, which may seem unusual or magical to them. I may sweep them off their feet with grand gestures, or I may be able to bring laughter into their life. We may feel as though we have incredible "chemistry" together, but we will need other planetary connections to stabilize and sustain our partnership. We may feel as though fate has brought us together. Although my partner may be mesmerized by me, I may tire of the fascination or outgrow it and want to move on to other things. If there are other aspects to our relationship holding my attention, I will stick around to explore them. I may feel as though my partner wants more from me than I am able to give. Or, if our bond is strong, I may be dismayed by how difficult it is for them to trust me. By being thoughtful, consistent, and patient, we can overcome the obstacles to trust. As long as we are able to be open with each other, we will find continual stimulation and surprise through this connection.

My partner's Uranus to my Venus will find me stimulated and aroused by my partner's nature. Their manner of expressing themselves will strike deep chords of interest in me, and I will respond with love. I may feel a touch of magic and mystery because my partner is able to awaken so deep a feeling in me. I may feel an inexpressible joy and awakening through our partnership. Although I never know what to expect, I always enjoy my partner's inventiveness and inspiration in love. The feeling that there is something "illegal" about our love makes it all the more exciting. However, I may have a different need for commitment than my partner does. They may sense that in me and pull away. Even if they want the relationship to work at a deeper level, I may have difficulty trusting them—they may seem too unpredictable to me. Once we overcome our trust issues, this contact can add the excitement we need to keep our relationship alive. Although we will need other connections between us to make our relationship long-term, this will provide the spark of interest that can open our hearts.

Our Uranus-Mars Combinations

My Uranus (♅) is in _____.

My partner's Mars (♂) is in _____.

My partner's Uranus (♅) is in _____.

My Mars (♂) is in _____.

Between our charts, my Uranus and my partner's Mars are:

_____ connected* or

_____ not emphasized.**

Between our charts, my partner's Uranus and my Mars are:

_____ connected* or

_____ not emphasized.**

*in resonance (the same sign), the same response type (modality), or the same polarity
**any other interrelationship

Uranus and Mars in contact can be extremely challenging—like a fire in an explosives factory (an undirected force) or lightning conducted down a metal pole (a directed force). Although we cannot control Uranus, we can direct its flow. By redirecting the force of the ego, Mars can be channeled as well. Although this is an extremely challenging, even contentious, combination, it can be harnessed as a powerhouse for good.

The value of a Mars-Uranus connection in a soul agreement is to pierce through our ego to the realms of the spirit. It often leads us to bring out our physical best. We can rise to challenges and experience extreme highs of energy when this combination is triggered. It may also indicate that there is a past (in previous lives) of violence that can be worked out in our partnership, or it may be that a more harmonious contact was ended abruptly, through an accident or unexpected event such as death. No matter what, we are sure to have chosen to stimulate the spiritual side of our nature. As this is generally considered to be a difficult combination, many relationships where this is a strong feature are of a short duration. It can be exciting, but it can also be contentious and volatile. There may be a lot of sexual stimulation that leads to the overwhelming urge for gratification before trust is built. Usually a relationship with this combination proceeds into long-term status only if there is a channel for the energies of Mars and Uranus in the relationship. For instance, the partners may have come together through martial arts training, hunting, archery, or another athletic pursuit. If this pursuit is given up, the partners will need to find another channel for this energy in order to avoid unhealthy conflict or violence. Still, if successfully tamed, such a combination can bring out the best in us, because to do so we must harness the ego, and this can lead the partners onto the path of spiritual development together.

When my Uranus contacts my partner's Mars, we may find our relationship very stimulating. I will keep my partner guessing by my style of expression; my partner's direct nature may trigger a strong reaction in me. We may enjoy interactions which challenge us to use our quick reactions and physical bodies. We may enjoy competing against each other. Teasing is one way to defuse some of this energy, but we must be careful not to let it go too far. We may enjoy a sense of danger or engage in high-thrill activities together, such as mountain climbing or skydiving. Sexual energy pulsing through our relationship may overwhelm our sense of caution and our tender feelings, or we may channel the energy through tantric sex. We may lose our sensitivity to each other when we are charged by Mars and Uranus. By directing these energies into healthful, "planned risk" pursuits, we can bring out the best in each other. We can feel the power of our spirit when we engage in these types of activities. As long as we balance this part of our relationship with other, more stable aspects of our combination, it can be used for the fulfillment of the soul's path to love.

My partner's Uranus in contact with my Mars will bring out the physical side of my nature. I may be overstimulated and irritated by their style, or I may feel the thrill of excitement through them. Although they may seem too reactionary, indirect, and outlandish compared to my direct and focused side, I can likely feel as if my partner is goading me, challenging me to excel in what I do. We may perform at a personal peak when we compete against each other. Our interaction may be rapid-fire, and I may have to guard against quick and powerful physical reactions to my partner when they prod me. Together, we can explore the realms at the edge of existence—it makes us feel life pounding through us. We can push the boundaries of our love, inspired by my partner's unique way of being. Sex can sweep us away, and we have to be careful not to let our drives run our lives. As long as we remember the other essentials of a good relationship, this connection can lead us into realms of ecstasy.

Neptune: Surrendering to Love

Neptune presents to us the veils we must penetrate to understand the true nature of reality. It appears to be all smoke and mirrors, but the illusion is meant to lead us into the magic theater, where we can see what is true from the perspective of the realms where physical form does not blind us. Neptune is spirit and the expression of spirituality. When we go into meditation, find the True Self, and experience it in our being, it is an experience that is truly indescribable. But even if we can't share it with others, it still exists. Neptune is notoriously difficult to express; it feels like a dream when we leave it because it's hard to validate in the physical world. Yet those who have familiarized themselves with its realms know it to be truer than what we call scientific reality.[21]

When we have a Neptune contact in a relationship, we experience heights of idealism and what others sometimes call illusion, because what we are experiencing is pure Spirit. It is quite frequently associated with "soul recognition" experiences, and the nature of the other planet involved determines the types of contacts in past lives. We can see the highest poten-

---

[21] Actually, what exists in the material world is an extension of the formless world of Neptune. They do not contradict each other once we see how they participate in a continuous reality, from dense form to subtle energy.

tial in our partner (or they in us). On that level, boundaries do not exist; yet on this level they must. If we dwell too much in Neptune's realm, we endanger our sense of self—our boundaries—and become merged (enmeshed) with each other. This is threatening to the integrity and individuality of each person and must be guarded against. Learning to balance spiritual wholeness with what appears in our day-to-day personality—and manifesting it in personality—is the challenge of Neptune.

The forces of Neptune ask us to surrender, because that's all we can do in a realm so large and formless. These forces bring change into our lives just as Uranus and Pluto do, but Neptune works by dissolving old forms rather than colliding with them. If we are not attuned to Neptune, we may not notice its work in our lives, except as a feeling of confusion or discontent with our circumstances. In our relationships, we may find that Neptune contacts trigger feelings of loss, neglect, or abandonment. Although these feelings are a part of being human, they typically arise when we cannot feel whole unto ourselves.

Our Neptune-Sun Combinations

My Neptune (♆) is in _____.
My partner's sun (☉) is in _____.

My partner's Neptune (♆) is in _____.
My sun (☉) is in _____.

Between our charts, my Neptune and my partner's sun are:
____ connected* or
____ not emphasized.**

Between our charts, my partner's Neptune and my sun are:
____ connected* or
____ not emphasized.**

*in resonance (same sign), the same response type (modality), or the same polarity
**any other interrelationship

When there is a sun-Neptune contact, the soul agreement is to develop an awareness of spiritual reality, including what we are like on a soul level. In past lives, we may have shared a spiritual path together. The Neptune person is now agreeing to stimulate the spiritual side of the sun person. In past lives, the sun person could have made sacrifices for the Neptune person. The Neptune person may have needed the sun person to give up or surrender to something for them. As the Neptune person becomes enthralled by the sun person, the sun person can easily get swept away by the image their partner sees. The Neptune person is seeing deep into their soul, and it is alluring for the sun person to think that they could be so wonderful. This leads both people into perceiving themselves and their relationship from the soul level.

The challenge is to bring that perception into our day-to-day lives in a way that preserves the soul's eminence in our relationship and our individual natures. Although we get better at it over time, this is a difficult balance to strike. When we see ourselves at the pure soul level, we have no doubt that we are perceiving truth—and we are. However, in our ordinary existence, that truth can seem dangerously irrelevant and may be confused with fantasy.

In contrast to the soul, the ego-centered personality wavers, wanders, weakens, and goes to extremes. No matter who has which planet, mistaken impressions as well as loss of boundaries and sense of self can result. In the personality, the soul-level truth may be difficult to sort out from fantasy (what we want to be true). Fantasy can mask the true spiritual nature of our beloved, obscuring love. If we naively follow our fantasies, we enter realms that may have little to do with who our partner really is in this world. This forces our partner into a situation where they cannot be themselves because they are not seen for who they are, taking away their humanness and their right to make mistakes, learn, and grow. The whole of chapter 2 is devoted to exploring the art of developing the attributes of soul-centered relationships in the "real world" and in many ways is about Neptune's realm.

My Neptune connected to my partner's sun tells how my spiritual nature receives focus through interaction with my partner, and how my partner is affected by my spirituality. For my partner, I may appear to be creative, imaginative, mystical, romantic. We may confuse each other because we don't seem to be the same people from meeting to meeting. My partner will inspire me, open me up to my spiritual side, and we may enjoy spiritual pursuits together. I may have a hard time figuring out just what my partner is like. I may idealize or idolize my partner and have unrealistic expectations of them and our relationship. I may not be able to see my partner's personality, the shadow side of their nature, because I am so filled with knowing them at a spiritual level or seeing them through my dreams and fantasies, the way I want them to be. I may know the soul, but not the person embodying it with their flaws and weaknesses. As the veils are removed and I see my beloved as a whole person, we will discover how we need to grow toward ensoulment. Together, we can embark on the journey of spiritual development.

If my partner's Neptune is in contact with my sun, spirituality flows throughout the relationship. My partner's interest in spirituality will be triggered by contact with me. They may lead me to explore my own deeper nature and to search for my purpose in living. We may, if I also accept this part of my nature, explore the inner realms together. We may inspire each other to creative and imaginative heights—we may stimulate an interest in the arts together. My partner may appear to be very spiritual to me, but at the same time, it may be hard to say just what they are like. They may seem mystical and full of romance. I may find that my partner puts me on a pedestal. This may be flattering but not realistic. They may not see my weaknesses, my humanness, and it can be difficult to live up to the standards they set. Eventually, the veil will be shed, and they will see other parts of my nature. My partner then may be able to help me, in more practical ways, to grow toward fulfilling my True Self and its purpose. At times, we could have difficulty knowing where one of us begins and the other ends. In Neptune's world, all thoughts and feelings are part of One Being, but in this world, to be healthy we must learn to maintain our individuality. By attuning myself to who I really am deep inside, I will be able to maintain my wholeness and assist my partner in surrendering to their higher nature instead of sacrificing for me or attempting to rescue me.

Our Neptune-Moon Combinations

My Neptune (Ψ) is in _____. My partner's moon ($\mathfrak{D}$) is in _____.

My partner's Neptune (Ψ) is in _____. My moon ($\mathfrak{D}$) is in _____.

Between our charts, my Neptune and my partner's moon are:
_____ connected* or
_____ not emphasized.**

Between our charts, my partner's Neptune and my moon are:
_____ connected* or
_____ not emphasized.**

*in resonance (the same sign), the same response type (modality), or the same polarity
**any other interrelationship

On the soul level, a Neptune-moon contact is meant to open us to the source of all feeling and emotion. Through it, the moon person can come to understand their shadow, the unacknowledged part of themselves. It is meant to help the Neptune person tune into their spiritual nature and feel the true source of their being. In past lives, there may have been many contacts where the individuals followed a spiritual path together. There could also be lifetimes of unfulfilled responsibilities or sacrifices to a family or other group, especially on the Neptune person's part. Feelings of abandonment or neglect may spill over from such other lifetimes into this one. The soul agreement may involve the release of any feelings lacking a spiritual origin, whether painful emotions or dreamy fantasies. A Neptune-moon contact opens the doors to spiritual expression because the contact feels good. Sometimes it feels so good, we are afraid to fully surrender to it.

The moon is especially attuned to pick up Neptune's signals, and the moon person may reflect back a truer image of the Neptune person than they can accept. Generally, this contact opens the partners to the world of spirituality and soul-level reality through the emotional and feeling aspects of their natures. This is one of the strongest "soul recognition" aspects, where it feels as though there is a deep, familial bond between the partners. However, this does not mean that this bond is stronger than other possible bonds, but only that the partners, especially the moon person, are likely to think so. With Neptune-moon, loss of boundaries between people is one of the most difficult issues, but daring to unravel the tangled threads of projections and expectations is well worth the effort.

When my Neptune is connected to my partner's moon, we live in a world of feeling. Dreams and emotions run very strong in our relationship. It may feel as though we are of one heart and share a mystical past, that we have deep roots or family bonds in common. These feelings may seem important to—and to come from—my partner. I may have more difficulty seeing them as part of my nature unless I have accepted and worked with the Neptune side of my nature. If Neptune is an unexplored and unaccepted part of me, the feelings my partner expresses could seem hard to grasp, or I may feel threatened by them. They may have a hard time articulating them, and they may think that I am unwilling to acknowledge their emotions, or my own. In spite of myself, I may feel overwhelmed by their response to me, and I may tap into unaccustomed levels of feeling in myself. I may feel as though I am in a dream world when I am with my partner; I may have difficulty seeing our relationship as a practical reality. If I am more comfortable and familiar with the realms of formlessness, I may enjoy exploring and experiencing this dream world, and it may inspire either or both of us to artistic expression. We may be led to the heights of spiritual ecstasy; our souls may truly meet and commune once we have dissolved the barriers to flowing into and out of that reality.

Sometimes we may encounter blockages due to family background and childhood conditioning. My partner may have had a difficult family life and I have a hard time understanding that; but if I do, I may feel drawn to assist my partner in healing old wounds. However, mistaken impressions can arise due to a loss of boundaries between us. For instance, my partner may see their mother in me, especially what they always wanted her to be. This may bring them to behave toward me in a childlike way, seeking my approval. Drugs, alcohol, or other addictive behaviors may be a problem for us. With tenderness and compassion, we can overcome any of these sensitive issues and grow together in our path to the Soul.

When my partner's Neptune is connected to my moon, the world of dreams and feelings seems to come from my partner. I may see them as very spiritual, and we may share a common interest in spiritual pursuits. Even if I didn't care about spirituality before our relationship, my beloved may trigger that interest in me. I may feel overwhelmed by emotion when I think about my partner—I may think the world of them. I may experience a high degree of creative inspiration, and if I am already inclined in that direction, I may write, act, or draw in an attempt to find an outlet for my feelings. Feelings of love can lead me to become too deeply attached, and my beloved may withdraw if they don't understand or feel comfortable with that. Ghosts from my childhood may seem to arise in their presence. In spite of my best efforts, I may treat my partner as if they were my mother, expecting them to care for me and being especially sensitive to their feedback. My partner may help me to understand and heal my past memories, painful and pleasant. I may experience old issues of abandonment and neglect through our interaction, whether or not my partner is abandoning me. Together we can develop the trust to explore where those feelings are coming from. My partner can help me to see the spiritual side of my experiences once we can open to each other. We can explore the intersection between feelings and spirituality through our bond.

Our Neptune-Mercury Combinations

My Neptune (♆) is in _____.

My partner's Mercury (☿) is in _____.

My partner's Neptune (♆) is in _____.

My Mercury (☿) is in _____.

Between our charts, my Neptune and my partner's Mercury are:

_____ connected* or

_____ not emphasized.**

Between our charts, my partner's Neptune and my Mercury are:

_____ connected* or

_____ not emphasized.**

*in resonance (the same sign), the same response type (modality), or the same polarity
**any other interrelationship

At its core, a Mercury-Neptune contact is meant to bring out soul-level communication. In past lives, we may have shared thoughts without speaking. Mercury, by its nature, is not a natural blend with Neptune, because Mercury wants things in little bite-sized chunks, while Neptune experiences life in large, subtly shifting energy patterns. So it requires a lot of work—developing fine communication skills and awareness of subtle levels of reality—for these two planets to connect well. If we have written a soul agreement that includes this contact, then we have decided to take on this mutual growth process. The Mercury person must become more refined in their way of perceiving the world, while the Neptune person must become more grounded, more expert at using language to describe what they know and experience. Poetry is one way to combine Mercury and Neptune; it may be helpful for each of us to practice writing poetry as a means of schooling ourselves in the art of really understanding each other at a deeper level. It is a challenging combination, but one that gives great rewards if we are willing to grow with it.

With my Neptune in contact with my partner's Mercury, when I want to feel things, my partner wants to talk about them. We may have difficulty communicating until we learn to blend spoken and unspoken forms of interaction, and to attune to subtle cues from each other. My partner's verbal communication may carry lots of hidden meaning that I will sense. Yet, when I ask them about it, they may not understand what I'm talking about—Mercury doesn't see the world that way! I may have to find a way to communicate what I want to convey using words, whether they are spoken or written. My partner may need to learn to look inside to find out where the things they say are really coming from in their nature. We may have a hard time telling who is thinking what—our thoughts may blend, our minds act as one. By learning to recognize and understand the many ways that we communicate with each other, we can become skilled at sharing on all levels of our nature in both subtle and bold ways.

If my partner's Neptune connects with my Mercury, I will probably have a hard time saying things to my partner that they can really understand. Their natural way of responding to me may not be verbal. If I want to get an idea across to them, I may have to rely on nonverbal means, write things down, or wait for them to take the initiative so they can communicate in their own way. They may hear things in my words that I didn't mean to say. They may have a hard time telling me—or knowing—what they think, because they really don't have an opinion about the things I say. When they do respond, it may not seem to follow from what I have been talking about. By carefully tuning into each other using other methods, we can come to bridge the gap between form and formless in our interaction.

Our Neptune-Venus Combinations

My Neptune (♆) is in _____.
My partner's Venus (♀) is in _____.

My partner's Neptune (♆) is in _____.
My Venus (♀) is in _____.

Between our charts, my Neptune and my partner's Venus are:
_____ connected* or
_____ not emphasized.**

Between our charts, my partner's Neptune and my Venus are:
_____ connected* or
_____ not emphasized.**

*in resonance (the same sign), the same response type (modality), or the same polarity
**any other interrelationship

The soul level expression of Neptune and Venus invites the expression of true spiritual love and suggests a soul agreement where the partners learn to sustain that love in their relationship on a day-to-day basis. This can come out as the most beautiful, heart-centered love flowing between the partners, as artistic expression, or as devotion to a larger cause. There is usually a feeling of deep soul recognition based on having loved each other many times before, recognized especially by the Venus person. Romantic feelings can result, encouraged by our modern culture, which teaches us to build our relationships on dependency and enmeshment. Sometimes this combination is meant to suggest a sacrifice of our personal love in favor of a greater purpose. We might imagine a situation where, in spite of the deep love felt between ourselves and our partner, we feel drawn to serve others in such a way that we find it difficult to be together. Or it may be that we serve that cause as a team, finding little time for enjoyment and expression of our personal love. No matter what, Neptune and Venus have much in common. The main challenge is to keep the overwhelming love feelings from clouding the other parts of our nature, or from preventing us from doing other things necessary to make life and love work.

Sometimes this combination can express as "unrequited love." If we find ourselves in such a relationship, it is important to hold onto our need for reciprocity. If our love is not returned, we know that another relationship will come to us where it is—if we hold ourselves open, and do not accept less than equality and reciprocal regard. By remaining mindful of our other needs, we can manage the pleasures of Venus-Neptune successfully.

If my Neptune is in contact with my partner's Venus, I may be surprised by the depth and expressiveness that my partner brings to our relationship. I may feel awe at how accurately they are able to express emotions that I feel as well. My partner can lead me into the realms of spirituality and depths of subtle emotion, of love, where we can merge into one consciousness. I can feel inspired by this, and we want to share these feelings without impediment. However, sometimes I may feel as though I need a breather, or my partner may just approach me with depth that I am not ready for. I may need to withdraw and get my bearings, especially if I am unfamiliar with these feelings and experiences. Given time, we may share our love with the world. More than anything, we may want to lose ourselves in our love, or there may be a secret love outside our relationship. These are neither practical nor healthy for us and our bond.

When my partner's Neptune is connected to my Venus, I could feel as though I have met my ideal mate. I feel deep love between us, a direct soul-to-soul interconnection. My partner may be surprised but not unwilling to share in this experience, or they may not accept my feelings—even think I'm irrational. It may seem to them as if I am able to bring to expression things they scarcely know how to feel, and yet when they open to me, they may feel its truth. This can produce a dizzy feeling, and one that leads us away from more "rational" expressions of our relationship. Alternatively, it can bring us to want to share our love with others through providing a service of some sort as a team. Sometimes, especially if my partner is unwilling or unable to acknowledge their subtle, spiritual side, I may bring more feeling to them than they can accept. I may feel as though I need to sacrifice myself for this love. There is the possibility that I will throw myself away, give myself completely to the relationship without regard for whether my love is being returned. As long as we remain in touch with other parts of our nature and develop a truly reciprocal relationship, this need not happen.

Our Neptune-Mars Combinations

My Neptune (♆) is in _____.

My partner's Mars (♂) is in _____.

My partner's Neptune (♆) is in _____.

My Mars (♂) is in _____.

Between our charts, my Neptune and my partner's Mars are:
_____ connected* or
_____ not emphasized.**

Between our charts, my partner's Neptune and my Mars are:
_____ connected* or
_____ not emphasized.**

*in resonance (the same sign), the same response type (modality), or the same polarity
**any other interrelationship

The soul agreement of the Neptune-Mars connection is that the Neptune person will help the Mars person to see the way they express their ego and to learn to sacrifice it to the larger Self. In past lives, the Neptune person may have sacrificed themselves for the Mars person, or one partner may have "conned" the other partner. Neptune and Mars are naturally dissimilar in their forms of expression. Mars has a one-pointed, direct focus and a need to express it actively. Neptune is diffuse, indirect, and constantly shifting in its nature—it is content to "be" its expression, receptively rather than actively. As with Mercury and Neptune, the blending of these energies comes through sustained effort toward their development. This is not an experience only for the Mars person. The Neptune person gains by having vigorous pressure placed on them to maintain their firmness, in spite of Mars's drive to change them into whatever suits the Mars person in the moment. This can strengthen Neptune's boundaries. Ultimately, the partners can team in an energetic expression of spirituality. Examples of this could include creating a spiritual path based on the release of the ego through physical activity, opening a martial arts school, or developing a sport such as Zen basketball.

If my Neptune connects with my partner's Mars, I may be surprised by how strongly my partner's forcefulness affects me. It may seem as though I can offer no defense, cannot protect myself in any way. I may feel that I have to change who I am or avoid confrontation with my partner in order to get along with them. They may feel as though I am wishy-washy or a pushover; they may be irritated by my lack of "backbone." I may see things in my partner that they would swear are not there; they may level accusations at me that I feel are just as invalid. We may both go into "protective mode." This challenging experience could lead me to question the value of the relationship, even who I am and how I express myself. If I am on a spiritual path, I may apply some of the concepts of my spiritual training to understand what is happening and to find ways to remain firm in my nature without pushing back. I may want to reach my partner and show them another way of experiencing life; if I am firm, this may be possible over time, but I must realize that I can't rescue them. Eventually, we may begin to relate through a common interest in softening the ego in both of us; we may find a way to express spirit through our physical nature.

If my partner's Neptune contacts my Mars, I will be challenged to redirect the force of my ego. My partner and I can benefit if I learn to be gentle. Otherwise, they may feel it necessary to hide their true nature. They may want to avoid me, or even mislead me, rather than face a conflict. I may have difficulty respecting their lack of interest in actively protecting themselves. It may seem that, no matter what I do, I can't get them to fight with me! Try as I might to trigger some energetic response, all they do is retreat. Eventually, I may come to see that this is not a healthy pattern to follow, and that I get a lot more response from my partner if I open up and let them reach out to me at their own pace. Then, they can inspire me to find more beneficial outlets for my extra energy. I may find that if I listen, they can help me find other ways of responding to life that are helpful in maintaining my balance and fulfilling my spiritual path. Together we can blend spiritual and physical activity through pursuits such as yoga, martial arts, or spiritually focused sexual interaction.

Pluto: Dying for Love

Pluto is the Lord of the Underworld. When we enter its realms, we are transformed. Such deep change often feels like death. All of us have accompanied Pluto on its journey into the depths of our hidden nature from time to time. Because these realms are unfamiliar to us, we often struggle with Pluto as it plows up our lives, and create more pain and difficulty for ourselves. The secret to working with the forces represented by Pluto is to understand the nature of the unconscious and the cycle of life and death.

Death is a form of change; it is half the cycle of life. Since life is eternal, death can only change the form that life takes. Death is not limited to the physical body—it can occur at any level of our existence. We may endure emotional death if we experience the death of a loved one or the end of a love relationship. We can undergo a mental death when some of our cherished beliefs are proven ineffective.

Since death recycles life, it is always followed by rebirth. Although dark clouds blacken our horizons, their winds and rains clear the air and refresh the landscape. So, too, does Pluto act in our lives. Just as we reach the depths of darkness, life bursts through—if we stop resisting the process. We can be lifted from the depths to the transcendent heights.

The depths probed during our Pluto journey are also called the unconscious. The unconscious is mysterious because we have learned to hide it from ourselves. Our primal urges and drives—to survive, to just be who we are, for sex, for love and nourishment—are often buried there. Our fears are there, including our fear of death, so if we feel that a part of us is dying, we are immediately drawn into the painful part of our unconscious, our wound, the core that is protected by the ego mask. Because Pluto triggers this most closely held fear, *no planet has the power to take us deeper into our wound.* Since it strips away the mask and brings to us what is real, no planet can give us a greater opportunity for growth.

A Pluto contact indicates that we cannot experience this relationship without being profoundly changed by it. Through this partnership, we can go into the depths of our nature and heal our wounds. A Pluto contact can unleash great power and drive, even compulsion, so that our wounds can be healed at the deepest level. When we touch that deeply into our wound, we usually experience discomfort, and we may find ourselves acting in ways that we never would normally. That is, we normally keep such behaviors deeply buried and guarded because we feel that they are unacceptable. The trademark characteristics of Pluto's touch are intense feeling and loss of control. We may experience feelings of being controlled, betrayed, or invaded. Patterns of abuse may be revealed. Pluto can also suggest power struggle in relationship, and in almost every relationship where Pluto is prominent, such a struggle for domination or control will need to be recognized and worked out. In positive expression, Pluto can represent rapid individual growth and profound healing. There is no doubt that it indicates a profound connection between the partners who find it in their combination. It can lead to reward beyond measure, as the True Selves of the partners emerge from the Underworld, where all the ego's masks and guises are burned away in the fires of love.

Our Pluto-Sun Combinations

My Pluto (♀) is in _____.
My partner's sun (☉) is in _____.

My partner's Pluto (♀) is in _____.
My sun (☉) is in _____.

Between our charts, my Pluto and my partner's sun are:
_____ connected* or
_____ not emphasized.**

Between our charts, my partner's Pluto and my sun are:
_____ connected* or
_____ not emphasized.**

*in resonance (the same sign), the same response type (modality), or the same polarity
**any other interrelationship

A Pluto-sun contact suggests a soul agreement in which the Pluto person is to provide a profound and intense transformation where the ego mask of the sun person is burned away, leaving only the True Self. This is usually a long-term and deeply felt experience, if the lovers can stay with it and not harm each other; and it is not always pleasant. However, the more we identify with the soul (True Self) and the spirit (God Self), the less threatening this will be. It is only the ego that will die in the fires if the energies are handled well. The relationship may be a process of constant healing, where painful experiences, past and present, will come to the surface. These may come from past lives—the reason for the soul agreement—and are frequently recreated in our childhood. The nature of what comes to the surface will be from the very core of our being. The help of skilled practitioners may be advisable in order to work out the profound and subtle ways in which the ego has masked the self. Part of resolving the challenges that arise will be to work through power issues. Pluto brings us the pure power of our Spirit; the ultimate challenge is learning to handle this incredible energy as it courses through us.

The Pluto person will give the sun person access to spiritual power, even as the Pluto person will feel their own power ignited. The sun person can find more profound and meaningful ways to fulfill their purpose in life, thus moving into a greater state of self-mastery. The Pluto person can learn about the depths of their own power and how to use it well, without the interference of the ego. Working through the issues that arise and bringing out our True Self is the ultimate reward.

When my Pluto is in contact with my partner's sun, I will feel my own power in ways I may never have felt before. My partner will feel similarly energized. We may enjoy the feel of it at first, and be awestruck at how deeply it affects us. As our egos reengage in our expression, however, we may struggle against each other instead of working as a team. We may spend a lot of time exploring the hidden realms of our unconscious together. I may be more comfortable with it than my partner—the sun wants to shine in the sky, not be buried in darkness. Many emotions and sensations may emerge from my partner which are uncomfortable for them. They may fight the stripping of the ego mask until they realize how wonderful it feels to experience the True Self that was buried underneath. I may share their discomfort if I am ill at ease with my own dark places. The test for me is to be aware of my power with my partner but, instead of using it with force, to lovingly support them in their transformative process. Although I can't go through it for them, I can make sure that I influence them responsibly and respond to them with patience and love. My partner may at times be unable to respond with a coherent self-image or consistent sense of self as they endure their metamorphosis.

If we don't realize or can't accept what is happening, we can spin our wheels fighting Pluto's irresistible forces. My partner may tell me that they feel overpowered or threatened by me, that they don't feel free to be who they are. They may feel as though I am distracting them from their path. I may feel as though they are behaving childishly, since I may not see how I am exerting any influence on them at all. If we feel inside our natures, we will know that much more is going on than meets the eye and it may require the help of others to rout out the difficulties. The more we are willing to be open to what Pluto brings us and to embrace its lessons, the more we will gain. What's at stake is our ascension from the ego to the True Self.

When my partner's Pluto is connected to my sun, I may feel overwhelmed by my partner's presence. I could feel as though my partner takes me deeper into my own nature than I am able to go without their influence. I may feel as though I am in an abyss, where I can see parts of myself I never knew existed or was afraid to acknowledge. I can find out what motivates me. I can learn to see how my past has taught me to create my present—what attitudes keep me from fulfilling my full potential. My partner is also affected by my experiences. Their insights into who I am lead to their own self-examination. As long as they use their influence to guide me and I don't feel used or manipulated, I can turn to them for support. As I allow these old ways of expressing myself to burn away, I can experience the joy and ecstasy of knowing my True Self, and feeling an overwhelming love for myself, beyond what I have ever felt before. However, if I fight the changes or misinterpret where they are coming from, I may think that my partner is manipulating me, and I may struggle against them. It can seem like they always know what's going on deep inside me—or that they see things that just aren't there! Every time I struggle against their strength, it brings up profound feelings in me. Once I learn that I can feel nothing that isn't already inside me, I can accept my experience for what it is. As long as my partner is a support and guide on my journey through my unconscious—as long as I feel safe with them—I can allow myself to gain new, powerful insights into myself and my path that bring indescribable joy.

Our Pluto-Moon Combinations

My Pluto (♀) is in _____.

My partner's moon (☽) is in _____.

My partner's Pluto (♀) is in _____.

My moon (☽) is in _____.

Between our charts, my Pluto and my partner's moon are:

_____ connected* or

_____ not emphasized.**

Between our charts, my partner's Pluto and my moon are:

____ connected* or

____ not emphasized.**

*in resonance (the same sign), the same response type (modality), or the same polarity

**any other interrelationship

When Pluto and moon connect, our soul agreement is to purge the moon person's old patterns of responding to, reacting to, or perceiving their world. The Pluto person must learn to be a compassionate and stable healing influence for the moon person. When there is such a soul agreement, it may suggest that in past lives there were emotional or family bonds and responsibilities that went unresolved. Death or catastrophe may have separated the partners, who may have been related by some other link than a love relationship. Often, when this happens, we make a vow to return to each other—such contact is now taking place. The challenge in this lifetime is to allow a catharsis to take place in a gentle and loving way. It is a universal law that we cannot foster change in someone else without ourselves experiencing a corresponding change; so the Pluto person will be transformed as deeply as the moon person. This is a connection that deeply affects the people involved. Neither can move through this relationship without being profoundly altered.

This is one of the most difficult combinations for a partnership to withstand, yet it is one that promises a treasure trove of benefits, if we do the self-work requested by it. As long as we remain constructive in this relationship, we are assured of reaping great rewards. Such a contact often, if not always, requires the help of a trained professional for the partners to truly heal the issues that arise. It is important to realize that both partners need to experience healing, not just one.

This can be one of the most sensitive contacts to exist between charts. The moon represents our most personal and private self—the part we may scarcely share with ourselves, let alone others. You will recall that the moon is associated with our memories, feelings, habits, emotional patterns, fears, needs, and ways of nurturing. Pluto probes with intensity into whatever it contacts—in this case all these tender areas. It specializes in bringing to our awareness anything buried in the unconscious, and since the moon partly represents the unconscious, this combination can be surprising and often uncomfortable as issues are resolved. To the moon person, even one who has done a lot of work digging into their unconscious, this can be threatening. To someone who is consciously unaware of what they are unleashing into their lives, it can feel as though everything they cling to for comfort and familiarity is being removed. They can enter a bewildering world through their partner.

Although the path can be difficult, the rewards are priceless. This is why we choose to enter into such a relationship. As challenging as it is, both our personal growth and our relationship will benefit from our increased clarity and our ability to respond to life without the shadow of our past. Out of the deepest shadows come our greatest awakenings. Once we reach the point where we are primarily identified with our God Self, we begin to cherish the joy such transformations bring in their wake. We become willing to go through the pain because it only strengthens our connection to who we really are.

Sometimes particularly painful family issues can surface. Memories of abuse can be revealed. We may find that our relationship with one of our parents, or the one between our parents, was toxic to us. Sometimes this interconnection can trigger a pattern of manipulation or abuse in our relationship. If this is happening, it is important to seek outside help and make sure that we are safe.

If my Pluto is in contact with my partner's moon, we share deep emotional experiences. Sometimes they can be wonderful and profound. Other times, they can be overwhelming and painful. Even though much of the painful emotion seems to come from my partner, I share in their anguish. I may find that my effect on them is surprisingly strong. Even some little things seem to trigger an emotional state in them. It may be hard for me to find a way to have an objective discussion with them. I may find that I need to understate my meaning. However, it is better to be gently up front about what I feel at the time, rather than leave it to explode with fury later because I bottled it up.

If we don't understand where this is coming from, we may steer our relationship in the wrong direction. When we get lost, it may be hard to sort out what's happening. My partner may think I'm causing their pain and trying to control them. I may not know what I am doing that gives them that impression, or be able to stop myself if I do. When we feel overwhelmed, we may withdraw; we may not know how to relate to each other. Fear, distrust, and doubt can isolate us from each other. We may fear being abandoned.

When we feel this way, we are in the depths of our unconscious. In the process of healing our relationship, we may resist each other's input and support. However, given time, we will come to understand what's going on. Sometimes I may tire of my partner's sensitivity, and withhold my feelings or withdraw in contempt. This will only make it more difficult to build trust, and break down the progress we have made toward mutual confidence and safety. It is important for me to practice self-control rather than attempting to control my partner. While it may be easier at times to slack off from trying to learn responsible use of power, the rewards of staying with the learning process will be a deeply intimate, powerful, and solid relationship. If we get stuck here, we can seek outside help to find out where our pain is coming from, and to help us release it. We can transform our relationship from anguish into overflowing love.

My partner's Pluto connected to my moon can bring out the best and the worst in us. My deepest fears and feelings seem to leap right out into the open. My partner may seem to know how to go more deeply into my nature than I can bear. This can feel overwhelming to me, and it may be hard for me to catch my emotional breath. I may have a hard time being objective when my partner approaches me—I may fear what they have to say. Many things can surface through our partnership. For instance, we may find buried in my memory painful childhood events. I may react strongly to any of my partner's efforts to guide me, feeling that they are efforts to control me. Or I might feel jealous of anyone my partner spends time with other than me. There could even be real issues of betrayal or domination between myself and my partner. These are all signs of deeper issues within each of us, and we may need to seek help in order to resolve them.

If my partner and I can use other parts of our relationship bond to build trust, we can open the door to very powerful healing processes for each of us. I will be able to reflect my partner's use of power and let them know when they are using it well. I can detect their manipulations when they occur and point them out, because I will be very sensitive to everything they do. They will be able to help me clear out old patterns that hold me back and keep me from being effective in my life. They may also be insightful when it comes to understanding my family and how I have been influenced. With my partner's gentle support, I can heal my emotional wounds and help my partner to do the same.

Our Pluto-Mercury Combinations

My Pluto (♀) is in _____.
My partner's Mercury (☿) is in _____.

My partner's Pluto (♀) is in _____.
My Mercury (☿) is in _____.

Between our charts, my Pluto and my partner's Mercury are:
_____ connected* or
_____ not emphasized.**

Between our charts, my partner's Pluto and my Mercury are:
_____ connected* or
_____ not emphasized.**

*in resonance (the same sign), the same response type (modality), or the same polarity
**any other interrelationship

The soul agreement between partners with a Pluto-Mercury combination usually involves deep study and the development of the mind, particularly for the Mercury person. They may have an agreement to share in learning about how powerful the mind can be when focused. They may have decided to be involved in investigation or research together. Each partner will benefit from the contact, which is often rather benign. Difficulties may arise if the Pluto person uses their influence with the Mercury person to affect their mind. It is a fine line between guidance and control or manipulation. Much depends on how aware the Mercury person is to begin with. If the Mercury person is naive regarding what the Pluto person presents to them, then the Pluto person's actions may seem controlling. The Pluto person may be able to tap the consciousness of the Mercury person and understand their thoughts and actions. They may be particularly effective in helping the Mercury person gain new self-understanding in an objective way.

They may be able to see the way they think, and understand the impact of their words in a new way. They may learn from the Pluto person about the influence of their attitudes on the rest of their life. The Pluto person can become aware of their own use of power through the Mercury person's ability to reflect it back to them through verbal communication. The Mercury person may give voice to things about the Pluto person that neither could express before. Usually the thought processes of both partners are deepened and enriched.

When my Pluto connects with my partner's Mercury, I may find that I have a particularly capable student to learn what I have to teach. My partner may be especially open and appreciative of my wisdom and use of power. They may be able to report to me how well I am able to teach and to convey information in general, and are likely to easily feel how I express my power. They may be inspired by my depth of awareness. I may be able to learn a great deal about my own use of power—whether everything that enters into our interactions with others is up-front, or whether there are unconscious cords and energies that I attach to my self-expression. Together we can learn how to create what we want from our mutual focus. We can learn to be stronger together than apart. Although there is a chance that I could control my Mercury partner, I can avoid this by understanding the importance of self-responsibility and reciprocity in relationships, and working hard to eradicate any form of control I might unconsciously indulge in.

If my partner's Pluto contacts my Mercury, I will feel a great deal of depth in their nature. They will lead me to see things at a deeper level, and we are likely to find mental pursuits very satisfying, if my partner does not try to control me. My mind will be stimulated to new studies, and to new levels of creativity. I may be inspired to probe more deeply into things now that my partner has opened my eyes. Generally, I may be comfortable with my partner's self-expression, although if I detect any manipulation, I may want to withdraw, resist, or fight back. I will probably find it difficult to communicate again until I understand what is going on. However, it may be challenging for me to see exactly what is happening, and I may need to observe our interaction for a while before I know what to communicate. I will probably find that we are mentally stronger when together than apart, and over time, we will develop power in our mutual focus. As long as we are able to practice reciprocity and self-responsibility, our combined forces should work well.

Our Pluto-Venus Combinations

My Pluto (♀) is in _____.
My partner's Venus (♀) is in _____.

My partner's Pluto (♀) is in _____.
My Venus (♀) is in _____.

Between our charts, my Pluto and my partner's Venus are:
_____ connected* or
_____ not emphasized.**

Between our charts, my partner's Pluto and my Venus are:
_____ connected* or
_____ not emphasized.**

*in resonance (the same sign), the same response type (modality), or the same polarity
**any other interrelationship

The soul agreement between partners with a Pluto-Venus combination involves a commitment to work through barriers to the expression of spiritual love. It will burn away the dross of ego-centered affections, leaving something that is real, deep, and true. The road to love for those with this combination may be "character-building," because that is what Pluto does best. Feelings will be intense and deep for both partners, although the Venus person may not maintain the intensity. Strong attachments may be aroused, and possessiveness or jealousy can be an issue. At its extreme, obsessive love or compulsive behavior may need to be cleared, in order for soul-centered love to prevail, along with the underlying fears of abandonment or betrayal. No matter how extreme, these must be uprooted for the relationship to last in balance. This is another connection suggesting powerful soul recognition. Intense feelings, from elation to fear, may accompany our first meetings. In past lives, cruelty, violence, or death may have played a role in our love. Perhaps we could not fulfill our love in those lifetimes, or express it without harming each other. In this lifetime, old patterns of loving must be washed away. We must go to the core of what brings us together and love each other from that place. Often this combination shows that the hearts must and will open. A blocked heart, usually a protection due to survival needs, may have been present in one or both partners. Its release will open the floodgates of love.

When my Pluto contacts my partner's Venus, I will probably find my desire for my partner powerfully aroused. I am likely to be sexually attracted and filled with intense emotion that could border on obsession. Through my partner, I can come to know love from the core of my being, but until we have built trust together, this can be a threatening experience. I may have a natural desire to protect my partner, yet at other times, I may feel fear, anger, or other painful emotions sweep through me, and I may have to struggle not to react powerfully to their ways of loving me. I may want to control or possess my partner because I'm afraid of losing them. However, in more rational moments, I can see that I must work through these sensitive areas, find out what's inside them, and move into the part of my Self where I can share in heartfelt, sensitive love.

If my partner's Pluto connects to my Venus, I may find that I have a profound effect on my partner. They may be overwhelmed by the emotions they associate with me. They may lead us both on a wild ride through a wide range of feelings, from fear to anger to hatred to love, all very intensely. Our sexual interaction is likely to be deep and complex. It may be difficult for me to open to my partner because I may feel frightened of their power and intensity. It may take time for me to feel safe with them, and for them to relax around me. As long as I am safe, I can help my partner understand their feelings by being patient and allowing them to grow. Once we learn to trust each other, we can explore the universe of our love through our sexuality. In time, we can truly open our hearts to each other and feel the love we share without barriers.

Our Pluto-Mars Combinations

> My Pluto (♀) is in _____.
> My partner's Mars (♂) is in _____.
>
> My partner's Pluto (♀) is in _____.
> My Mars (♂) is in _____.
>
> Between our charts, my Pluto and my partner's Mars are:
> _____ connected* or
> _____ not emphasized.**
>
> Between our charts, my partner's Pluto and my Mars are:
> _____ connected* or
> _____ not emphasized.**
>
> *in resonance (the same sign), the same response type (modality), or the same polarity
> **any other interrelationship

Pluto and Mars are volatile together, but with care and delicacy, we can develop great strength through this combination. They can be likened to the uncontrolled forces of a flooding river—if redirected well, the rechanneled river can provide water for crops or lights for a city. In a Pluto-Mars soul agreement, intense spiritual growth processes can occur in both partners. Mars pierces the veils or shells which lie between ordinary and spiritual realities. Pluto represents the intense powers that are unleashed as a result of the piercing. In more mundane terms, this can result in the forceful release of energy blockages, stored emotions, and mental obstructions. Such releases can affect both the Mars and the Pluto persons. Usually, this connection indicates a provocative, even tumultuous, relationship. Both partners will be challenged to cleanse themselves of their ego guises; this is the only way that the relationship can exist in trust, safety, and love.

In past lives, there may have been violent or abusive contact; sometimes this is found between those who have battled and killed. In this lifetime, the impulse to react, possibly to overreact, is strong. This energy can be channeled into vigorous pursuits that blend the transformative processes of Pluto with the physical activity of Mars. These may include power-oriented sports, massage, psychotherapy, healing, or similar approaches. To stay together, both partners must eradicate their egos; therefore, the treasures are boundless, although the path may be difficult to follow. The Mars person is likely to act out the Pluto person's motivations or manipulations. So, if there are problems, the Mars person may seem to be the source—the provoker—but a closer examination will reveal that the Pluto person plays an important, though less obvious, role.

If either partner's Pluto contacts either partner's Mars, we may be surprised at the strength and intensity of the reactions we provoke in each other. We may become very competitive with each other, or we could decide to unite forces against a common foe. We will tend to be warriors in some way, but whether we can harness the energy of our combination for a common good is the challenge that we must meet. It may be difficult to build trust in our relationship; we may start off with lots of sexual energy, which begs for expression before we have built a foundation. The intensity of our emotions can be more difficult to handle if we don't come together slowly. The strength of the energetic connection can lead us down the path of fear if we don't build a feeling of safety first. If either partner has not learned a gentler approach to life, either partner could become abusive or aggressive. However, for most relationships, the power of these two planets need not clash. They can be channeled for good—for self-healing, for healing the relationship, and for piercing through to the core of the Self, where love and joy reside.

Chiron: Clearing Love's Wounds

We've all felt hurt. After the first unfettered impulse of love, we often withdraw in fear of the risk involved. We don't trust, because we have felt pain before. Then, gradually, we come to develop mutual trust and learn to love again. The process of building trust and love involves the clearing of old wounds if we are going to love well, by the soul's method.

All the wild-card planets take us into our wounded areas, because they bring to the surface things we had long ago buried, or could not look at. So every one of the planets explored in this chapter can be wound-healers. However, Chiron is specifically about our core wound and shows an open doorway where we can heal the wounds that stand in love's way. By looking at how our Chiron and our partner's connect in each other's charts, we can see where this partnership can heal us.

Our Chiron-Sun Combinations

My Chiron (⚷) is in _____.

My partner's sun (☉) is in _____.

My partner's Chiron (⚷) is in _____.

My sun (☉) is in _____.

Between our charts, my Chiron and my partner's sun are:

_____ connected* or

_____ not emphasized.**

Between our charts, my partner's Chiron and my sun are:

_____ connected* or

_____ not emphasized.**

*in resonance (the same sign), the same response type (modality), or the same polarity
**any other interrelationship

A sun-Chiron connection suggests a soul agreement to engage in a mutual healing process. It may be time for the sun person to heal their wounds related to self-expression. The Chiron person receives the benefit of the sun person's light and vitality pouring through their door to healing. In past lives, the partners may have been in a wounding relationship, where the sun person was unable to express their true solar nature. The Chiron person may have wounded others, particularly (but not necessarily) the sun person. Now the sun person may have come back to support the Chiron person's healing process. This placement invites the sun person to open to their True Self. Their basic issues may be self-expression, self-discovery, and self-acceptance. They may be able to redefine and refine their identity, and better know where to exert their solar force. They may become more courageous and gain more zest for life.

Since we are here to learn through all our planetary placements, we always have room to grow with every planet. Even a well-expressed sun can open to new layers of truer self-expression and -mastery. The sun person may learn to express its sign qualities at a more evolved level. The Chiron person will find their need to heal their own nature, particularly their core wound, of tantamount importance as the sun person highlights this part of their nature. The value of this to the soul cannot be underestimated. The core wound keeps us from being able to express who we are at the highest levels of being. As the wound is healed, we move into self-mastery—the full manifestation of the God Self in our personality. We can love fully, give completely, and fulfill our purpose more profoundly. We live our lives with more joy.

If my Chiron contacts my partner's sun, I will find my need to heal receiving the full glow of their being. Their confidence and ease of self-expression may trigger pain for what I myself am unable to express or experience. I may admire them or feel envious—or their style or mannerisms may simply bring my pain to the surface. Inside, I see myself reflected in their nature, perhaps a part of myself that I would rather not see. Perhaps I buried this part a long time ago; perhaps someone told me that I was inadequate, or that this part of me was a weakness. My partner will find that they are drawn to scrutinize more carefully their ways of expressing who they think they are. They may notice that some behaviors they had always thought acceptable now seem, when they think about it, to be things they want to modify in some way. They may find that they want to refocus their ways of expressing their motivations in order to fulfill their heart's path. At times, I may feel duty bound to rescue my partner, yet they may feel that I am trying to fix them even though they aren't broken. It is important for us to remember that, when the healing becomes forced, it is no longer healing.

When my partner's Chiron is linked to my sun, I may find myself thinking about who I am in new ways. I may probe into the question, "Who am

I?" from new angles and with new insights because of the stimulation my partner gives me. I may feel pained at the ways I have expressed myself in the past, as I recognize how I can be more responsible, fulfill a higher purpose, and indulge in less pride. I may find that my partner helps me open to who I am deep inside by helping me to feel forgiven. I may feel healed and made whole through continued contact with them. My partner may show some surprising parts of their nature, areas of pain and hurt that neither of us knew were there. It may seem strange to me, since I feel so confident about those things. By maintaining my humility—remembering that I too have room to grow—I can assist my partner in clearing their deepest difficulties when they are ready. Sometimes we may feel as though there is just too much pain, and neither of us can bear to deal with it. When this occurs, we know it's time to back off and return to it another time, or get assistance.

Our Chiron-Moon Combinations

My Chiron (⚷) is in _____. My partner's moon (☽) is in _____.

My partner's Chiron (⚷) is in _____. My moon (☽) is in _____.

Between our charts, my Chiron and my partner's moon are:
_____ connected* or
_____ not emphasized.**

Between our charts, my partner's Chiron and my moon are:
_____ connected* or
_____ not emphasized.**

*in resonance (the same sign), the same response type (modality), or the same polarity
**any other interrelationship

When Chiron and moon are connected in two charts, the soul agreement involves the clearing of wounds related to the past, especially in the moon person's attitudes and early conditioning. There may have been past-life experiences of emotional wounding between the partners. Perhaps they shared a path in the healing arts or medical professions. In this combination, the Chiron person gains the benefit of learning by observing and experiencing their partner's healing process.

The moon person may find that they are spurred to explore their family background, both in this lifetime and in past lives. They may be drawn to explore their genealogy and their cultural background. The Chiron person may find themselves wanting to explore their life in the same manner, or they may go in another direction based upon what is needed to heal their core wound at the time. The moon person can lead the Chiron person to heal their wound through their senses, feelings, and emotions. The moon person can be a mirror reflecting back the Chiron person's core wound. Difficulties can arise if either person mistakes the mirror—their partner—for the source of the wounding. The Chiron person is likely to feel pain when they see their wound reflected back to them, and often the tendency is to feel as though their partner is causing the pain.

The greatest danger with this connection is loss of perspective. Its highest manifestation is the complete release of any woundedness having to do with emotions and past conditioning, and with a sustained focus on clearing, such a breakthrough can occur. Although self-healing is a process that never ends, the partners can also team up to heal others, by teaching what they have learned in their own experiences.

My Chiron to my partner's moon will put the focus on clearing my partner's pain associated with family background, past conditioning, and even past-life experiences. As they go deep inside themselves, I may find that I get in touch with my core wound through their experience. I may be able to help my partner release many painful experiences, and I may want to rescue them from their hurt. The challenge for me is to allow them to have their experience and to support them in a general, nonjudgmental way. Observing them in the throes of change will trigger my own releases. Where I have pain, it will surface. I must also allow myself to experience healing, not just to be the "healing support" of my partner. Sometimes we may feel overwhelmed by the pain of the moment, but it helps to realize that this pain really comes from the past and has little to do with us in the here and now.

If the pain is too difficult to clear on our own, or we begin to feel unsafe with each other, I may be the first recognize that we are out of our league and could use the help of someone with the right training.

My partner's Chiron connected to my moon draws me into the wounds of my past. I may find myself unwittingly reviewing my childhood, heritage, cultural background, and past lives. This may be painful as well as joyful for me, especially if my childhood included circumstances of emotional, psychological, or physical abuse. Subtle emotional suppression is likely to come up. I may examine in particular the role of my mother in my current self-expression, successes, and challenges. If my partner is female, I will be especially likely to see my mother mirrored in her, and I may have a hard time seeing her for who she really is. Whatever their gender, my partner may want to be as supportive as possible, even wanting to rescue me. However, if they crowd me, I am likely to react, because underneath it all, I recognize that what's being healed has nothing to do with them. My self-work may trigger something deep within my partner. They may be so strongly affected by my discoveries and emotional experiences that they go into their own healing process. If we each take responsibility for our own growth processes, we will be able to help each other. If we blame each other for our pain, we will drag each other down. By working together, we can make our relationship into a nourishing and supportive environment for each other.

Our Chiron-Mercury Combinations

My Chiron (⚷) is in _____.
My partner's Mercury (☿) is in _____.

My partner's Chiron (⚷) is in _____.
My Mercury (☿) is in _____.

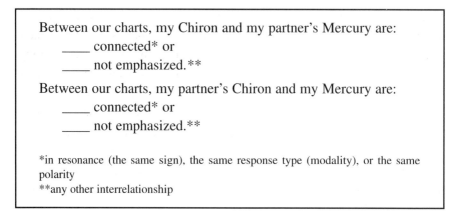

Between our charts, my Chiron and my partner's Mercury are:
____ connected* or
____ not emphasized.**

Between our charts, my partner's Chiron and my Mercury are:
____ connected* or
____ not emphasized.**

*in resonance (the same sign), the same response type (modality), or the same polarity
**any other interrelationship

The soul agreement suggested by a Chiron-Mercury contact can go in two directions. Since Mercury and Chiron are both "conductors" of energy—they both bring to us the processes suggested by other planets—this agreement can involve being a vehicle for change, either for each other, or as a team for other people. This combination may also suggest the healing of communicative and perceptual faculties, particularly within the Mercury person. In past lives, the partners may have had a hand in miscommunication or misrepresentation. They may have agreed to rectify misunderstandings that arose then. Either one or both of the partners may be "injured." Both partners will have the opportunity to develop their Mercury function, even though only one has Mercury connected.

Pain related to schooling, intelligence, language function and abilities, skill in communication, and ways of thinking can be revealed. The Mercury person may be able to help the Chiron person become aware of their own woundedness by talking about it. The wound may be revealed through misunderstandings that arise because of the way the Mercury person tends to communicate; however, this is not the core problem. By delving into what's really going on behind the surface irritation, the true wound will show itself. Often this has to do with experiences in the first three years of life, related to exploring the world and connecting with others through speech. As long as the partners respect each other's sensitive territories, this combination can blend well.

When my Chiron contacts my partner's Mercury, my wound may be triggered by my partner's way of communicating. I may completely misread what they are trying to say. My partner may feel misunderstood, even if I am able to comprehend their words. I may not be responding to their meaning in the way they feel they need. We may have a hard time talking to each other without experiencing pain. It may seem as though my partner has a knack for tweaking my insecurities with their words. It could feel to me as if they are clumsy or unrefined in their speech or education. Something in my past may have led me to become sensitive in the area they unintentionally stumbled into. My partner may feel as though they don't measure up to my standards of intelligence and communicative skills. When we encounter these challenges, it is a sign that we are triggering each other's woundedness. My partner may be able to reflect my own wound to me and show me new ways of seeing life in that area. I may be able to support my partner in communicating more compassionately. By treading gently in tender areas and finding other ways to communicate, we can overcome these difficulties.

When my partner's Chiron connects with my Mercury, it may seem as though I can't say anything without getting a reaction from my partner. I may find that I need to think very carefully about the possible repercussions of my words before I speak. Deep inside, my partner is feeling insecure about their ability to think things through and talk about them. My perspective, and way of sharing it, may lead my partner into areas made sensitive by their past experiences. I may start to examine the things I have learned throughout life, identifying wounds to my intelligence and finding weaknesses in what I know. I may be reluctant to involve myself in sensitive mental pursuits with my partner until our trust is built. The pain I am experiencing tells me that I have the opportunity to overcome my mental weaknesses and insecurities. My partner can help me grow in those areas and can also benefit from my perspective on their wounded areas of expression. My thoughtful objectivity may help them to see what their wound is about and how to release it. I may be able to model an alternative approach and behavior pattern for them. We can use dialogue to clear our issues and come to a united understanding.

Our Chiron-Venus Combinations

My Chiron (⚷) is in _____.
My partner's Venus (♀) is in _____.

My partner's Chiron (⚷) is in _____.
My Venus (♀) is in _____.

Between our charts, my Chiron and my partner's Venus are:
_____ connected* or
_____ not emphasized.**

Between our charts, my partner's Chiron and my Venus are:
_____ connected* or
_____ not emphasized.**

*in resonance (the same sign), the same response type (modality), or the same polarity
**any other interrelationship

Our Chiron-Venus contact suggests a soul level agreement to heal wounded love. In past lives, a relationship between the partners may have been unfulfilled, due either to an internal impediment to their relationship or to external factors. Before incarnating in this lifetime, the partners may have decided that healing through love and interaction with each other is the best way to approach their wound. The Venus person may have decided to assist the Chiron person in their healing experience, and in the process may learn to love in a more spiritual way. In some way, the Chiron person's nature can be healed through the love of the Venus person. The Venus person may see the woundedness of the Chiron person, and may feel obligated to assist in the healing process. The Chiron person's sensitivity puts a spotlight on the Venus person's ability to love. Both may benefit by learning to love in a new way. The purpose of the contact is nearly always to heal the love nature of both individuals, although the Chiron person's healing experience may provide the keynote, and the Venus person be more the guide.

When my Chiron combines with my partner's Venus, I may have difficulty opening to the love that my partner offers. I may feel as though some invisible block keeps my heart from opening to them. I may be afraid of what I will feel, of being overwhelmed, or of getting hurt. I may be unable to trust, and I may recoil from my partner's efforts to assuage my fears. The development of our relationship may proceed only very slowly due to my woundedness. My partner will also learn to refine their loving nature, perhaps learning to be more patient as I navigate through my own metamorphoses. My partner may want to rescue me because they are impatient to proceed in the relationship, or they don't want to explore their own woundedness. They may also unconsciously be trying to control the relationship through their rescue efforts. The challenge for my partner is to learn to love selflessly and have faith in the process of the relationship. We both may need to learn how to let each other find our own ways of healing our pain, and offer guidance only when asked.

If my partner's Chiron contacts my Venus, I may feel that my partner does not love me as much as I love them. They may seem withdrawn and distrustful. Or they could seem to love too much; I may be unable to get away from them as much as I want to. Either way, they are not loving in a truly reciprocal and sensitive way; this indicates that underneath they are not yet able to trust me. They may have been hurt in relationships in the past, and they may be reluctant to open up now. Their heart may be energetically sealed over for protection, and it may take extra time for us to build trust. If I have the same difficulties, my partner will trigger them in me as I watch them grow. We can succeed through patience and through each allowing the other to grow at their own pace, retreating slightly when our partner is not ready for what we have to offer. Once we have learned to rely on each other's stability and sensitivity, we will be able to open our hearts to each other, and an incredible love with flow forth, the result of healing our love wounds.

Our Chiron-Mars Combinations

My Chiron (⚷) is in _____.

My partner's Mars (♂) is in _____.

My partner's Chiron (⚷) is in _____.

My Mars (♂) is in _____.

Between our charts, my Chiron and my partner's Mars are:
      _____ connected* or
      _____ not emphasized.**

Between our charts, my partner's Chiron and my Mars are:
      _____ connected* or
      _____ not emphasized.**

*in resonance (the same sign), the same response type (modality), or the same polarity
**any other interrelationship

On a soul level, a Chiron-Mars connection is a warrior's wound. In past lives, the partners may have shared an experience of physical injury or attack. Sometimes this can indicate past-life betrayal; if so, this issue will arise in the relationship so it can be cleared. The Chiron person is likely to have been injured by the Mars person, but the reverse may also be true. Chances are good that, if a victim-attacker pattern shows up in this form, both partners have experienced each role at various times, probably with each other. The challenge in this lifetime is for the Mars person to learn how to temper their defend-attack behavior patterns, and for the Chiron person to learn how to avoid falling into a victim role. The Chiron person may show more evidence of woundedness, but each person is equally wounded. Defend-attack behavior can be transformed into compassionate response based on inner independence once the ego is brought into harmony with the

True Self. The result can be an understanding of conflict resolution, especially how to heal abusive relationships. Abusiveness can occur with this combination, although it can be overcome, as with any wound. If you are abused or abusing, seek the help you need to protect and heal yourself.

If my Chiron contacts my partner's Mars, I may fear getting hurt by them. I may feel exceptionally sensitive to their energies, and they may have a hard time controlling their impulses with me—they may be triggered in inexplicable ways when they are in my presence. We may seem to go on "automatic" when we are together, or when either of us engage in certain behaviors that challenge our equilibrium. If we can handle our own energies well enough to share this part of our nature with each other, we can each heal. My partner can help me to gently explore my fears; I can help my partner learn to soften their impulses and attend to others' needs. Together, we can develop an understanding of how relationships become hurtful, and then perhaps we can help others outside our relationship.

When my partner's Chiron connects with my Mars, I may have a hard time controlling my impulsive side around my partner. It may seem that my partner does things just to get to me. Even though I want to be more gentle and loving, I may fly off the handle without knowing why. They may become fearful of me, or take their own defensive or protective measures. If I have learned to recognize and temper my ego responses, I may be able to help my partner heal their wound, by going into it in a gentle way when they are ready. As my partner works on healing their core wound, they may be able to help me understand what in me triggers my forceful behavior patterns, or we may need to seek the help of others. Together, we can develop new insights into the challenges of softening direct action, and defusing the use of force in relationships, a skill that we can then share with others if desired.

The North and South Nodes: Turning Up the Volume

You may remember that we looked at the North and South Nodes in chapter 3 as an expression of a basic polarity in our charts. The nodes can also provide us with a major key to our soul agreements. Simply put, they are *intensifiers*. If any planets connect with the nodes by resonance or response type, the nodes turn up the volume of those planet(s). They also emphasize the feeling of leftover karma from other lifetimes that we must now work with. Since the nodes are always in polarity to each other, a planet that contacts one node will contact the other. If a planet is resonant with one, it will be in polarity with the other, and if a planet shares a response type with one, it will also share it with the other.

To add the North and South Nodes to your interpretation:

1. Find the nodes (☊, ☋) in each person's chart.

2. Fill out the form below or in the appendix (page 320).

3. Consider all planets that contact the nodes, no matter which chart they are found in. All of them will be emphasized in your relationship.

4. Look up the polarity and the nature of each planet that is involved. These will tell you what issue(s) can be resolved through these connections, and the way you are likely to experience them.

My nodes (☊, ☋) are found in the polarity of

_____ - _____.

My partner's nodes (☊, ☋) are found in the polarity of

_____ - _____.

My planets that contact my own nodes are

_____.

My planets that contact my partner's nodes are

_____.

My partner's planets that contact their own nodes are

_____.

My partner's planets that contact my nodes are

_____.

Healing a Difficult Connection

Although some of the combinations that we find between our charts might be more difficult than others, every one of them can be brought to the soul level, where they can express without conflict. In some instances, we may find that merely knowing how the soul expression can work will trigger our growth in that direction. At other times, we may need a long-term focus on learning specific skills in order to achieve our goals. Finally, there may be times when we need the help of skilled healers and other practitioners to bring about the changes we desire.

Keep in mind that, as creative and unique as we all are, we are fully capable of working out our own pathways to loving each other from our True Selves. We can improve our individual expression of the problem energies. We can work out the ways we misunderstand a given combination. We can bring a third connecting planet (which represents another personal skill) into the mix. By developing certain skills as the building blocks for our relationship, and attuning to the archetypes suggested by the planets and signs in our astrological charts, we can surely find the best way to express how we were born to be together.

CHAPTER NINE

WHERE DO WE GO FROM HERE?

B y now, I hope that you have gained some deeper insights about your
relationships by entering the magical world of astrology. Even so, we
know that this is not the end of the road. Perhaps you can see the work set
before you. Perhaps you find your faith in your relationship confirmed.
Perhaps you can detect where you made a detour from love, and now it is
time to get back on the right path.

As much as books can do for us, they cannot always be as individual
or as personal as we need. Sometimes, it is advisable to seek the support
of skilled professionals. There's nothing like sharing your pain with someone who has been there before, and who knows how to lead you through
it. This does not betray your partner or your relationship: by improving
your self-understanding and healing your wounds, you can be of greater
assistance to your partner as well. Even if your partner is not open to the
healing that you are experiencing, you may find that by setting a sincere
example, your partner will find the courage to learn about themselves in
their own way.

We can only be as strong in relationships as we are in ourselves. We
can't bring more to the relationship than we find in ourselves. This is why
it is important to work on ourselves, even as we seek to grow with our partner, or as we seek love if we have not yet found it. If every time we feel

pain, we take responsibility for it; if every time we see a problem, we look for its solution within; if every time we find that our partner is not reciprocating, we retreat slightly; then we will find that our relationship naturally returns to balance.

More than anything, we must listen to our inner voice, the guidance of the Higher Power, and the messages from our inner connection with our beloved. We should never let written words override our own good, sound, inner direction or knowing about ourselves.

When to Go for Help

It is time to seek help when we:

- feel unsafe with our relationship.

- feel overwhelmed or unable to function.

- want to harm our partner in any way: emotionally, verbally, physically, or spiritually.

- want to harm ourselves.

There are many people who can help you. Accept the guidance of someone you trust, if you aren't sure you can trust your own judgment or fulfill your own needs. Depending on your symptoms and situation, those who can help you may include psychotherapists, astrologers, energetic healers and other healers, massage therapists and other body workers, spiritual counselors, psychiatrists, support networks, shelters, and law enforcement agencies. If all else fails, your local government should be able to refer you to services you can afford if you yourself do not know where to turn.

What to Do Next

I hope that this book has increased your understanding of astrology, and whetted your appetite to know more about yourself and your partner through astrology. Here are some things you can do:

- Read other books on astrology. You can start with the suggested reading list in the appendix.

- Have your chart read by a competent astrologer. There are astrologers in every part of the world.

- Study astrology yourself. Classes are likely to be in your area if you live in a city. If you can't find classes in your area, home study courses are available. See the appendix for more information.

Whatever you decide, I wish you all the best in pursuing your path to soul-centered love. Thanks for reading!

APPENDIX

The Signs

This is a small selection of possible characteristics. You choose which qualities you will act out.

♈ **Aries the Identity Seeker**
Seeking the answer to "who am I," initiating, pioneering, inspiring, energetic, focused; impulsive, selfish, ungrounded, may not follow through

♉ **Taurus the Revealer of Beauty**
Creating/building beauty, artistic, manifesting, stable, strong, earthy, anchored, persistent; security-seeking, materialistic, possessive, desire-ruled, stubborn

♊ **Gemini the Experimenter**
Collecting knowledge, wanting to know, quick, communicative, dual-natured, intellectual, versatile, imitative; superficial, undisciplined, fickle, nervous

♋ **Cancer the Nurturer**
Nurturing the family or "tribe," sensitive, caring, instinctive, receptive, protecting, healing, psychic; defensive, insecure, moody, overprotective

♌ Leo the Giver

Expressing divine love and creativity, generous, warm, strong-willed, enthusiastic, dramatic, sociable; approval seeking, snobbish, selfish, proud

♍ Virgo the Harvester

Applying spirit (inner nature) into matter, skilled, logical, efficient, dedicated, humble, discerning; critical, anxious, tense, messy, weak health

♎ Libra the Harmonizer

Balancing opposites to find harmony and beauty, fair, cooperative, charming, artistic, intellectual; manipulative, indecisive, lazy, vain, false

♏ Scorpio the Transformer

Manifesting death and rebirth, bringing the depths to light, sincere, intense, deep, driving, powerful, psychic; driven, manipulative, secretive, destructive, reclusive

♐ Sagittarius the Seeker

Seeking universal knowledge and awareness, philosophical, direct, honest, open-minded, humanitarian; dogmatic, fanatical, moralistic, tactless, judgmental

♑ Capricorn the Protector

Providing wise leadership (to protect and serve), wise, realistic, effective, hard-working, sincere, careful; depressive, pessimistic, fearful, restrictive, cold

♒ Aquarius the Maverick

Manifesting group consciousness, independent, inventive, futuristic, objective, humanitarian, politically aware, socially responsible; eccentric, rebellious, cold, scattered

♓ Pisces the Visionary

Healing and uniting the whole, spiritual, empathic, healing, inspirational, flexible, imaginative; self-sacrificing, wishy-washy, confused, escapist, ungrounded

The Planets

☉ **Sun**
Giver of life and light, the Spirit/God Self, how we want to be a hero, our purpose; our way of seeing our father, male partner, gods, heroes

☽ **Moon**
Nurturing quality, feelings, emotions, sensations, memory, past conditioning, habits, Soul memory, subconscious mind, instincts, moods; our way of seeing our mother, older women, family, heredity

☿ **Mercury**
The communicator, connector; the logical mind, intelligence, way of perceiving reality; siblings, agents, catalysts, interpreters, companions, counselors

♀ **Venus**
The goddess of love and beauty, bonding, attraction, resources, values, self-love and self-esteem, relationships; female peers, friends, lovers, artists, craftspeople

♂ **Mars**
The warrior, action and energy, desire, sex drive, the will to survive, assertiveness, aggression, anger; male peers, athletes, soldiers/police, surgeons, meatcutters

♃ **Jupiter**
Expansion and integration, learning, travel, society and social class, expansion of consciousness, humor, philosophy; teachers, the permissive father, leaders, judges

♄ **Saturn**
Limitation, structure, protection, aging, wisdom, responsibility, traditions, maturity; teachers, authority figures, government, the restrictive father

⚷ Chiron

The wounded healer, opening the doorway to spiritual growth, transitions, the healing arts, healing trauma, shamanism; healers, astrologers, oracles, therapists

♅ Uranus

The awakener, intuition, shocking or unusual events (accidents and miracles), electricity, electronics; technologists, electronics technicians, intuitive counselors

♆ Neptune

The unseen realms, pure Spirit, spiritual love, unity with the whole, inner truth, imagination, illusion, confusion, magnetism; healers, spiritual leaders, con artists

♇ Pluto

The transformer, profound long-term change, rebirth, regeneration, the deep unconscious; depth therapists and astrologers, healers, plutocrats, controlling or domineering people

Response Type Tally Grid

Instructions:

1. Count every placement in your chart, including the North and South Nodes, the Ascendant, the Descendent, the MC, and the IC. Give the Sun and Moon 3 points each. Give everything else 1 point.
2. Count the points in each column. There should be a grand total (across columns) of 22 points.
3. For one response type to be strong, it must have at least 5 points more than the other types.
4. If any of the scores are within 4 points of each other, you are a mixed type, and you will respond in different ways at different times. The one with the highest score will be accordingly more dominant.
5. If you are an evenly mixed type, you can look at the Sun and Moon by themselves to see what your strongest response type is. If they are in different types, give the Moon the most weight if you are female and the Sun the most weight if you are male.

Planet	Cardinal	Fixed	Mutable
☉ Sun			
☽ Moon			
☿ Mercury			
♀ Venus			
♂ Mars			
♃ Jupiter			
♄ Saturn			
♅ Uranus			
♆ Neptune			
♇ Pluto			
⚷ Chiron			
Ascendant			
Descendent			
MC			
IC			
Total			

What Response Type Are You?

Score yourself, and your partner, from 0 (not at all) to 3 (nearly always).

When you are facing life's big issues or are feeling overwhelmed, do you:
1. _____ feel as though you lose your focus or direction?
2. _____ wonder who you are?
3. _____ feel like the rug's been pulled out from under you, like you're losing control?
4. _____ get down on yourself?
5. _____ feel scattered?
6. _____ feel ungrounded?

When someone brings up a new idea to you:
7. _____ at first, do you try to make it your own idea?
8. _____ do you take action, or take control of the situation, if you like the idea?
9. _____ at first, do you resist, or withdraw to think about it?
10. _____ after giving it some thought, do you probe and test the new idea?
11. _____ at first, do you say "Okay, whatever"?
12. _____ after giving it some thought, do you reconsider your response, then feel regret for your easy commitment?

Do you respond more positively when:
13. _____ someone makes suggestions, but lets you take the lead?
14. _____ someone is patient and gives you time to think about it?
15. _____ someone accepts it when you change your mind?

Do you:
16. _____ get excited about things easily, but lose interest just as fast?
17. _____ start lots of projects that you never seem to finish?
18. _____ make changes easily if it's your own idea or have some control or self-interest?
19. _____ need encouragement to stick to something?
20. _____ like to try new things?

21. _____ need to take the lead?
22. _____ tend to take over other people's ideas?
23. _____ like to be up front with people?
24. _____ tend to hold things in?
25. _____ tend to be slow to change?
26. _____ need time to get used to new ideas?
27. _____ stick with something to the end once you accept it?
28. _____ keep your feelings to yourself?
29. _____ hate to admit to your weaknesses?
30. _____ need support and trust with anything new?
31. _____ become stubborn if pushed or manipulated?
32. _____ tend to be basically flexible, wanting to make things work?
33. _____ have frequent ups and downs?
34. _____ easily take on and throw off new ideas and situations?
35. _____ feel open to newness, but lack the discipline to follow
           through?
36. _____ live chaotically, without a rhythm to your life?
37. _____ feel sensitive to those around you?
38. _____ want instant results, because you become easily discouraged?
39. _____ tend not to follow through, due to distractions or feeling
           scattered?

Scoring: Group your scores into three sets using the list below. Tally your
points within each type. The wider the difference between your scores on
each response type, the stronger your emphasized type.

> Score yourself as:
> **cardinal** on questions 1–2, 7–8, 16–23
> **fixed** on questions 3–4, 9–10, 24–31
> **mutable** on questions 5–6, 11–12, 32–39

Approach Type Tally Grid

Instructions:

1. Count every placement in your chart, including the North and South Nodes. Also count the Ascendant, Descendent, MC, and IC. Give the Sun and Moon 3 points each. Give everything else 1 point each.

2. Count the points in each column, for a grand total of 22 points.

3. For one approach type to be strong, it must have at least 4 points more than the other types.

4. If any of the scores are within 3 points of each other, you are a mixed type, and you will respond in different ways at different times. The approach type with the most points will be slightly more dominant.

5. If you are an evenly mixed type, you can look at the Sun and Moon by themselves to see what your strongest response type is. If they are in different types, give the Moon the most weight if you are female and the Sun the most weight if you are male.

Planet	Fire	Earth	Air	Water
☉ Sun				
☽ Moon				
☿ Mercury				
♀ Venus				
♂ Mars				
♃ Jupiter				
♄ Saturn				
♅ Uranus				
♆ Neptune				
♇ Pluto				
⚷ Chiron				
Ascendant				
Descendent				
MC				
IC				
Total				

What Approach Type Are You?

Score yourself (and your partner) from 0 (not at all) to 3 (nearly always).

I primarily identify with:
1. _____ action
2. _____ sensation (touching)
3. _____ thinking
4. _____ feeling

I most often say:
5. _____ nothing —I act before speaking and just let my actions speak for themselves.
6. _____ I feel or sense that...
7. _____ I think that...
8. _____ I feel that...

When you first see something new, do you want to:
9. _____ touch it?
10. _____ read or think about it?
11. _____ search your feelings about it?
12. _____ try it out, see what you can do with it?

Do you:
13. _____ like to do active things—sports or other physical activities?
14. _____ like to have another, steadier person around?
15. _____ have a feeling of optimism, no matter what?
16. _____ approach life with enthusiasm and humor?
17. _____ enjoy excitement?
18. _____ anger easily?
19. _____ have difficulty seeing things from another's point of view, in the heat of the moment?
20. _____ find it difficult to be patient?
21. _____ have to work at being receptive or passive?
22. _____ like to build or plan things?
23. _____ enjoy working to reach a goal?
24. _____ act and move slowly; enjoy walking rather than running?

25._____ tend toward stability in your life?
26._____ love touching and being touched?
27._____ do better at building on others' ideas, rather than coming up with your own?
28._____ consider yourself practical?
29._____ tend to "stuff" your emotions in favor of reality?
30._____ find it difficult to be flexible?
31._____ enjoy the stimulation of interacting with others?
32._____ love to talk?
33._____ thrive on making things happen for others, on "making the connection"?
34._____ love to get around?
35._____ have to be where things are "happening"; love a crowd?
36._____ like all people and find something in common with everyone?
37._____ think, act, and move quickly?
38._____ love to dabble, but lose interest in things quickly?
39._____ find it difficult to deal with other people's intensity or emotion?
40._____ seem to flow through life?
41._____ live in a world of feelings and emotions?
42._____ easily become like those people around you?
43._____ tend to "go with the flow"?
44._____ tend to be aware of how others feel?
45._____ experience insecurity, moodiness, and/or depression?
46._____ have an artistic side to your nature?
47._____ find it difficult to be objective?
48._____ have difficulty placing practicality before feelings?

Scoring: Group your scores into four sets using the list below. Tally your points within each type. The wider the difference between your scores on each approach type, the stronger your emphasized type.

> Score yourself as:
> **fire** on questions 1, 5, 12, 13–21
> **earth** on questions 2, 6, 9, 22–30
> **air** on questions 3, 7, 10, 31–39
> **water** on questions 4, 8, 11, 40–48

Chart of Sign Interrelationships

Signs	Aries	Taurus	Gemini	Cancer	Leo	Virgo
Aries	resonance	dissimilarity	companionship	response type	approach type	dissimilarity
Taurus	dissimilarity	resonance	dissimilarity	companionship	response type	approach type
Gemini	companionship	dissimilarity	resonance	dissimilarity	companionship	response type
Cancer	response type	companionship	dissimilarity	resonance	dissimilarity	companionship
Leo	approach type	response type	companionship	dissimilarity	resonance	dissimilarity
Virgo	dissimilarity	approach type	response type	companionship	dissimilarity	resonance
Libra	polarity/response type	dissimilarity	approach type	response type	companionship	dissimilarity
Scorpio	dissimilarity	polarity/response type	dissimilarity	approach type	response type	companionship
Sagittarius	approach type	dissimilarity	polarity/response type	dissimilarity	approach type	response type
Capricorn	response type	approach type	dissimilarity	polarity/response type	dissimilarity	approach type
Aquarius	companionship	response type	approach type	dissimilarity	polarity/response type	dissimilarity
Pisces	dissimilarity	companionship	response type	approach type	dissimilarity	polarity/response type

Signs	Libra	Scorpio	Sagittarius	Capricorn	Aquarius	Pisces
Aries	polarity/response type	dissimilarity	approach type	response type	companionship	dissimilarity
Taurus	dissimilarity	polarity/response type	dissimilarity	approach type	response type	companionship
Gemini	approach type	dissimilarity	polarity/response type	dissimilarity	approach type	response type
Cancer	response type	approach type	dissimilarity	polarity/response type	dissimilarity	approach type
Leo	companionship	response type	approach type	dissimilarity	polarity/response type	dissimilarity
Virgo	dissimilarity	companionship	response type	approach type	dissimilarity	polarity/response type
Libra	resonance	dissimilarity	companionship	response type	approach type	dissimilarity
Scorpio	dissimilarity	resonance	dissimilarity	companionship	response type	approach type
Sagittarius	companionship	dissimilarity	resonance	dissimilarity	companionship	response type
Capricorn	response type	companionship	dissimilarity	resonance	dissimilarity	companionship
Aquarius	approach type	response type	companionship	dissimilarity	resonance	dissimilarity
Pisces	dissimilarity	approach type	response type	companionship	dissimilarity	resonance

Use this chart to determine what interrelationship exists between each sign pair. Response type is the same as modality. Approach type is the same as element. If signs show approach type or polarity, they will also share companionship.

My Astrological Profile

Before we begin, please note: *The answers to these questions are purely a matter of our preference. Our responses are part of how we decide to be creative with our chart. No chart indicators can tell us for sure how we will answer them.*

_____ I enjoy the challenge and excitement of my relationships. I do better in relationships with a stronger element of complementarity.

OR

_____ I enjoy the comfort and ease of my relationships. I do better in relationships with a stronger element of similarity.

My Planetary Positions

My planets are in the following signs:

My sun (☉) is in _____.
My moon (☽) is in _____.
My Mercury (☿) is in _____.
My Venus (♀) is in _____.
My Mars (♂) is in _____.
My Jupiter (♃) is in _____.
My Saturn (♄) is in _____.
My Chiron (⚷) is in _____.
My Uranus (♅) is in _____.
My Neptune (♆) is in _____.
My Pluto (♇) is in _____.
My North Node (☊) is in _____.
My South Node (☋) is in _____.

The General Indicators (Response and Approach Types)

My strongest response type (modality) is _____. (I am likeliest to experience challenge/conflict with others in the same response type.)

My strongest approach type (element) is _____. I am most harmonious with the same approach type, am comfortable with _____, am stimulated by _____, and will probably be most challenged by _____.

Approach Types

COMFORTABLE:
Fire ~ Air
Earth ~ Water

STIMULATING:
Fire ~ Earth
Air ~ Water

CHALLENGING:
Fire ~ Water
Earth ~ Air

The Sun and Moon

My Sun (☉) is in _____.
My Moon (☽) is in _____.

In my chart, they are in:
_____ resonance (the same sign),
_____ companionship (two signs apart),
_____ the same response type (three signs apart),
_____ the same approach type (four signs apart),
_____ polarity, or
_____ dissimilarity (none of the above).

Venus and Mars

My Venus (♀) is in _____.

My Mars (♂) is in _____.

In my chart, Venus and Mars are in:

_____ resonance (the same sign),

_____ companionship (two signs apart),

_____ the same response type (three signs apart),

_____ the same approach type (four signs apart),

_____ polarity, or

_____ dissimilarity (none of the above).

My Partner's Astrological Profile

Note: *The answers to these questions are purely a matter of their prefer-ence. Their responses are part of how they decide to be creative with their chart. No chart indicators can tell us for sure how they will answer these questions. It is best to ask our partner personally about how they feel.*

_____ They enjoy challenge and excitement in their relationships. They do better in relationships with a stronger element of comple-mentarity.

OR

_____ They enjoy comfort and ease in their relationships. They do better in relationships with a stronger element of similarity.

My Partner's Planetary Positions

My partner's planets are in the following signs:

My partner's sun (☉) is in _____.
My partner's moon (☽) is in _____.
My partner's Mercury (☿) is in _____.
My partner's Venus (♀) is in _____.
My partner's Mars (♂) is in _____.
My partner's Jupiter (♃) is in _____.
My partner's Saturn (♄) is in _____.
My partner's Chiron (⚷) is in _____.
My partner's Uranus (♅) is in _____.
My partner's Neptune (♆) is in _____.
My partner's Pluto (♇) is in _____.
My partner's North Node (☊) is in _____.
My partner's South Node (☋) is in _____.

The General Indicators (Response and Approach Types)

Their strongest response type (modality) is _____.
(They are likeliest to experience challenge/conflict with others in
the same response type.)

Their strongest approach type (element) is _____.
They are most harmonious with the same approach type, are
comfortable with _____, are stimulated by
_____, and will probably be most challenged by
_____.

Approach Types

COMFORTABLE:	STIMULATING:	CHALLENGING:
Fire ~ Air	Fire ~ Earth	Fire ~ Water
Earth ~ Water	Air ~ Water	Earth ~ Air

The Sun and Moon

My partner's Sun (☉) is in _____.
My partner's Moon (☽) is in _____.

In their chart, the sun and moon are in:
　　_____ resonance (the same sign),
　　_____ companionship (two signs apart),
　　_____ the same response type (three signs apart),
　　_____ the same approach type (four signs apart),
　　_____ polarity, or
　　_____ dissimilarity (none of the above).

Mars and Venus

My partner's Venus (♀) is in _____.
My partner's Mars (♂) is in _____.

In their chart, Venus and Mars are in:
_____ resonance (the same sign),
_____ companionship (two signs apart),
_____ the same response type (three signs apart),
_____ the same approach type (four signs apart),
_____ polarity, or
_____ dissimilarity (none of the above).

When We Combine Our Charts

The General Indicators (Response and Approach Types)

My strongest response type (modality) is _____.
My partner's strongest response type is _____.
(People are likeliest to experience challenge/conflict with others in the same modality.)

My strongest approach type (element) is _____.
My partner's strongest approach type is _____.
Our approach types are:
_____ harmonious (same type)
_____ comfortable (fire-air or earth-water)
_____ stimulating (fire-earth or air-water)
_____ challenging (fire-water or earth-air)

Our Sun–Moon Combinations

My sun (☉) is in _____.
My partner's sun (☉) is in _____.

My moon (☽) is in _____.
My partner's moon (☽) is in _____.

Between our charts, my sun to my partner's moon is in:

_____ resonance (in the same sign),

_____ companionship (two signs apart),

_____ the same response type (modality),

[response type: _____]

_____ the same approach type (element),

[approach type: _____]

_____ the same polarity, [polarity: _____] or

_____ dissimilarity (none of the above).

Between our charts, my moon to my partner's sun is in:

_____ resonance (in the same sign),

_____ companionship (two signs apart),

_____ the same response type (modality),

[response type: _____]

_____ the same approach type (element),

[approach type: _____]

_____ the same polarity, [polarity: _____] or

_____ dissimilarity (none of the above).

Between our charts, my sun to my partner's sun is in:

_____ resonance (in the same sign),

_____ companionship (two signs apart),

_____ the same response type (modality),

[response type: _____]

_____ the same approach type (element),

[approach type: _____]

_____ the same polarity, [polarity: _____] or

_____ dissimilarity (none of the above).

Between our charts, my moon to my partner's moon is in:

_____ resonance (in the same sign),

_____ companionship (two signs apart),

_____ the same response type (modality),

[response type: _____]

_____ the same approach type (element),

[approach type: _____]

_____ the same polarity, [polarity: _____] or

_____ dissimilarity (none of the above).

Our Venus-Mars Combinations

My Venus (♀) is in _____.
My partner's Venus (♀) is in _____.

My Mars (♂) is in _____.
My partner's Mars (♂) is in _____.

Between our charts, my Venus to my partner's Mars is in:
_____ resonance (in the same sign),
_____ companionship (two signs apart),
_____ the same response type (modality),
[response type: _____]
_____ the same approach type (element),
[approach type: _____]
_____ the same polarity, [polarity: _____] or
_____ dissimilarity (none of the above).

Between our charts, my Mars to my partner's Venus is in:
_____ resonance (in the same sign),
_____ companionship (two signs apart),
_____ the same response type (modality),
[response type: _____]
_____ the same approach type (element),
[approach type: _____]
_____ the same polarity, [polarity: _____] or
_____ dissimilarity (none of the above).

Between our charts, my Venus to my partner's Venus is in:
_____ resonance (in the same sign),
_____ companionship (two signs apart),
_____ the same response type (modality),
[response type: _____]
_____ the same approach type (element),
[approach type: _____]
_____ the same polarity, [polarity: _____] or
_____ dissimilarity (none of the above).

Between our charts, my Mars to my partner's Mars is in:
_____ resonance (in the same sign),

_____ companionship (two signs apart),

_____ the same response type (modality),

[response type: _____]

_____ the same approach type (element),

[approach type: _____]

_____ the same polarity, [polarity: _____] or

_____ dissimilarity (none of the above).

Our Jupiter-Saturn Combinations

My Jupiter (♃) is in _____.

My partner's Jupiter (♃) is in _____.

My Saturn (♄) is in _____.

My partner's Saturn (♄) is in _____.

Between our charts, my Jupiter to my partner's Saturn is in:

_____ resonance (in the same sign),

_____ companionship (two signs apart),

_____ the same response type (modality),

[response type: _____]

_____ the same approach type (element),

[approach type: _____]

_____ the same polarity, [polarity: _____] or

_____ dissimilarity (none of the above).

Between our charts, my Saturn to my partner's Jupiter is in:

_____ resonance (in the same sign),

_____ companionship (two signs apart),

_____ the same response type (modality),

[response type: _____]

_____ the same approach type (element),

[approach type: _____]

_____ the same polarity, [polarity: _____] or

_____ dissimilarity (none of the above).

Between our charts, my Jupiter to my partner's Jupiter is in:
_____ resonance (in the same sign),
_____ companionship (two signs apart),
_____ the same response type (modality),
[response type: _____]
_____ the same approach type (element),
[approach type: _____]
_____ the same polarity, [polarity: _____] or
_____ dissimilarity (none of the above).

Between our charts, my Saturn to my partner's Saturn is in:
_____ resonance (in the same sign),
_____ companionship (two signs apart),
_____ in the same response type (modality),
[response type: _____]
_____ the same approach type (element),
[approach type: _____]
_____ the same polarity, [polarity: _____] or
_____ dissimilarity (none of the above).

Our chart combination seems to contain mostly _____similarity, or _____complementarity, or _____a balance of the two.

Wild-Card Planet Connections

Our Uranus-Sun Combinations

My Uranus (♅) is in _____.
My partner's sun (☉) is in _____.

My partner's Uranus (♅) is in _____.
My sun (☉) is in _____.

Between our charts, my Uranus and my partner's sun are:
_____ connected* or
_____ not emphasized.**

Between our charts, my partner's Uranus and my sun are:
_____ connected* or
_____ not emphasized.**

*in resonance (the same sign), the same response type (modality), or the same polarity
**any other interrelationship

Our Uranus-Moon Combinations

My Uranus (♅) is in _____.
My partner's moon (☽) is in _____.

My partner's Uranus (♅) is in _____.

My moon (☽) is in _____.

Between our charts, my Uranus to my partner's moon are:
_____ connected* or
_____ not emphasized.**

Between our charts, my partner's Uranus and my moon are:
_____ connected* or
_____ not emphasized.**

*in resonance (the same sign), the same response type (modality), or the same polarity
**any other interrelationship

Our Uranus-Mercury Combinations

My Uranus (♅) is in _____.
My partner's Mercury (☿) is in _____.

My partner's Uranus (♅) is in _____.
My Mercury (☿) is in _____.

Between our charts, my Uranus and my partner's Mercury are:
_____ connected* or
_____ not emphasized.**

Between our charts, my partner's Uranus and my Mercury are:
_____ connected* or
_____ not emphasized.**

*in resonance (the same sign), the same response type (modality), or the same polarity
**any other interrelationship

Our Uranus-Mars Combinations

My Uranus (♅) is in _____.
My partner's Mars (♂) is in _____.

My partner's Uranus (♅) is in _____.
My Mars (♂) is in _____.

Between our charts, my Uranus and my partner's Mars are:
_____ connected* or
_____ not emphasized.**

Between our charts, my partner's Uranus and my Mars are:
_____ connected* or
_____ not emphasized.**

*in resonance (the same sign), the same response type (modality), or the same polarity
**any other interrelationship

Our Neptune-Sun Combinations

My Neptune (♆) is in _____.
My partner's sun (☉) is in _____.

My partner's Neptune (♆) is in _____.
My sun (☉) is in _____.

Between our charts, my Neptune and my partner's sun are:
_____ connected* or
_____ not emphasized.**

Between our charts, my partner's Neptune and my sun are:
_____ connected* or
_____ not emphasized.**

*in resonance (same sign), the same response type (modality), or the same polarity
**any other interrelationship

Our Neptune-Moon Combinations

My Neptune (♆) is in _____. My partner's moon (☽)
is in _____.

My partner's Neptune (♆) is in _____. My moon (☽)
is in _____.

Between our charts, my Neptune and my partner's moon are:
_____ connected* or
_____ not emphasized.**

Between our charts, my partner's Neptune and my moon are:
_____ connected* or
_____ not emphasized.**

*in resonance (the same sign), the same response type (modality), or the same polarity
**any other interrelationship

Our Neptune-Mercury Combinations

My Neptune (♆) is in _____.
My partner's Mercury (☿) is in _____.

My partner's Neptune (♆) is in _____.
My Mercury (☿) is in _____.

Between our charts, my Neptune and my partner's Mercury are:
_____ connected* or
_____ not emphasized.**

Between our charts, my partner's Neptune and my Mercury are:
_____ connected* or
_____ not emphasized.**

*in resonance (the same sign), the same response type (modality), or the same polarity
**any other interrelationship

Our Neptune-Venus Combinations

My Neptune (♆) is in _____.
My partner's Venus (♀) is in _____.

My partner's Neptune (♆) is in _____.
My Venus (♀) is in _____.

Between our charts, my Neptune and my partner's Venus are:
_____ connected* or
_____ not emphasized.**

Between our charts, my partner's Neptune and my Venus are:
_____ connected* or
_____ not emphasized.**

*in resonance (the same sign), the same response type (modality), or the same polarity
**any other interrelationship

Our Neptune-Mars Combinations

My Neptune (♆) is in _____.
My partner's Mars (♂) is in _____.

My partner's Neptune (♆) is in _____.
My Mars (♂) is in _____.

Between our charts, my Neptune and my partner's Mars are:
_____ connected* or
_____ not emphasized.**

Between our charts, my partner's Neptune and my Mars are:
_____ connected* or
_____ not emphasized.**

*in resonance (the same sign), the same response type (modality), or the same polarity
**any other interrelationship

Our Pluto-Sun Combinations

My Pluto (♀) is in _____.
My partner's sun (☉) is in _____.

My partner's Pluto (♀) is in _____.
My sun (☉) is in _____.

Between our charts, my Pluto and my partner's sun are:
    ____ connected* or
    ____ not emphasized.**

Between our charts, my partner's Pluto and my sun are:
    ____ connected* or
    ____ not emphasized.**

*in resonance (the same sign), the same response type (modality), or the same polarity
**any other interrelationship

Our Pluto-Moon Combinations

My Pluto (♀) is in _____.
My partner's moon (☽) is in _____.

My partner's Pluto (♀) is in _____.
My moon (☽) is in _____.

Between our charts, my Pluto and my partner's moon are:
    ____ connected* or
    ____ not emphasized.**

Between our charts, my partner's Pluto and my moon are:
    ____ connected* or
    ____ not emphasized.**

*in resonance (the same sign), the same response type (modality), or the same polarity
**any other interrelationship

Our Pluto-Mercury Combinations

My Pluto (♇) is in _____.
My partner's Mercury (☿) is in _____.

My partner's Pluto (♇) is in _____.
My Mercury (☿) is in _____.

Between our charts, my Pluto and my partner's Mercury are:
_____ connected* or
_____ not emphasized.**

Between our charts, my partner's Pluto and my Mercury are:
_____ connected* or
_____ not emphasized.**

*in resonance (the same sign), the same response type (modality), or the same polarity
**any other interrelationship

Our Pluto-Venus Combinations

My Pluto (♇) is in _____.
My partner's Venus (♀) is in _____.

My partner's Pluto (♇) is in _____.
My Venus (♀) is in _____.

Between our charts, my Pluto and my partner's Venus are:
_____ connected* or
_____ not emphasized.**

Between our charts, my partner's Pluto and my Venus are:
_____ connected* or
_____ not emphasized.**

*in resonance (the same sign), the same response type (modality), or the same polarity
**any other interrelationship

Our Pluto-Mars Combinations

My Pluto (♀) is in _____.
My partner's Mars (♂) is in _____.

My partner's Pluto (♀) is in _____.
My Mars (♂) is in _____.

Between our charts, my Pluto and my partner's Mars are:
_____ connected* or
_____ not emphasized.**

Between our charts, my partner's Pluto and my Mars are:
_____ connected* or
_____ not emphasized.**

*in resonance (the same sign), the same response type (modality), or the same polarity
**any other interrelationship

Our Chiron-Sun Combinations

My Chiron (⚷) is in _____.
My partner's sun (☉) is in _____.

My partner's Chiron (⚷) is in _____.
My sun (☉) is in _____.

Between our charts, my Chiron and my partner's sun are:
_____ connected* or
_____ not emphasized.**

Between our charts, my partner's Chiron and my sun are:
_____ connected* or
_____ not emphasized.**

*in resonance (the same sign), the same response type (modality), or the same polarity
**any other interrelationship

Our Chiron-Moon Combinations

My Chiron (⚷) is in _____. My partner's moon (☽) is in _____.

My partner's Chiron (⚷) is in _____. My moon (☽) is in _____.

Between our charts, my Chiron and my partner's moon are:
_____ connected* or
_____ not emphasized.**

Between our charts, my partner's Chiron and my moon are:
_____ connected* or
_____ not emphasized.**

*in resonance (the same sign), the same response type (modality), or the same polarity
**any other interrelationship

Our Chiron-Mercury Combinations

My Chiron (⚷) is in _____.
My partner's Mercury (☿) is in _____.

My partner's Chiron (⚷) is in _____.
My Mercury (☿) is in _____.

Between our charts, my Chiron and my partner's Mercury are:
_____ connected* or
_____ not emphasized.**

Between our charts, my partner's Chiron and my Mercury are:
_____ connected* or
_____ not emphasized.**

*in resonance (the same sign), the same response type (modality), or the same polarity
**any other interrelationship

Our Chiron-Venus Combinations

My Chiron (⚷) is in _____.
My partner's Venus (♀) is in _____.

My partner's Chiron (⚷) is in _____.
My Venus (♀) is in _____.

Between our charts, my Chiron and my partner's Venus are:
_____ connected* or
_____ not emphasized.**

Between our charts, my partner's Chiron and my Venus are:
_____ connected* or
_____ not emphasized.**

*in resonance (the same sign), the same response type (modality), or the same polarity
**any other interrelationship

Our Chiron-Mars Combinations

My Chiron (⚷) is in _____.
My partner's Mars (♂) is in _____.

My partner's Chiron (⚷) is in _____.
My Mars (♂) is in _____.

Between our charts, my Chiron and my partner's Mars are:
_____ connected* or
_____ not emphasized.**

Between our charts, my partner's Chiron and my Mars are:
_____ connected* or
_____ not emphasized.**

*in resonance (the same sign), the same response type (modality), or the same polarity
**any other interrelationship

My nodes (☊, ☋) are found in the polarity of
_____ - _____.

My partner's nodes (☊, ☋) are found in the polarity of
_____- _____.

My planets that contact my own nodes are
_____.

My planets that contact my partner's nodes are
_____.

My partner's planets that contact their own nodes are
_____.

My partner's planets that contact my nodes are
_____.

BIBLIOGRAPHY

Anthony, Carol K. *Love, An Inner Connection.* Stow, Mass.: Anthony Publishing Company, 1993.

Brennan, Barbara. *Hands of Light.* New York: Bantam, 1988.

———. *Light Emerging.* New York: Bantam, 1993.

Eisler, Riane. *The Chalice & the Blade.* San Francisco: Harper & Row, 1987.

Forrest, Steven. *The Inner Sky.* San Diego: ACS Publications, 1988.

Gimbutas, Marija. *The Language of the Goddess.* San Francisco: Harper & Row, 1989.

Newton, Michael, Ph.D. *Journey of Souls: Case Studies of Life Between Lives.* St. Paul, MN: Llewellyn Publications, 1995.

SUGGESTED READING

Anthony, Carol K. *Love, an Inner Connection.* Stow, Mass.: Anthony Publishing Company, 1993.

Forrest, Stephen. *The Inner Sky.* San Diego, CA: ACS Publications, 1988.

Hand, Robert. *Horoscope Symbols.* San Diego, CA: ACS Publications, 1991.

Rogers-Gallagher, Kim. *Astrology for the Light Side of the Brain.* San Diego, CA: ACS Publications, 1995.

RESOURCES

Chart Services (to get a copy of your natal chart)
Astrological Software
Rectification of Birth Time Services (for those who do not have a birth time)
Astrological Services (counseling, etc.)

For the above services, please contact:
Terry Lamb Astrological Services
(619) 589-1774 (Mon. – Fri. 9 A.M. – 7 P.M. Pacific time)
P.O. Box 553
La Mesa, CA 91944-0553
www.flash.net/~tlamb

Chart Services (to get a copy of your natal chart)
Astrological Software

For the above services, please contact:
Astro Communication Services
(800) 888-9983
www.astrocom.com

ABOUT THE AUTHOR

Terry Lamb is a nationally known astrologer, healer, writer, and speaker who specializes in helping others with business and personal growth using her background in linguistics (M.A., UCSD), healing and natural health, psychology, and spiritual studies. Her insights into life's forces have helped hundreds of clients find their path to fulfillment and success. A teacher and tutor since her college days, she founded *The Astrological Certification Program* in 1992 for in-person and home study. Active in several professional organizations, she is also published in various magazines and journals, and on the Internet she has her own website, www.flash.net/~tlamb. Terry is available for bookings and counseling sessions at (619) 589-1774 or tlamb@flash.net.

✷✷✷

We hope you enjoyed
this Hay House Astro Room book.
If you would like to receive a free catalog featuring additional
Hay House books and products, or if you would like information about
the Hay Foundation, please contact:

Hay House, Inc.
P.O. Box 5100
Carlsbad, CA 92018-5100

(760) 431-7695 or **(800) 654-5126**
(760) 431-6948 (fax) or **(800) 650-5115 (fax)**

Please visit the Hay House Website at: **www.hayhouse.com**

✷✷✷